Schooling Indifference

This book is concerned with re-imagining Religious Education (RE) as this is practiced in schools, colleges and universities throughout the UK and in a wide variety of international educational contexts.

On the basis of a critical analysis of current theory and practice in RE, the authors argue that this educational framing is no longer plausible in the light of new theoretical developments within the academy. A new educational approach to RE is outlined that challenges students to think and practice differently. This includes a 'becoming ethnographer' approach that can acknowledge socio-material relations and engage the broader literacies necessary for such study.

Part One examines how RE has been constructed as a discipline in historical and spatial terms that abstract its study from material concerns. Part Two offers some new starting points: Spinoza, Foucault and feminist theory that differently foreground context and relationality, and 'Islam' read as a discursive, located tradition rather than as 'world view'. Finally, Part Three proposes a new trajectory for research and practice in RE, with the aim of re-engaging schools, colleges and universities in a dialogue that promotes thinking and practice that—as educational—is continually in touch with the need to be critical, open-ended and ethically justifiable.

John I'Anson is currently Associate Dean in the Faculty of Social Sciences at the University of Stirling, having, until recently, been Director of Initial Teacher Education. He gained his Ph.D. at the University of Lancaster and has previously taught as a Principal Teacher of Religious, Moral, and Philosophical Studies in the North East of Scotland. He has undertaken empirical research projects that include aesthetic education, film and digital literacies, children's rights and participation, and issues in the transition from initial teacher education to the induction year. His publications include philosophy of education, Religious Education, and children's rights. He is Convener of the Research on Children's Rights in Education at the European Educational Research Association.

Alison Jasper is the co-founder of the University of Stirling's programme in Gender Studies and, currently, Programme Director in Religion within the Faculty of Arts and Humanities. She gained her Ph.D. at the University of Glasgow and has previously taught RE at a number of schools in the North East of England and in Glasgow. She has participated in research projects on RE and is the author of *The Shining Garment of the Text* (Sheffield: Sheffield Academic Press, 1998) and *Because of Beauvoir: Christianity and the Cultivation of Female Genius* (Baylor UP, 2012).

Gender, Theology and Spirituality

Edited by Lisa Isherwood, University of Winchester, UK

For a full list of titles in this series, please visit www.routledge.com

11 **Being the Body of Christ**
Towards a Twenty-First Century Homosexual theology
for the Anglican Church
Chris Mounsey

12 **Catholics, Conflicts and Choices**
An Exploration of Power Relations in the Catholic Church
Angela Coco

13 **Baby, You are My Religion**
Women, Gay Bars, and theology Before Stonewall
Marie Cartier

14 **Radical Otherness**
Sociological and Theological Approaches
Lisa Isherwood and David Harris

15 **Public theology and the Challenge of Feminism**
Edited by Anita Monro and Stephen Burns

16 **Searching for the Holy Spirit**
Feminist theology and Traditional Doctrine
Anne Claar Thomasson-Rosingh

17 **God and Difference**
The Trinity, Sexuality, and the Transformation of Finitude
Linn Marie Tonstad

18 **Christian Goddess Spirituality**
Enchanting Christianity
Mary Ann Beavis

19 **Schooling Indifference**
Re-Imagining RE in Multi-Cultural and Gendered Spaces
John I'Anson and Alison Jasper

Schooling Indifference
Re-Imagining RE in Multi-Cultural and Gendered Spaces

John I'Anson and Alison Jasper

NEW YORK AND LONDON

First published 2017
by Routledge
711 Third Avenue, New York, NY 10017

and by Routledge
2 Park Square, Milton Park, Abingdon, Oxon OX14 4RN

Routledge is an imprint of the Taylor & Francis Group, an informa business

© 2017 John I'Anson and Alison Jasper

The right of John I'Anson and Alison Jasper to be identified as authors of this work has been asserted by them in accordance with sections 77 and 78 of the Copyright, Designs and Patents Act 1988.

All rights reserved. No part of this book may be reprinted or reproduced or utilised in any form or by any electronic, mechanical, or other means, now known or hereafter invented, including photocopying and recording, or in any information storage or retrieval system, without permission in writing from the publishers.

Trademark notice: Product or corporate names may be trademarks or registered trademarks, and are used only for identification and explanation without intent to infringe.

British Library Cataloguing-in-Publication Data
A catalogue record for this book is available from the British Library

Library of Congress Cataloging-in-Publication Data
A catalog record for this book has been requested

ISBN: 978-1-138-18469-5 (hbk)
ISBN: 978-1-315-15780-1 (ebk)

Typeset in Sabon
by Apex CoVantage, LLC

Printed and bound in Great Britain by
TJ International Ltd, Padstow, Cornwall

Contents

Acknowledgements	ix
Introduction	1

PART 1
Diagnostic ⟶ 9

1 Diagnosing Indifference—An Historical Analysis ⟶ 11

   (i) Introduction 11
   (ii) After Smart 14
   (iii) The Business Case? 19
   (iv) The Definition of Religion 21
   (v) Conclusion 22

2 Assembling RE—Spaces, Relations and Translations ⟶ 29

   (i) Introduction 30
   (ii) Religion and Education? 30
   (iii) RE and the Spatialities of Knowledge Production 32
   (iv) 'Religion': Felicity Conditions 36
   (v) Objectivity and Scientific Practice: Mapping
       Translations 39
   (vi) RE and the Work of Translation 41
   (vii) Forms of Translation: The Concept of Belief 42
   (viii) Examining RE 43
       (a) The Qualifications Framework: Sameness and
           Equivalence 44
       (b) Examination Practices: Acts of Writing 45
       (c) Curriculum Arrangements: Ordering Practices 45
       (d) Producing Religion, Subjectivity and Truth 49
   (ix) Conclusion 51

vi *Contents*

PART 2
Thinking Otherwise—Resisting Indifference   57

3   **Thinking Otherwise—Spinoza and Foucault**   59

   (i) Introduction 59
   (ii) The Rhetoric of Neutrality: A Metaphorical Critique 59
   (iii) Privileging the Visual: Some Consequences 62
   (iv) Imaginaries 64
   (v) Re-Imagining Cultural Difference: Spinoza 65
   (vi) Spinoza's Contribution 67
      (a) Orientation to Analysis: Conatus *67*
      (b) Mode of Analysis: Ethology 68
      (c) Access to Truth: Philosophy and Spiritual
         Exercise (Askêsis) *70*
   (vii) Conclusion: Towards Uncommon Sense? 72

4   **Thinking Otherwise—Gender in the Mix**   77

   (i) Introduction 77
   (ii) Transcendence Incarnate 81
   (iii) Neighbourliness 88
   (iv) Re-Vising Spirituality 94
   (v) Becoming Undone 100
   (vi) Conclusion 108

5   **Thinking Otherwise—The Anthropology of Islam**   115

   (i) Introduction 115
   (ii) Points of Departure 116
   (iii) Islam as a Tradition 119
      (a) Al-Ghazālī 119
      (b) Do Dreams Matter? 120
      (c) Different Types of Dreams 121
      (d) Are Jinn Actants? 123
   (iv) Case Study: Jinn and Multiple Ontologies 125
   (v) The Work of Imagining 127

PART 3
Remediation—Beyond Indifference?   133

6   **Remediation—Imagining Otherwise**   135

   (i) Introduction 135
   (ii) Mapping into Knowledge: From Epistemology
     to Ontology 136

Contents vii

    (iii) William James's Relational Universe: Towards a
        Radical Empiricism 138
    (iv) Some Ontological Implications of James's
        Radical Empiricism 140
     (v) Towards an Ontology of the Virtual 141
    (vi) Towards a Heuristic for Re-Connecting Higher
        Education and Schools 143
   (vii) Three Elements of RE: Towards a Heuristic 144
        (a) The Critical Element 145
        (b) The Experimental Element 149
        (c) The Ethical Element 151
  (viii) The Three Elements in Practice 152
    (ix) Re-Thinking Educational Practice Beyond Indifference:
        Towards Empirical Practice 154

7   Teasing Out the Cross-Cutting Themes   **163**

In Conclusion 169

Index   173

Acknowledgements

We acknowledge with gratitude, all those who, over the years, have encouraged our ongoing interest in developing a new way to think about RE. We have benefitted from working in an institution that has always brought students of 'religion' together with students of 'professional education' in a joint degree, so that we have gained enormously from the interest and enthusiasm of students in both areas who have worked with us as educators and researchers. We are grateful to the whole range of scholars, past and present, who have provided us with ideas and inspiration, as well as to current and former academic colleagues at Stirling, noting in particular Jeremy Carrette, Mary Keller, Gavin Flood, Tim Fitzgerald, Michael Marten, Andrew Hass, Sabine Dedenbach-Salazar Saenz, Francis Stewart, Fiona Darroch, Pamela Sue Anderson, Lisa Isherwood, Ian Munday, Heather Lynch, Tara Fenwick, Richard Edwards, James MacAllister, Gert Biesta, Louise Scott and Kitt Curwen.

We would also like to thank the Trustees of the Carnegie Fund for their generosity in awarding us a research grant that enabled us to engage with a large number of stakeholders within the field.

Finally, we thank our families and friends for their patience and support. In particular, we would like to mention David, Lesley-Anne, Jaimie and Patrick, Hannah, Ruth and May.

Introduction

This book begins with a critical reading of the present situation of religious education (RE) in schools, colleges and higher education, especially within the UK, but also in many international sites where this subject area is found in the curriculum. We will use the term RE in what we discuss to cover the many different forms of provision available. Although the cognate disciplines are referred to variably as Religion, RS (Religious Studies) or sometimes—when run concurrently with programmes in Christian theology in universities—TRS (Theology and Religious Studies), we think that all areas of study are subject to many of the same pressures and influences, and part of our project in any case is to encourage a new dialogue between educational contexts. Whilst we accept that different things will be happening in these respective spaces, we want to offer a diagnosis of what we see as generally problematic in the present situation and to suggest some new directions of travel in the broadest terms, a vision of programmatic change that we hope has implications for both research and educational practice.

Our intention is to open up thinking around a new and distinctively educational account of RE. We hope to stimulate thinking in the direction of new critical, ethical and experimental opportunities within a field that is arguably, at present, foreclosed by an existing settlement that was achieved some time ago. Our hope is that we can generate new insights into the challenges involved in making sense of the differences that are commonly engaged within RE, whilst also resisting the closures that restrict opportunities for change and transformation. In order to do this, we will make references to a broad range of theoretical insights from the academy—the world of the universities—including developments in feminist theory, critical religion, the anthropology of the good, Science and Technology Studies and critical re-readings in the philosophy of education. We also draw on our own experience as educators and researchers in both schools and university sectors for more than 20 years and on conversations we have undertaken with stakeholders in these sectors since 2012.[1]

The aim is to make RE come alive and to represent it as a more dynamic and challenging educational activity—as an intellectually grounded, yet adventurous, process that is attentive and hospitable to existing as well as to a range of radically new practices going along together (Verran, 1999) in

2   Introduction

a neighbourly fashion. We want to call forth an openness and responsiveness to events, ideas and invitations that betoken change and transformation. Whilst practices that may lead to measurable social and economic benefits are perhaps the preferred outcomes of present policy and curricula discussions at both government and institutional levels (Brown and Carasso, 2013; Collini, 2012; McGettigan, 2013), our focus of concern is framed differently. The upshot of the process through which we take our readers in this book is directed towards an educational heuristic in terms of the critical, ethical and experimental, whose purpose is to provide a way of determining the kinds of imaginative work that will best provide motivation and practices for living well and hospitably within an increasingly complex global situation.

In Part One, we start in an empirical frame of mind by looking at how contemporary RE has been constructed as a discipline over more than four decades. We begin, grounding our study in the current situation, coming out of a set of specific historical (Chapter One) and spatial (Chapter Two) circumstances. In historical terms, the present settlement emerged first, from an understanding of what 'religion' and 'education' meant within British culture after the end of the Second World War. Subsequently, RE became associated, in the UK, with the contributions of Ninian Smart and an assemblage of theories that drew upon a long tradition of European and American strands of thinking, notably including phenomenology.[2] In relation to spatial circumstances, we reflect on how RE tends still to be located in terms of abstractions from material or embodied positions, an orientation that has been the particular target of recent feminist and gender theory (Lloyd, 1984; Price and Shildrick, 1999; Pedwell, 2012). Still focusing on how things and relations are presently choreographed in the world of RE, our analysis of its spatial circumstances also draws on Ian Hacking's theoretical work (1992) on styles of reasoning. Hacking (1992, 12) used the term 'styles of reasoning' to introduce and suggest new ways in which something could be held to be 'a candidate for truth or for falsehood' and consequently reveal or bring about new objects, evidences or possibilities (11). We argue that the present framing of RE has been informed by styles of reasoning that index a particular spatial imaginary, drawing upon a Western, Cartesian legacy that has imported an arbitrary subject/object division into the discipline or subject area. This constructs students as non-implicated observers, exercising a detached rationality, a style of reasoning that additionally makes it very difficult to address forms of alterity, or the affective and existential dimensions that such an engagement often elicits (Crang and Thrift, 2000; Law and Lin, 2010; I'Anson and Jasper, 2011). In adopting an approach that has thus more in common with a Jamesian perspective positing a relational universe (Carrette, 2013), we are, of course, claiming that something is missing from the current account of RE. We are saying, *inter alia*, that whilst the RE educator, researcher or student is constantly negotiating embodied encounters with different humans/non-humans and others in the course of

Introduction 3

their lived experience of teaching or being in school/university spaces, this dynamic remains, at present, largely invisible and unexplored, even though it necessarily impacts on the nature of what they are teaching or how they are being educated. We suggest that the current settlement is still struggling to recognise these crucial dimensions of embodiment and relationality and has yet to establish ways in which to start bringing them into play.

Following on from this initial diagnostic, in Part Two we entertain a variety of different ways forward—three thought experiments—that we hope will provide practitioners with starting points and encouragement for making changes or moving beyond existing framings into less familiar territory. These are three distinct trajectories that will hopefully encourage readers to think and imagine in new terms. Chapter Three, which considers Spinoza's philosophy (and his subsequent influence on Foucault), invites us to engage with a different philosophical tradition that foregrounds relationality, embodiment and the significance of the imagination for our collective ways of making sense. Chapter Four engages with feminist theorising and methodology in its radical challenge to styles of reasoning that privilege (male normative) abstract and disengaged approaches that discriminate against (female-associated) embodied and relational matters of concern. Tools are offered that afford a radical questioning—and disruption—of settled forms of thought where injustice, in relation particularly to gender, remains invisible. In Chapter Five, we then consider 'Islam' as a discursive tradition rather than as a 'world view' and consider some of the complexities that are routinely excluded in its Western forms of presentation. This enables us to acknowledge other forms of difference—whether these are conceptual, relating to the significance of dreams, or different ontologies that have 'real life' effects that can present challenges, for example, within health care contexts, where competing ontologies may collide. Such approaches, we hope, illustrate and enable different framings that are both critical and based in empirical experience—of being a Muslim in a Western context or of being female in a patriarchal, male-normative context—and allow new questions that are both relational and embodied, and therefore more ethical and experimental in orientation, to arise.

Having considered a variety of different ways forward from the current settlement, in Part Three, we go on to propose a new theoretical framing together with new practices of inquiry that practitioners may wish to take up and engage with in their own specific contexts. This re-orientation and framing also suggests a new trajectory for research in RE. Given the relatively limited discussion of 'religion' as a concept within current framings of RE, it also becomes desirable to re-engage this issue. We therefore hope to promote an educational heuristics that has the capacity to develop this and other significant exchanges between schools, colleges and universities in future, framing an approach and a tradition of inquiry that are continually in touch with the need to be critical, open-ended and ethically justifiable.

4 Introduction

We could sum up one of the chief aims of our book as being the attempt to avoid 'indifference' in RE. Such indifference goes hand-in-hand with a mobilisation of abstracted uniformities that are presented in ways that have little or no consequence for the student inquirer. The educational matters of concern[3] are, in this scenario, presented as non-affecting—and so it is not surprising if the student remains largely un-affected by their activities in the classroom. As practitioners, we acknowledge that we do not always follow our own best insights; it is hard to encourage provocation for change on a consistent basis, and the present settlement has been powerfully forged in the midst of key debates about the possibility of studying 'religion' at all (Strhan, 2015), achieved through the bracketing out of personal identification or of any claims to truth in regard to 'religion'. This, we argue, has placed limits upon the educational scope of the subject, and these limitations become especially noticeable if education is understood as a process of drawing out or of leading students into new places that have not yet been identified, sampled, measured or mapped (Masschelein, 2006; 2010a, b). Perhaps our best insights foreground the student's own articulation of their imaginary—their way of conceiving of human existence and their place within that wider context—and the ethical work involved in bringing this into relationship with different people and circumstances. The messiness of actual living demands styles of reasoning that are rather different from those being promoted at present in RE. Of course, knowledge production based on experimental encounters, going somewhere new and unpredictable is, by its very nature, hard to plan for. We maintain, nevertheless, that the present framing of RE continues to veer towards the 'an-educational' insofar as the plane on which it is practised has been so severely limited already that students are only permitted an engagement within excessively predefined terms.

If, instead, we open up the field of engagement, there is no doubt that we raise challenges to our own understanding of the ontological ground on which we thought we stood securely (Steiner, 1978). This, then, is the potentially radical proposal, opening the subject of RE up to unsettling questions about its very *raison d'être* as this is currently understood. Nonetheless, we are not alone in thinking that there is an urgent need to move beyond what is currently identified as RE. There is wide acknowledgement that we must address the ambiguities and tensions of a hugely enhanced technical capacity to mobilise complex ideologies and of unprecedented movement of peoples around the world (Benjamin and Dervin, 2015). As educators, researchers and students of RE, we need to articulate and practice what we do in fresh ways, showing how we can become skilled in using critical and imaginative tools to handle the dynamic conditions of contemporary cultures and whatever is mobilised under the heading of 'religion' in such conditions. Thus, in terms both of styles of reasoning and practice, we want to move, for example, from treating 'Islam' or 'Hinduism' or the 'not religious' as fixed entities in time, towards a critical engagement with those individuals, communities, discourses and bodies which are currently identifying themselves in these

Introduction 5

ways and with their embodied and material conditions. And at the same time—in this encounter with differences—we need to become more critically aware of our own distinctive commitments, assumptions and of the relations that sustain them (Latour, 2013). The skills attained by taking on the different approach or style we are suggesting would thus, we hope, increase the capacity of educators, researchers and students to engage in new forms of diplomacy; that is, negotiations on the ground about how best to live within the global and local (Dekoven, 2001; Sarroub, 2009) matrix of relationships and engaged practices (Ingold, 2011) that is our contemporary context.

In sum, in this book, instead of treating RE as a *known* body—as if it were something we could come to stable conclusions about—we envisage RE more as a dynamic, fluid and shifting relational matrix. Conceived as a dynamic field of play, it only makes sense within multi-faceted forms of engagement that are alive to difference, complexity and the inevitably ethical implications of making and sustaining relationships. Restyled as such, RE could then be aligned with other practices across the curriculum that are also concerned with ways to achieve a greater fullness of inter-relational engagement.

Notes

1. The authors held a series of interviews between 2012 and 2014 with a number of stakeholders (teachers, both new and established; educational administrators and policy makers; teacher educators; representatives of Churches and non-Christian traditions; academics). They are grateful both to these interviewees and correspondents and to the Trustees of the Carnegie Fund, whose generous donation allowed them to widen their circle of conversation partners beyond the Scottish context.
2. The 'phenomenology of religion', as a concept, ultimately derives from the work of European scholars like Cornelis Tiele (b. 1830), Max Müller (b. 1823) and Rudolf Otto (b. 1869). Through the 19th and into the 20th centuries, these influences came together in various 'schools' in which the term 'phenomenology of religion' was often regarded as interchangeable with the 'history of religions' or 'comparative religion'. These schools—predominantly the Dutch (including William Brede Kristensen and Geradus van der Leeuw), the American (including Joachim Wach and Mircea Eliade) and the British (including Geoffrey Parrinder and Andrew Walls)—had their characteristic differences of approach. Nevertheless, in more general terms, they all ascribed to the idea that data collected from all over the world could be classified as different expressions of a common phenomenon—'religion'(Strenski, 2006). Another aspect of the phenomenology of religion that was key for Smart was that it was distinguished by a gradual movement away from evolutionary thinking; these so-called 'phenomenological' thinkers were less interested than previous scholars of 'religion', in the idea of progression from 'primitive' to 'civilised' forms. They tended to be more interested in understanding the experience of others rather than wanting to stand fully outside it and explain its cause. It marks the growth of a concern for 'empathy' and the attempt to experience the world as others do—to stand in their shoes. Another important influence at the time was the later work of philosopher Ludwig Wittgenstein, especially on language, where the study of intra-religious logics provided a further rationale for attending to the discourse of religion 'as such'.

6 Introduction

3. Ripley *et al.* (2009, 6) provide a useful characterisation of 'matters of concern' as deployed by Latour (2008), which they describe in the following terms:

> 'Latour proposes the notion of "matters of concern" in distinction to the more common scientific category of "matters of fact". While matters of fact, in our reading of Latour, are developed without consideration of desire (moral, ethical, or other), matters of concern embrace and are centered in those desires. While matters of fact exist without context, in an attempt to uncover the indisputable, matters of concern gather context(s) into themselves, disputing both the possibility and the efficacy of indisputability. What results is an approach that engaged with its own inherent contradictions and controversies, a "multifarious inquiry launched with the tools of anthropology, philosophy, metaphysics, history, sociology to detect how many participants are gathered in a thing to make it exist and maintain existence" (Latour, 2004, 246)'.

Bibliography

Benjamin, S. and Dervin, F., 2015. *Migration, Diversity and Education: Beyond Third Kids*. Basingsoke Hampshire and New York: Palgrave Macmillan (Religious Literacy Partnership and Programme).

Brown, R. and Carasso, H., 2013. *Everything for Sale?: The Marketisation of UK Higher Education (Research in Higher Education)*. London and New York: Routledge.

Carrette, J., 2013. *William James's Hidden Religious Imagination: A Universe of Relations*. London and New York: Routledge.

Collini, S., 2012. *What Are Universities For?* London: Penguin.

Crang, M. and Thrift, N., eds., 2000. *Thinking Space: Critical Geographies*. London and New York: Routledge.

Dekoven, M., 2001. *Feminist Locations: Global and Local, Theory and Practice*. New Brunswick, NJ and London: Rutgers University Press.

Hacking, I., 1992. '"Style" for historians and philosophers'. *Studies in History and Philosophy of Science, Part A*, vol. 23, no. 1, pp. 1–20.

I'Anson, J. and Jasper, A., 2011. '"Religion" in educational spaces: Knowing, knowing well, and knowing differently'. *Arts and Humanities in Higher Education*, vol. 10, no. 3, pp. 295–313.

Ingold, T., 2011. *Being Alive: Essays on Movement, Knowledge and Description*. London and New York: Routledge.

Latour, B., 2004. 'Why has critique run out of steam? From matters of fact to matters of concern'. *Critical Inquiry*, vol. 30, no. 2, pp. 225–248.

Latour, B., 2008. What is the Style of Matters of Concern? Spinoza Lectures at the University of Amsterdam, 2005. Amsterdam: Van Gorcum. Available from www.bruno-latour.fr/sites/default/files/97-SPINOZA-GB.pdf

Latour, B., 2013. *An Inquiry Into Modes of Existence: An Anthropology of the Modern*. Cambridge, MA: Harvard University Press.

Law, J. and Lin, W.-Y., 2010. 'Cultivating disconcertment'. *The Sociological Review*, vol. 58, no. S2, pp. 135–153.

Lloyd, G., 1984. *The Man of Reason: 'Male' and 'Female' in Western Philosophy*. London: Methuen.

McGettigan, A., 2013. *The Great University Gamble*. London: Pluto Press.

Masschelein, J., 2006. 'Experience and the limits of governmentality'. *Educational Philosophy and Theory*, vol. 38, no. 4, pp. 561–576.

Masschelein, J., 2010a. 'The idea of critical e-ducational research: E-ducating the gaze and inviting to go walking'. In: I. Gurzeev ed., *The Possibility/Impossibility of a New Critical Language in Education*. Rotterdam: Sense, pp. 275–291.

Masschelein, J., 2010b. 'E-ducating the gaze: The idea of a poor pedagogy'. *Ethics and Education*, vol. 5, no. 1, pp. 43–53.

Pedwell, C., 2012. *Feminism, Culture and Embodied Practice*. London and New York: Routledge.

Price, J. and Shildrick, M., 1999. *Feminist Theory and the Body: A Reader*. Edinburgh: Edinburgh University Press.

Ripley, C., Thün, G. and Velikov, K., 2009. 'Matters of concern'. *Journal of Architectural Education*, vol. 62, no. 4, pp. 6–14.

Sarroub, L.K., 2009. 'Glocalism in literacy and marriage in transnational lives'. *Critical Inquiry in Language Studies (Special Issue: Immigration, Language, and Education)*, vol. 6, no. 1–2, pp. 63–80.

Steiner, G., 1978. *On Difficulties and Other Essays*. Oxford: Oxford University Press.

Strenski, I., 2006. *Thinking About Religion: An Historical Introudction to Theories of Religion*. Oxford: Blackwell Publishing.

Strhan, A., 2015. PE SGB Keynote: 'Enchanting rationalities'. Available from www.philosophy-of-education.org/files/events/conference-papers-2015/PESGB%20 2015%20Keynote%20Panel%20-%20Strhan.pdf.

Verran, H., 1999. 'Staying true to the laugher in Nigerian classroom'. In: John Law and John Hassard eds., *Actor Network Theory and After*. Oxford, UK: Blackwell Publishing, pp. 136–155.

Part 1
Diagnostic

Introduction to Part One

The focus of Part One is an analysis of how the 'religion slot' within education settings came to be conceived and established in the way it did: the conditions, that is, of its articulation, production and institutionalisation, such that *this* rationale for RE became *the* default way of making sense of 'religion' both within UK and, more broadly, in a variety of international educational contexts.

Chapter One is concerned with understanding how the rationale for RE was established through a consideration of broadly historical factors through time. Having identified how historical approaches to religion within the field of education became problematic, Chapter Two then attempts to map the rhetorical strategies, spatial imaginaries and practices of translation across time that together constituted the approach to RE that remains deeply influential at the present time.

Having accomplished this, we will then be in a position the better to explore some of the ontological, epistemological and ethical limits associated with this still dominant framing, as a prelude to proposing some possible new ways forward, in Part Two.

1 Diagnosing Indifference—An Historical Analysis

(i) Introduction

In this first chapter, we identify some of the historical vectors that have had a material influence upon the development of RE as a distinct subject area or discipline through time. More specifically, we consider how RE was accommodated within the context of school and university education in the UK from around the middle of the 20th century, with far-reaching consequences for the practice of RE internationally. We argue that since the establishment of this framing—which largely settled the scope and disciplinary identity of RE some 40 years ago—there has been relatively little change as regards the subject's theoretical rationale and *modus operandi*, notwithstanding considerable investment in new pedagogical approaches and technologies.

One of our major concerns about the present settlement concerning RE's aims and purposes is that it has tended to downplay any ongoing relationship between school spaces and academic study identified with 'religion' in universities—especially as regards the possibility of dialogue developing new theoretical understandings and the pedagogical innovations that these might enable. We feel the challenges and possibilities of this relationship are insufficiently acknowledged in the work of teacher education, in school RE or even at universities, where there is, at least for the present, less standardisation of curricula and thus perhaps more scope for developing the kind of open-ended and experimental approaches we are advocating. In school contexts, however, communication of stable ideas and content tends to predominate. Responsibility for the theoretical analysis of these framings, ideas and contents, as an aspect of day-to-day practice, tends to be seen at school level as something that is located elsewhere: separated from what goes on in the classroom or in departmental RE meetings. It is regarded, rather, as the proper concern of examination boards who may consult with academics in their deliberations but whose work is, practically speaking, somewhat set apart from the sphere of the universities. At the same time, limitations on what can be taught in schools and colleges are arguably disproportionately restrictive in comparison with the still much greater freedom of university academics to decide on what they will teach,[1] and this seems odd within what is now an almost exclusively graduate profession, even within the school or college context.

12 *Diagnostic*

A key purpose of this book is, therefore, to try to promote an educational heuristic that gives some impetus to expanding sites of intersection between these different communities of researchers, educators and students who seemingly have so much in common and yet who rarely communicate. This is in order to move towards the possibility of innovation and new translations rather than a continuation of approaches that have been accepted—more or less without question—for many years and that have arguably led to a certain closure in school RE and a misalliance in the provision of teacher education at the HE level (I'Anson, 2004; I'Anson and Jasper, 2011). In the chapters that follow, we identify a number of areas for discussion within the highly interdisciplinary contexts of the humanities and social sciences that might become sites of vital exchange for all RE subject areas, from school to university. Before such an exploration can begin, however, it is necessary to map how present understandings were formed and how the disconnect between educational sectors we have identified came about.

The existing settlement rests largely on an understanding of 'religion' dating back to the 1960s and 70s. Introduced without much discussion about how it could actually be taught in schools or universities, the highly significant *Working Paper 36* (Schools Council, 1971) formed the basis of much reflection on school RE teaching from that date and was all about new perspectives and multiple approaches. Although the lack of consideration for its pedagogic implications could be regarded as a shortcoming, what was arguably more problematic was the fact that the initiative failed to convince stakeholders of the need to *continue* working with both expert translators and experienced practitioners. In general, once the process of initial translation from those exciting new approaches into school practice had been completed, it took on a normative character, becoming a fixed content or form of knowledge to be transferred from educators to students, largely unaltered. In the intervening years, we would contend that there has been insufficient reflection on how to re-think the subject of RE afresh, as something that is good for us and our students, and rather more discussion about how a fairly static content can be transferred more effectively or made to appear more relevant. We want to move towards a more complex notion of *considered practice* (not to be confused with the now more conventional notions of 'reflective practice') where critical attention is given to both substance and methodology—or, to put it another way, to what is taught, how this is practised and its effects. We hope by describing this process of consideration that we can encourage more experimentation, leading to new and different kinds of practice and action. A key concern, then, is to try to reconnect (at least) two educational spaces that have, over time, become disconnected and to consider the consequences of doing this.

Turning, then, to the historical context in the UK in order to offer one kind of diagnosis or understanding of the situation in more detail, we note continuing public interest in RE in schools. This is often expressed through the media, where is it not always distinguished from forms of 'religious observance' (RO)—or acts of collective worship—that have tended to bring the historical involvement of Christian communities to the fore. This generalised concern raises questions about how far affiliations categorised as 'religious' should be allowed to influence the running of schools within the publicly funded sector (Paton and Gilligan, 2014; Richardson, 2015; Alderson, 2016; McIvor, 2016). Informed by the wide absorption of secularisation theories (Bruce, 2002; Houtman and Aupers, 2008) and, more recently, by the emergence of a popularist 'new atheism' (Dawkins, 2006; Dennett, 2007; Hitchens, 2007; Wynne-Jones, 2009), some people are perplexed that such a subject persists within the curriculum at all. One view, critically analysed by Timothy Fitzgerald (2015), suggests that what has distinguished what is called 'religion' within modernity is precisely its perceived status as a private concern with personal faith and piety, feeding what thus seems to be a common sense argument that anything designated 'religious' should be separated from public ('secular') settlements—in education, as in all other respects.

However, ambivalence about the role of RE is not simply something external to the school system; it is also part of the official account itself. The Education Act of 1944, the Education (Scotland) Act of 1945 and all subsequent legislation relating to RE (such as the Education (Scotland) Act of 1980 and the 1988 Education Reform Act (in England)) continue to impose a statutory duty on all local authorities in the UK to provide RE whilst at the same time giving parents the right to withdraw their children. There is a similar internal ambivalence about RO. Following the 1988 Education Reform Act, every Local Education Authority (LEA) in England and Wales had to appoint a Standing Advisory Council on RE (SACRE) to oversee the provision of both RE and RO. The following extract from guidance issued by one English council (*Essex SACRE*, 2013, 4) expresses something of the discomfort experienced by these bodies when attempting to respond to the statutory requirement to provide collective acts of worship:

> In view of the changes to British society (and schools) that have occurred since 1944, many people hold the view that collective worship is now an outmoded concept. Many prefer the term 'spiritual reflection', which supports the requirement for schools to promote pupils' spiritual development. The notion of spiritual reflection lends itself to the 'stimulus/response' model for collective worship which is the preferred model of Essex SACRE (see page 17 below). In providing structured time for daily spiritual reflection, schools will be providing something important for the wellbeing of pupils and other participants; something that is unique and distinctive; something that is different from but complementary to 'assembly'.

In spite of any ambivalence about the statutory provision, however, the subject area in schools, at any rate, appears to be surprisingly resilient, continuing to provoke those who favour a more so-called 'secular' approach (Weldon, 2016).

14   *Diagnostic*

One reason for RE's apparent resilience may be that moves to incorporate it into the public examination system have already been very effective in containing or controlling input that might appear confessional. RE is a relative newcomer to the ranks of subjects that can be publicly examined, and this change was initially welcomed as a way of giving it a place within the curriculum alongside other academic subjects whose status in relation to the defining religion/secular binary would not have been at issue. The exam-based settlement seems thus, on the one hand, to have addressed concerns in a formal way about making proper provision for RE (something that remains a concern for a significant minority within the UK (Church of England, 2006)) whilst, on the other hand, to have retained statutory and thus 'secular' control over content and approach. In this way, the current official settlement represents a framework that accords with contexts of governance and sovereignty as Stack *et al.* (2015) outline it. Nonetheless, by privileging one particular form of examinable knowledge that powerfully reflects a particular Western, male-normative, text-based ethos of 'secular' rationality and disembodied objectivity, the examination system has also closed down the potential of this educational space. In Chapter two, reflecting some wider contemporary concerns about the impact of an 'examination-driven curriculum' (Conroy *et al.*, 2013, 220), we will look at this issue in greater detail.

(ii) After Smart

Arguably the most important influence for change in relation to the official account of RE in a UK context since the 1940s has been the work of Ninian Smart (Barnes, 2000). Although Smart's work from the 1950s–70s focused largely on higher education (Masefield and Wiebe, 1994), it was also hugely influential in the school sector (Smart, 1957; 1968), perhaps most significantly through the publication of *Working Paper 36* (Schools Council, 1971), whose production Smart directed. Innovative and exciting in its time, Smart wrote with the deliberate intention of being accessible, seeking to reach as wide an audience as possible (Smart, 1969; 1973a; 1983). He acted on a growing realisation that the RE context encompassed more than a simple choice between confessional Christianity and non-believers. Legislation relating to RE, confirming its statutory status in schools in 1944 and 1945, had been passed at a time when a majority of the population were regular churchgoers. By the 1970s, of course, adherence to Christianity was decreasing rapidly, at least in terms of church-going (Brown, 2000, 2009; Brown and Woodhead, 2016). At the same time, British communities with their origins in former colonies were expanding and identifying themselves as 'non-Christian' in very different ways from home-grown secularists and humanists with their roots in European traditions of liberalism, rationalist philosophy and empirical science as they were then understood. In response, Smart introduced 'Religious Studies' at Lancaster University as a degree subject separate

Diagnosing Indifference—An Historical Analysis 15

from (Christian) theology and tried to increase awareness of the much more varied ways in which people could be, in his terms, 'religious'. Notably, he resisted the tendency to reduce the experiences he identified as religious dimensions into classically scientific—psychological or sociological—terms. He acknowledged these experiences as 'facts' with powerful consequences for how people acted (Smart, 1973b).

Smart was thus a key figure within a liberalisation of UK RE. Although his work on religious experience (that drew upon European traditions of phenomenology) was not matched by comparable pedagogical research, it was, nonetheless, an accessible, ethical project characterised by empathetic hospitality to 'the other' (I'Anson and Jasper, 2006), that clearly had wide appeal. Smart's contribution was nevertheless, in our view, a victim of its own success. Its defining 'dimensions' of religion (e.g., Smart, 1969) were easily aligned to categories that facilitated comparisons, serving the ends of assessable uniformity and sameness as much as those of empathy and respect for difference. Moreover, in an era before structuralism and post-modernity entered into Western consciousness and vocabulary, Smart's systematic analysis still implied a guarantee of objectivity or stable 'neutrality' in the encounter with difference. This meant that in spite of its rich and varied insights, the project he initiated continued to serve a hegemonic ontology and outlook (I'Anson and Jasper, 2006; 2011), no matter how new and exciting the content that was being introduced.

Of course, we are not alone in proposing some kind of critique of Smart's work. A whole range of questions has been raised about it since it first emerged. For example, one downside of his legacy (Wright, 2006, 333) might appear to be a lack of desirable cohesion. Whilst in a previous era, locally agreed syllabuses could express a basic agreement, for example, as to the nature of Christianity and how it could be taught in schools:

> [w]ith the advent of forms of liberal RE operating in a multi-faith context and seeking to cultivate religious understanding in an open non-confessional manner, this consensus quickly fragmented. Liberal religious educators faced the daunting task of interpreting religion in a pluralistic context in which there was no shared understanding of the nature of religion.

A host of other writers and scholars have commented on the official account of RE established after Smart (Jackson, 1997; 2004; 2006; 2008; 2010; Grimmitt, 2000; 2010; Wright, 2004; 2006; 2008; 2016; De Souza *et al.*, 2006; Conroy *et al.*, 2013), although, once again, the debate has tended to be more about how uncontested forms of knowledge can be taught more convincingly than about drawing students into the production of new knowledge. Some contestants have been conservative in orientation. This is not to say they have advocated a simplistic return to Christian confessionalism, but they have tended to take up the cudgels against more recent academic

16 *Diagnostic*

themes such as 'postmodernity' (Wright, 2004) or the 'practice of "social constructivism"' (Conroy *et al.*, 2013, 222). In response, we might suggest, however, that both of these—post-structuralism and social constructivism—tend towards the unsettling of established privilege and authority (Butler, 1990; 2004) in a revolutionary mode (Kristeva, 2002). And, for this reason, it would not be unreasonable to suggest, perhaps, that recent calls to be sensitive to 'foundationally distinct religious and metaphysical world views' or to avoid depriving the subject of 'key elements such as authority and propositional content' (Conroy *et al.*, 2013, 222) appear to be referencing more traditional outlooks, rather than endeavouring to address current realities in new and different terms.

One important example of a conservative approach to RE in the post-Smartian period is Andrew Wright's critical realism. Wright suggests that in response to complex contemporary cultural situations, RE students should be equipped as well-informed and skillful critical thinkers. Whereas the Smartian legacy of ideological neutrality—understood positively—was the attempt to avoid evaluating one kind of experience against another, in favour of an ethically motivated project of empathetic engagement, Wright boldly characterises the range of contemporary cultures as a 'diversity of religious truth claims' (Wright in Jackson, 2004, 77). Whatever the truth is, and he does not claim to be able to pin it down, the processes of rational enquiry aligned with a growth in 'religious literacy' represent for Wright the best means we have to reach it. Arguably, however, this does not address the way in which—empirically speaking—truth claims are formed within culturally specific frameworks rather than across a single level playing field, something feminist theory has been very successful in establishing (Crenshaw, 1991; Hartsock, 1998; Harding, 2004). To address this critique, it would be necessary, for example, to consider Wright's authorial positionality or to consider that this approach discounts a good deal of recent critical work that identifies the masculine privilege and sense of entitlement in notions of rationality and objectivity as they have been constructed in the past (Lloyd, 1984; Le Dœuff, 1989; Anderson, 1998).

There is also a tendency within more recent theory about RE to reflect Michel de Certeau's classic thesis (1984) about the textual focus of Western thinking as a whole. This is present in all approaches focused on interpretation and representation. Whilst recent interpretative approaches (Jackson, 1997; 2004; 2008) clearly acknowledge what might be called the hermeneutics of suspicion and draw on texts, including oral traditions, narrative and mythology, that might have been ignored or marginalised in the past, the focus of analysis remains primarily textual. Conroy *et al.* (2013) go so far as to say that the difficulties faced by practitioners of RE in UK contexts can in large part be explained by an 'eschewal of the text' (221). In response to approaches that focus on literacies, texts and their interpretation, we suggest, however, that the value of any textual focus crucially depends upon how the 'literacies' in question are being conceived and translated. Too

Diagnosing Indifference—An Historical Analysis 17

restricted (and uncritical) an understanding of literacy has the potential simply to re-inscribe existing knowledge practices; that is, ones that are generally centred on abstraction and memorisation and often those that are most easily measured through examinations. As an aside too, we note that Smart's understanding of RS moved decisively away from the limitations inherent in the classical association of the study of religions with sacred texts. Whilst textual study clearly has a place within a multi-dimensional approach such as he advocated (1969; 1989 etc.), his approach was distinctive precisely because it included the study of practice through a concern with ritual and other forms of 'experience': an aspect of Smart's intellectual legacy, it should be noted, that has continued to find acknowledgement in work in the area of RE (Cunningham, 2001).

Another interesting and important approach in play within the academic body of work on RE 'after Smart', Michael Grimmitt's work emphasises the distinction between *learning about* and *learning from* (2010, 273–8). His use of the distinction emerges first in *RE and Human Development* (1987), where the work of *learning about* is 'intended to contribute to pupils' understanding of how human beings develop as a result of their interaction with each other in communities and societies' (Grimmitt, 2010, 273). From our perspective, even more interestingly, the work of *learning from* (2010, 274) encourages

> . . . pupils to think through their own beliefs, values and attitudes and to examine and clarify these (and possibly, affirm or reject them) in the light of the beliefs and values they had been learning about in the religious traditions they had studied.

Grimmitt's distinctive language moved into the context of *Agreed RE Syllabuses*, which comprise arrangements for RE made within schools administered by LEAs (in England and Wales) via *Model Syllabuses*. These were documents drafted in response to criticism of the 1988 Education Act in England and Wales and directed against perceived imbalances between Christianity and 'other faiths' (Grimmitt, 2010, 269). Nevertheless, whilst *learning from* took its place as an educational priority within a wider vision of interactional learning in RE, Grimmitt notes that this element was 'often reduced to a short and superficial plenary reflection at the end of a lesson' (2010, 275). It indicates, we would suggest, a wider unwillingness to engage with types of 'work on the self' (Foucault, 1986) that may be a necessary condition for accessing discourse that challenges taken-for-granted framings—betokening both the challenge of the experimental and—in relation to 'the other'—the ethical. In recent work, Grimmitt appears to have been more concerned with the role of RE in processing 'truth claims' (2010, 9). Thus, although he argues that there has been a 'seismic shift in the social, political, religious, moral and ethnic landscape of the UK' following on from the events of 9/11 (2010, 9), he continues to view RE as a context for working towards

18 *Diagnostic*

fundamentally cohesive and integrated ends (2010, 14), again, without real acknowledgment of the lack of a level playing field on which policymaking or work with students might actually take place. Grimmitt certainly advocates critical discussion 'of religion and religions witin their globalised and politicised context' (2010, 17) and encourages ideological self-criticism, but does not appear to see his own commitment to 'truth, reconciliation and peace' (2010, 18) as similarly ideological. The issue here, it should be said, is not that reconciliation and peace are unworthy topics or aims for RE, but that a common understanding of these concepts cannot be achieved without considerable initial work on ideological presuppositions on all sides.

Recently, highly interdisciplinary, so-called dialogical approaches in RE have sought to develop students' discursive and critical competencies by drawing on a much wider diversity of elements as educational material, typically including the experiences of the young people themselves. These approaches are therefore naturally attentive to contextual factors that other post-Smartian approaches to UK RE, touched on above, tend to pass over. Dialogical approaches often employ anthropological or ethnographic methodologies to help open up RE spaces to these contextual factors (Jackson, 2004). Making use of the students' own experiences of the world, these forms of RE, developed in UK contexts by Julia Ipgrave (2001), for example, rely much less on testing knowledge and memory of fixed contents. Nonetheless, this approach still has a tendency to translate knowledge practices into the literary or textual. In other words, having enlarged the matters of concern (Latour, 2004a; 2004b) within an RE context, to encompass practices and phenomena beyond text, outcomes are often recuperated in a predominantly textual way.

Robert Jackson's account of Norwegian educationalist Heide Leganger-Krogstad's dialogical approach (Jackson, 2004) provides another illustration. This interesting description of RE practice involves the exploration of a school's local area and its variable characteristics. Leganger-Krogstad organises visits to places or communities whilst representatives of these different communities are invited to visit the children's school. In the dialogical aspect of her practice, children are encouraged to reflect on these and other source materials in the light of their own awareness of each other, their families and local history in order to begin to recognise the relationship between themselves and their wider contextual frameworks. Notably, however, Jackson's commentary still tends to frame the children's responses to this initiative in terms of 'analyzing', 'looking at', 'reporting back' and 'distancing'. Reflexivity and the skills of ethnography thus appear focused on a process of implicitly neutral observation (Jackson, 2004, 112). This particular example in Jackson (2004) is itself also vulnerable to the level playing field question in that no critique is developed of the normative values—perceived entitlements, forms of mastery, ontological presuppositions or positionality—embedded in the exercise as a whole. In a similar sense, Julia Ipgrave's work on pupil-to-pupil dialogue

Diagnosing Indifference—An Historical Analysis 19

(2001), whilst exciting and innovative, does not engage in any depth with the positionality or context of its authors or researchers.

We can thus conclude that little if any of the discussion surrounding an official account of RE from the time of Smart onwards expresses a commitment to critical reflexivity *vis-à-vis* the practices that inform its analysis and understanding as a practice *in itself*. Even in discussions about whether its subject matter should be primarily informed by philosophical or anthropological approaches—such as in the debates staged between Andrew Wright and Robert Jackson (Jackson, 2008; Wright, 2008)—they do not extend to the idea that anthropological approaches might inform or even be constitutive of RE practices as such, with students becoming experimenters rather than seeking out evidences for preconceived projects or theories. Thus, on the anthropological side of the debate, as argued by Jackson, it is empirical work *previously conducted by others* (and adults at that) that is the primary focus of concern. What this suggests is that there is a common, shared assumption that inquirers in RE settings are primarily engaging with texts, rather than being inducted into practices that are concerned with producing knowledge as such or, as Stengers (1997) describes it, themselves 'mapping into knowledge'.

We return to the possibility that one reason for this is a continuing disconnection between school education and the academy. It would appear that the ethos presently supporting RE is more oriented to policy requirements than theory and practice driven. In terms of resources for thinking through the issue of what is good for us and our students and why we are doing this in schools or universities, there are more silences than informed discussions between practitioners and university academics and scholars of religion about rationale. The position taken here is that universities are, or should be, fundamental to what is taught in schools and perhaps particularly in relation to their role in complexifying knowledge (Williams, 23 April 2016). What we want to do, then, is to invite people to engage more fully in questions of meaning and purpose, multiplying the range of theories and perspectives in thinking educationally about the subject in order to open up new and fruitful pathways.

(iii) The Business Case?

If Smart mapped out the ground for RE at Lancaster University in the 1960s and 70s, the account of RE he produced, whilst it still determines key categories and provides markers for certain unchallenged assumptions, has in other ways been eroded over time and replaced in part by another (Bloomer, 1997; I'Anson and Jasper, 2006). This newer prescribed account is characterised, not by the attentive exploration of difference/s or even by a preoccupation with texts, but by increasing conformity to standards that focus on clarity and self-identity (Law, 1999, 10). As already noted, there is an irony in the fact that elements of Smart's work on RE have suited the aims of this

20 Diagnostic

superseding account very well. As that account fosters measurable forms of exchangeable and assessable knowledge, the understanding of 'religious dimensions' (Smart, 1969) has been widely taken up to satisfy this requirement. These are patterns that continue to underpin most books published on the general topic of 'religion' and RE textbooks to this day. The preoccupation with measurability and the commodification of knowledge/s has become a more or less standard characteristic of educational and indeed of policy structures more broadly, and schools, universities and educational research have been typically required to conform to a view of education as a means to quantifiable outcomes. This approach goes hand in hand with one form of corporatisation of education: establishing students and other stakeholders including government agencies as potential or actual customers within forms of capitalist exchange (Collini, 2012; Brown and Carasso, 2013; Mcgettigan, 2013). Current research into education is now typically shaped by national governments in partnership with private sector practices and needs (Brooks *et al.*, 2012, 10). This leads to there being less funding available for the kind of research that engages with social and cultural diversity for the sake, for example, of knowing well and knowing differently (Law, 2004; Lather, 2010; I'Anson and Jasper, 2011; Marten, 2013). In Marten's words (2013, 213) this is characterised by knowing in the sense of

> ... understanding the diversity and confusion that manifest [themselves] to us once we encounter Other worldviews, directing us towards knowing what we are seeing in a different way.

Arguably more scientistic—that is, more concerned with measurement than with posing questions—than scientific (Lather, 2007, 2), this approach has the potential to eradicate anything that fails to conform to the official rationale and to serve the agenda of those who, in policy terms, seek to minimise challenging differences.

Against this trend, social scientist and feminist theorist Patti Lather strongly advocates the value of 'getting lost' or of engaging in 'messiness' as important alternative pathways towards new knowledge/s. For instance, undertaking research with women living with HIV/AIDS (Lather and Smithies, 1997), instead of focusing on eradicating the problem as understood from her own perspective, Lather tried to take the women's experiences seriously on their own terms. In this context, it was empathy with the women's sense of powerlessness that was, for Lather, the most important element of the research. In her view, we need 'to learn about getting lost in terms of what it means to not be in control and to try to figure out a life, given that' (Lather, 2007, vii). Acknowledging and exploring the complex roots of powerlessness was thus just as significant an outcome of the research as re-inscribing normative values and privileges by simply jumping in and establishing a solution from the hegemonic perspective.

Diagnosing Indifference—An Historical Analysis 21

Educational theorist Gert Biesta (2009, 33) also criticises current educational process and strategy for its uncritical preoccupation with measureable outcomes that address issues of funding but fail to give due consideration to what we might desire in educational terms (2009, 43–44):

> I have tried to make a case for the need to reconnect with the question of purpose in education. I have shown that we now live in an age in which discussions about education are dominated by measurement and comparisons of educational outcomes and that these measurements as such seem to direct much of educational policy and, through this, also much of educational practice.

According to Biesta (2009, 43–44), the danger is that we 'end up valuing what is measured rather than that we engage in measurement of what we value'. It is a concern with what 'good' education consists of, rather than a limited and limiting concern with effectiveness within these terms, that needs to be seen as the focus of a distinctively *educational* enquiry.

(iv) The Definition of Religion

Something also needs to be said from the beginning about the term 'religion' that has in recent years become the focus of intense debate (McCutcheon, 1997; Fitzgerald, 2007; Stack *et al.*, 2015). As authors, we acknowledge a strong impetus not to use the term at all because the essentialising tendencies of what Fitzgerald has called this 'power category' act reductively and contentiously to link and exclude (Fitzgerald, 2007; 2011; 2015) according to a variety of interests and agenda that are largely invisible and may be highly suspect. Trevor Stack elegantly summarises complex debates about the history of the term (Stack *et al.*, 2015, 1–4) in the introduction to an edited collection on the category of religion, suggesting in broad terms that as governments everywhere have developed their range and power, the classifications of institutions, practices and persons as 'religious' or 'non religious' has been part of that expansion of sovereignty or 'power to authorise' (4). In other words, by delineating a binary between 'religion' and 'the secular' or 'religion' and 'politics', governments have thus not so much described an area or body of knowledge as mobilised the dynamics of power in terms of ideologically inflected inclusions/exclusions.

In this book, we do still use the term 'religion'. Our somewhat sparing and critical use of the term reflects the fact that it continues to be widely used in daily language and, of course, in RE. Within this RE context, 'faith' and 'beliefs' and 'religion' often also function as interchangeable synonyms for a huge range of disparate human experiences (Tweed, 2006). There is, then, arguably, considerable scope here for ambivalence relating to the fundamental term or terms of this debate, although this aspect of the subject has

22 *Diagnostic*

seemingly only become more visible to practitioners and theorists within the field more recently. Drivers for this theoretical and analytical challenge are, once again, the changes that have taken place within the academy over the last half century towards a more relational and contextual analysis and, subsequent to Smart's work, the growth of post-colonial and subaltern analysis, drawing attention to the ways in which the term 'religion' itself arguably belongs to a predominantly Western, heterocisnormative governance or sovereignty (Fitzgerald, 2007; Stack *et al.*, 2015). On the one hand, this debate might support the views of those who object to the subject being within the curriculum at all; 'religion' and its synonyms represent a power category upholding Western neoliberal structures and therefore have nothing to do with education. On the other hand, the words remain in circulation, producing effects; far from innocent, 'religion' and its synonyms are freighted with variable connotations. Yet, rather than attempt to remove this altogether, we argue that it is better continually and critically to assess the terms when they arise and perhaps in the longer term, even to examine whether and how they could be reused.

(v) Conclusion

In conclusion, this approach to the historical context of the dominant framing of RE is intended to identify significant directions of travel and to indicate how more recent developments within the academy interrupt and challenge some of its ruling lexicon—for example, that of text or literacy. These terms are still stuck within a modernist tradition of Western, heteronormative understandings of knowledge, playing a particular role within the wider liberal economy. Whilst acknowledging the pragmatic concerns of practitioners and policy makers, our job, as we see it, is not to fit the subject to the framework but to raise critical questions. Our fundamental concern might be conceived as work that *fissures* stable strata (Winquist, 2003). Reading texts from howsoever many different 'religious' contexts will have no overall effect on our capacity to negotiate in a complex world if we continue to ignore, for example, the fact that textuality and text-based forms of analysis are not fundamental to all people at all historical points. Even given the text-based Western traditions (Certeau, 1984) underpinning Christianity, Judaism and Islam, there is always more than text at play.[2]

To sum up: Ninian Smart took advantage of a move observable in the 1960s and 70s away from the older confessional or narrowly moral certainties that had characterised 'Religious Instruction' or 'Scripture' in the early years that followed after the first Education Acts of 1944 and 45 were passed. The approach (at school and higher education levels) to which he contributed was in tune with a rhetoric of openness to difference/s, yet demonstrably still aligned with privileged ontologies—expressed in normative, Western and masculinist discourses—that are still widely believed to be neutral. In other words, what is key here is that this dominant approach—still detectable in

Diagnosing Indifference—An Historical Analysis 23

what we have described as the official account of RE—remains intellectually aligned within some quite rigid categorisations—for example, in relation to the familiar Western notions of 'religion' and 'beliefs'. In the academy, things have changed. There has been movement—mediated through a diffusion of broadly post-structuralist approaches—towards the recognition of much more relational ontologies whereby what is crucial is acknowledgement of context and the significance of the web of relations that any specific context entails (Irigaray, 2004; Wildman, 2010), and this has shifted understanding from a basis in essentialised approaches towards contextualised knowledge practices. Yet, at the same time, schools, universities and educational research more generally have been required increasingly to conform to structures whereby education is seen as a means to achieving strictly measurable economic or socio-economic benefits with students and stakeholders often configured as a type of customer.

The contradictions between these forces—and between substantive and relational ontologies that underpin such competing orientations—have clearly now led to a crisis of plausibility (Berger, 1971)[3] in relation to the official account of RE; a fundamental failure on the part of policy makers particularly, but perhaps also on the part of academics and practitioners, to think through the complex implications of these newer relational ontologies. And this, arguably, is exemplified in the evident disconnections between how RE is viewed and understood at school level and the many forms of critical theology and religion at higher education levels (I'Anson, 2004; I'Anson and Jasper, 2011).

Another way to describe the situation is to say that the official settlement is densely striated (Deleuze and Guattari, 1987), that is to say, hierarchical and horizontal relationships are indicated by the arrangements of objects, bodies, movements, costs, spaces, boundaries and immobilities that construct the field of RE. A multiplicity of external influences also produces restricted grid-like structures that impinge on the space, reducing movement even further. For example, the educational 'Ur texts' produced by, *inter alia*—NASACRE (National Association of Standing Advisory Councils on RE), SACRE (Standing Advisory Council on RE), Ofsted (Office for Standards in Education), SQA (Scottish Qualifications Authority), National Curriculum (England and Wales), *Curriculum for Excellence* (Scotland) and others—align what happens within the classroom to other privileged agenda having to do with a wide range of pastoral, disciplinary and legal (Hunter, 1994; 1996) regulations concerned with planning, academic disciplinary, benchmarking and quality assurance issues. These striated spaces become a bottleneck whose purpose is seemingly, like any other social sorting mechanisms, to achieve a certain range of controllable subjects and a more or less docile social body through a 'strict regiment of disciplinary acts' (Foucault, 1975). In a contemporary British context, we could say that these disciplinary acts drive us all towards notions of subjectivity that tend to be individualistic, rational, predominantly masculinist, disembodied and, as has

24 *Diagnostic*

been said already, aligned with forms of neoliberalism that together package RE as a more or less commodifiable and purely voluntary form of diversity within very closely demarcated limits.

In further chapters, we will embark on some new thinking that proposes, for example, more robustly educational as distinct from ideological or neoliberal justifications for maintaining space for a discussion and engagement with 'religion' in the curriculum. We will explore the possibility of RE as a space for critical attentiveness to challenging difference/s and a response to what Biesta (2009) has termed 'learnification', defined precisely as a resistance to the relational element in the educator/student relationship. We hope this will help keep challenging the assumption that we can encounter knowledge in purely 'neutral' terms. This will necessitate some acknowledgement of the ways in which engaging with cultural differences will lead to, and call forth, changes to our own characteristic ways of carrying on. Finally, in future chapters, we will also begin to argue that we need to engage urgently with the question of what is educationally desirable to broaden the understanding of socialisation and to consider the implications for present-day cultural horizons.

Notes

1. In UK TRS, subject benchmarks are drawn up by the Quality Assurance Agency detailing an agreed syllabus, but the terms of these benchmarks are advisory rather than prescriptive. Available from www.qaa.ac.uk/en/Publications/Documents/Subject-benchmark-statement-theology-and-religious-studies.pdf.
2. Our understanding of 'reading' in this book should be taken as generally inclusive of traditional textual associations but also sometimes gestures towards multimodal understandings of text and sense-making, especially in relation to ethnographic practices.
3. The notion of plausibility crisis is especially associated with the work of Peter Berger in the sociology of religion. According to Berger, when the legitimations that support a plausibility come under strain, a crisis in plausibility is likely to follow. In devising this understanding, Berger drew upon the sociology of knowledge associated with the Hungarian-born sociologist, Karl Mannheim.

Bibliography

Alderson, R., 29 February 2016. 'Humanists call for end to religious influence in school'. BBC News Scotland. Available from www.bbc.co.uk/news/uk-scotland-35674059.

Anderson, P.S., 1998. *A Feminist Philosophy of Religion: The Rationality and Myths of Religious Belief*. Oxford: Blackwells.

Barnes, L.P., 2000. 'Ninian Smart and the phenomenological approach to religious education'. *Religion*, vol. 30, no. 4, pp. 315–332.

Berger, P.L., 1971. *A Rumour of Angels: Modern Society and the Rediscovery of the Supernatural*. Harmondsworth: Penguin.

Biesta, G., 2 December 2009. 'Good education in an age of measurement: On the need to reconnect with the question of purpose in education'. *Educational Assessment, Evaluation and Accountability*, vol. 21, pp. 33–46.

Diagnosing Indifference—An Historical Analysis 25

Bloomer, M., 1997. *Curriculum Making in Post-16 Education: The Social Conditions of Studentship*. London: Routledge.

Brooks, R., Fuller, A. and Waters, J., 2012. *Changing Spaces of Education: New Perspectives on the Nature of Learning*. London and New York: Routledge.

Brown, A. and Woodhead, L., 2016. *That Was the Church That Was: How the Church of England Lost the English People*. London: Bloomsbury.

Brown, C.G., 2000, 2009. *The Death of Christian Britain: Understanding Secularisation 1800–200*. London and New York: Routledge.

Brown, R. and Carasso, H., 2013. *Everything for Sale?: The Marketisation of UK Higher Education (Research in Higher Education)*. London and New York: Routledge.

Bruce, S., 2002. *God Is Dead: Seculaization in the West (Religion in the Modern World)*. Malden, MA, Oxford and Carlton, Victoria: Blackwell Publishing Ltd.

Butler, J., 1990, 1999. *Gender Trouble: Feminism and the Subversion of Identity*. London and New York: Routledge.

Butler, J., 2004. *Undoing Gender*. New York and London: Routledge.

Certeau, M.de, 1984. *The Practice of Everyday Life*. Berkeley, Los Angeles and London: University of California Press.

Church of England, 2 February 2006. 'The importance of religious education: Joint statement'. The Church of England Media Centre. Available from www.church ofengland.org/media-centre/news/2006/02/pr2106b.aspx.

Collini, S., 2012. *What are Universities For?* London and New York: Penguin Books.

Conroy, J.C., Lundie, D., Davis, R.A., Baumfield, V., Barnes, L.P., Gallagher, T., Lowden, K., Bourque, N. and Wenell, K., 2013. *Does RE Work? A Multi-dimensional Investigation*. London: Bloomsbury.

Crenshaw, K., 1991. 'Mapping the margins: Intersectionality, identity politics and violence against women of color'. *Stanford Law Review*, vol. 43, pp. 1241–1279.

Cunningham, A., 2001. 'Obituary for Ninian Smart'. *Religion*, vol. 31, pp. 325–326.

Dawkins, R., 2006. *The God Delusion*. 2007 ed. London: Black Swan (Transworld Publishers).

Deleuze, G. and Guattari, F., Les Editions de Minuit, Paris, 1987. *A Thousand Plateaus: Capitalism and Schizophrenia*. 1988 ed. London and New York: Continuum.

Dennett, D.C., 2007. *Breaking the Spell: Religion as a Natural Phenomenon*. London: Penguin.

Essex Standing Advisory Council on Religious Education (SACRE), 2013. *Guidance on Collective Worship in Schools*. Essex: Essex County Council.

Fitzgerald, T., 2007. *Religion and the Secular: Historical and Colonial Formations*. London and Oakville, CT: Equinox.

Fitzgerald, T., 2011. *Religion and Politics in International Relations: The Modern Myth*. New York: Continuum.

Fitzgerald, T., 2015. 'Critical religion and critical research on religion: Religion and politics as modern fictions'. *Critical Research on Religion*, vol. 3, no. 3, pp. 303–319.

Foucault, M., 1975. *Discipline and Punish: The Birth of the Prison*. 1995 ed. London and New York: Vintage Books and Gallimard, Paris.

Foucault, M., 1986. *The Care of the Self: The History of Sexuality 3*. New York: Pantheon Books.

Grimmitt, M., 1987. *Religious Education and Human Development*. McCrimmon Publishing Co. Ltd.

26 Diagnostic

Grimmitt, M., 2000. 'Contemporary pedagogies of religious education: What are they?'. In: M. Grimmitt ed., *Pedagogies of Religious Education*. Great Wakering: McCrimmon Publishing Co. Ltd, pp. 24–52.

Grimmitt, M., 2010. 'Living in an era of globalised and politicised reiigion: What is to be religious education's response?'. In: M. Grimmitt ed., *Religious Education and Social and Community Cohesion: An Exploration of Challenges and Opportunities*. Great Wakering, Essex: McCrimmons, pp. 8–25.

Harding, S., 2004. *The Feminist Standpoint Theory Reader: Intellectual and Political Controversies*. London and New York: Routledge.

Hartsock, N.C.M., 1998. *The Feminist Standpoint Revisited and Other Essays*. Boulder, CO and Oxford: Westview Press.

Hitchens, C., 2007. *God Is Not Great: How Religion Poisons Everything*. New York: Warner Twelve.

Houtman, D. and Aupers, S., 2008. 'The spiritual revolution and the New Age gender puzzle: The sacralization of the self in late modernity (1980–2000)'. In: K. Aune, S. Sharma and G. Vincett eds., *Women and Religion in the West: Challenging Secularization*. Aldershot and Burlington, VT: Ashgate, pp. 99–118.

Hunter, I., 1994. *Rethinking the School: Subjectivity, Bureaucracy, Criticism*. St Leonards, NSW: Allen and Unwin pty Ltd.

Hunter, I., 1996. 'Assembling the school'. In: A. Barry, T. Osbourne and N.S. Rose eds., *Foucault and Political Reason: Liberalism, Neo-liberalism and Rationalities of Government*. Chicago and London: University of Chicago and London: UCL, pp. 143–166.

I'Anson, J., 2004. 'Mapping the subject: Student teachers, location and the understanding of religion'. *British Journal of Religious Studies*, vol. 26, no. 1, pp. 41–56.

I'Anson, J. and Jasper, A., 2006. 'New lines of flight: Negotiating religions and cultures in gendered educational spaces'. *Discourse: Learning and Teaching in Philosophical and Religious Studies*, vol. 5, no. 2, pp. 75–98.

I'Anson, J. and Jasper, A., 2011. '"Religion" in educational spaces: Knowing, knowing well, and knowing differently'. *Arts and Humanities in Higher Education*, vol. 10, no. 3, pp. 295–314.

Ipgrave, J., 2001. *Pupil-to-Pupil Dialogue in the Classroom as a Tool for RE: Occasional Papers II*. Warwick: Warwick Religions and Education Research Unit.

Irigaray, L., 2004. *Key Writings*. London and New York: Continuum.

Jackson, R., 1997. *Religious Education: An Interpretive Approach*. London: Hodder Education.

Jackson, R., 2004. *Rethinking Religious Education and Plurality: Issues in Diversity and Pedagogy*. London and New York: RoutledgeFalmer.

Jackson, R. 2006. 'Promoting Religious Tolerance and Non-discrimination in Schools: A European Perspective', *Journal of Religious Education*, 54(3): 30–38.

Jackson, R., 2008. 'Contextual religious education and the interpretive approach'. *British Journal of RE*, vol. 30, no. 1, pp. 13–24.

Jackson, R., 2010. Religious diversity and education for democratic citizenship: The contribution of the council of Europe. In: K. Engebretson, M.d. Souza, G. Durka and L. Gearon eds., *International Handbook of Inter-RE, Volume 4: Religion, Citizenship and Human Rights*. Dordrecht, the Netherlands: Springer Academic Publishers, pp. 1121–1151.

Kristeva, J., 2002. *Revolt, She Said: An Interview by Philippe Petit*. S. Lotringer ed. Los Angeles and New York: Semiotext(e).

Diagnosing Indifference—An Historical Analysis 27

Lather, P., 2007. *Getting Lost: Feminist Efforts Towards a Double(d) Science*. New York: SUNY.

Lather, P., 2010. *Engaging Science: Policy From the Side of the Messy*. New York Washington, DC, Baltimore, Bern, Frankfurt am Main, Berlin, Brussels, Vienna and Oxford: Peter Lang.

Lather, P. and Smithies, C., 1997. *Troubling the Angels: Women Living With HIV/ AIDS*. Boulder, CO: Westview Press.

Latour, B., 2004a. *Politics of Nature: How to Bring the Sciences Into Democracy*. Cambridge, MA: Harvard University Press.

Latour, B., Winter 2004b. Why has critique run out of steam? From matters of fact to matters of concern. *Critical Inquiry*, vol. 30, no. 2, pp. 225–248.

Law, J. 1999. 'After ANT: complexity, naming and topology'. *The Sociological Review*, 47, S1, pp. 1–14.

Law, J., 2004. *After Method: Mess in Social Science Research*. Abingdon, Oxon and New York: Routledge.

Le Dœuff, M., 1980. Editions Payot. *The Philosophical Imaginary, L'Imaginaire Philosophique*. 1989 ed. London and Stanford, CA: Athlone Press and Stanford University Press.

Lloyd, G., 1984. *The Man of Reason: 'Male' and 'Female' in Western Philosophy*. London: Methuen Young Books.

McCutcheon, R.T., 1997. *Manufacturing Religion: The Discourse on Sui Generis Religion and the Politics of Nostalgia*. Oxford and New York: Oxford University Press.

McGettigan, A. 2013. *The Great University Gamble: Money, Markets and the Future of Higher Education*. London: Pluto Press.

McIvor, J., 12 September 2016. 'Humanists' legal challenge to school religious observance'. BBC News. Available from www.bbc.co.uk/news/uk-scotland-37336340.

Marten, M., 2013. 'On knowing, knowing well and knowing differently: Historicising Scottish missions in 19th century and early 20th century Palestine'. In: E. Fleischmann, S. Grypma, M. Marten and I.M. Okkenhaug eds., *Transnational and Historical Perspectives on Global Health, Welfare and Humanitarianism*. Kristiansand, Norway: Portal.

Masefield, P. and Wiebe, D., 1994. *Aspects of Religion: Essays in Honour of Ninian Smart*. New York: Peter Lang.

Paton, G. and Gilligan, A., 2 May 2014. 'Head teachers raise "serious concerns" over Islamic School take-over'. The Telegraph. Available from www.telegraph.co.uk/ education/educationnews/10804289/Head-teachers-raise-serious-concerns-over-Islamic-school-take-over.html.

Richardson, H., 12 November 2015. 'Schools' religious assemblies should be scrapped'. BBC News. Available from www.bbc.co.uk/news/education-34802820.

Schools Council, 1971. *Religious Education in Secondary Schools (Schools Council Working Paper 36)*. London: Methuen Educ. and Evans Bros.

Smart, N., 1957. *The Teacher and Christian Belief*. 1966 ed. London: Clarke.

Smart, N. 1968 *Secular Education and the Logic of Religion*. London: Faber and Faber.

Smart, N., 1969. New York: Charles Scribner's Sons. *The Religious Experience of Mankind*. 1971 ed. Glasgow: Fontana.

Smart, N., 1973a. *The Phenomenon of Religion*. London: Macmillan.

Smart, N., 1973b. *The Science of Religion and the sociology of Knowledge: Some Methodological Questions*. Princeton, NJ: Princeton University Press.

28 Diagnostic

Smart, N., 1983. *World Views: Crosscultural Explorations of Human Beliefs*. 1995 ed. London: Prentice-Hall.

Smart, N. 1989. *The World's Religions: Old Traditions and Modern Transformations*. Cambridge: Cambridge University Press.

Souza, de M., Durka, G., Engebretson, K., Jackson, R. and McGrady, A., 2006. *International Handbook of the Religious, Moral and Spiritual Dimensions in Education (Part One)*. Dordrecht: Springer.

Stack, T., Goldenberg, N. and Fitzgerald, T., 2015. *Religion as a Category of Governance and Sovereignty*. Leiden and Boston: Brill.

Stengers, I., 1997. *Power and Invention: Situating Science*. Minneapolis, MN: University of Minnesota Press.

Tweed, T.A., 2006. *Crossing and Dwelling: A Theory of Religion*. Cambridge, MA and London: Harvard University Press.

Weldon, V., 2 February 2016. 'Landmark report: Influence of religion on Scottish schools increasing'. *The Sunday Herald*. Available from www.heraldscotland.com/news/14308275.Landmark_report__Influence_of_religion_on_Scottish_schools_increasing/?ref=erec.

Wildman, W.J., 2010. 'An introduction to relational ontology'. In: J. Polkinghorne and J. Zizioulas eds., *The Trinity and an Entangled World: Relationality in Physical Science and theology*. Grand Rapids: Eerdmans, pp. 55–73.

Williams, Z., Saturday 23 April 2016. 'Mary Beard: "The role of the academic is to make everything less simple"'. *The Guardian* (Saturday Review). Available from www.theguardian.com/books/2016/apr/23/mary-beard-the-role-of-the-academic-is-to-make-everything-less-simple.

Winquist, C.E., 2003. *The Surface of the Deep*. Aurora, CO: The Davies Group.

Wright, A., 2004. *Religion, Education and Post-modernity*. London: RoutledgeFalmer.

Wright, A., 2006. 'Critical realism as a tool for the interpretation of cultural diversity in liberal religious education'. In: M. de Souza, G. Durka, K. Engebretson, R. Jackson and A. Mcgrady eds., *International Handbook of the Religious, Moral and Spritiual Dimension in Education (Part One)*. Dordrecht: Springer, pp. 333–348.

Wright, A., 2008. 'Contextual religious education and the actuality of religions'. *British Journal of RE*, vol. 30, no. 1, pp. 3–12.

Wright, A., 2016. *Religious Education and Critical Realism: Knowledge, Reality and Religious Literacy*. Abingdon, Oxford and New York: Routledge.

Wynne-Jones, J., 25 April 2009. 'Atheists target UK schools'. Available from www.telegraph.co.uk/education/educationnews/5219687/Atheists-target-UK-schools.html.

2 Assembling RE—Spaces, Relations and Translations

Having, in Chapter one, outlined a genealogy of contemporary practice in RE that is primarily concerned with the ways in which theory and practice have been assembled *through* time, this chapter offers a spatial analysis of practice *across* time so as to highlight some of the key dynamics and assumptions that inform present-day practice. The joint aim of these chapters is to offer a diagnosis of what we refer to as the contemporary plausibility crisis in RE, which we describe as one of indifference.

Through offering an analysis that focuses upon the relations between the different ideas, concepts and tropes (such as metaphors) that together make up the present understanding of RE, this chapter aims to foreground how RE is discursively positioned—and in turn positions its would-be students—as an educational subject area. We will explore how these concepts and tropes draw upon a distinctive understanding of space insofar as the way they are related and the way that the student is positioned in relation to them (as variously near, above, alongside, far etc.) implies a particular spatial configuration. We argue that these spatial constructions have had, and continue to have, far-reaching implications for the kinds of relations, practices and knowledges that are valued as educational. Such an analysis provides further insight into the ways that current framings became settled and some of the possible reasons for this.

These points are illustrated through a case study based upon a recent examination paper that draws out how the trope of neutrality (and associated assumptions regarding knowledge) inflects current thinking about the educational purpose of RE.

Once the trope of neutrality—for a long time, a key catch-word, separating the new dispensation RE from its former 'confessional' guise—is regarded as no longer plausible, either as a point of departure or as the means through which knowledge is gathered and organised—it becomes necessary to inquire into the kinds of philosophical framings and assumptions that are brought to this form of inquiry. This framing will have far-reaching implications as regards *what* is attended to, *how* inquiry follows on from this and *why* this might conceivably count as an appropriate educational response within these terms.

30 *Diagnostic*

(i) Introduction

This chapter is concerned with outlining the 'explicative order' of RE, or, to put this another way, with attempting to map the diverse practices, translations, assumptions and orientations that routinely inform its practices of sense-making. The chapter begins by outlining some of the ways in which the official account of RE, through its appeal to the trope of neutrality, draws upon a particular spatial imaginary that both legitimates its positioning *vis-à-vis* other possible ways of going on, whilst also informing the kinds of practices that are deemed appropriate and inappropriate to this. The current settlement, we argue, privileges the production of *distance* as a theoretical goal, appropriate to a would-be scientific practice that tries to avoid difficulties associated with confessional approaches, which can be seen as privileging 'insider' perspectives that are too closely aligned with a particular point of view. We then explore some of the consequences of the orientation to sense-making taken up in this dominant approach to RE, before calling into question whether such an account affords an educationally significant engagement with 'religion', defined here as an educational matter of concern.

In terms of our diagnosis of the present crisis in relation to what we have defined as indifference, our argument is twofold. Firstly, we argue that although in terms of the legitimation of knowledge, the present settlement achieved its purpose (insofar as it produced an approach to RE that could be included within 'secular' educational contexts), this was at the expense of the *non-affectingness* of the objects of inquiry/matters of concern. Put another way, the price for inclusion within a 'secular' curricular framework is that the approach to studying 'religion' neither makes a claim upon students, nor does it make a difference to their lives. In short, we contend that the present settlement in RE is *insufficiently educational* since education necessarily implies the possibility of a subject open to change and becoming (Masschelein, 2010a, b). Secondly, we argue that theoretical developments within the academy during the past 40 years have moved beyond the framings that inform the present settlement and that, in the light of these, it is necessary to re-think RE as an educational matter of concern. We argue that since the time of RE's current inauguration in the 1970s, there have been a series of theoretical re-orientations within the academy, coupled with cultural and policy shifts (Strhan, 2015) that have created a crisis of plausibility in regards to the taken-for-granted framings and knowledge practices associated with making sense of 'religion'.

(ii) Religion and Education?

When it was first introduced, the present RE settlement engaged the questions 'what is religion?' and 'what form might its analysis take?' (e.g., Schools Council, 1971).[1] However, of much lesser import within this account is the

Assembling RE—Spaces, Relations and Translations 31

question as to 'what is education?' and the difference that thinking through this question might make. Raising *both* the question of 'religion' and that of 'education', we contend, leads to a questioning of the ways in which the intersection between 'religion' and 'education' has been conceived and, as a consequence, how this might be choreographed in future. In this chapter, we consider the implications of trying to take seriously *both* questions, i.e., in what practices RE consist *and* what the educational implications of this study are. Such a framing enables us to move beyond the limitations in regarding education as simply a negative constraint—as with, for example, the assumption that this amounts simply to avoiding approaches that involve some form of confessionalism—and, instead, work toward offering a more positive rationale for what an educational approach might consist in.

The present default approach to RE within educational contexts is centred around the question 'what is religion?', to which various 'dimensions' and definitions are typically proposed in response (Flood, 2012). Insofar as such accounts aim to demarcate an 'object' of concern in a definite and stable form, these tend towards a substantive ontology where such a focus can be clearly identified—such as a ritual, belief or rite of passage (Wildman, 2010). If we turn to some of the foundational texts (such as the Schools Council, 1971, and Smart, 1968), it is presumed that 'religion' can be identified through the specification of clear contents and that the account offered is educational *on account of its neutrality*. Here, a plane of sense-making is constructed that does not presume a committed standpoint; indeed, it explicitly eschews such a confessionalism as being educationally inappropriate. Within these terms, RE, under the sign of neutrality, is presented in a manner that presumes that it will not affect—or have consequences for—the student engaged in its study. To this extent, a 'neutral' framing, where particular commitments are set aside, is assumed, *ipso facto*, to be educational. What is rather surprising, however, is that *questions concerning the nature and purposes of education* have very little presence in this discussion, with education functioning largely as a negative constraint (simply ruling out framings and assumptions), rather than issuing in more positive trajectories. To be properly educational, within these terms, is for students to make sense in ways that both leave behind their own set of concerns and identifications and which avoid the possibility of any change in these concerns and identifications being elicited through such study.

It is also noteworthy in this connection that the very term 'RE' does not initially promote a questioning approach or enquiry into the forms that 'Religious' and 'Education' might take in relation to one another; the two placeholders are simply juxtaposed together without comment or further ado. There is, in other words, no discussion of the relationship between the 'R' and the 'E' in RE: hence the insertion of a preposition that relates the two, such as religion *with* education, or a conjunctive, such as religion *and* education, might invite a questioning as to *how* precisely the two terms 'religion' and 'education' are, or might be, related in practice and whether there

32 Diagnostic

might be some affinities and tensions between the two discourses. Were the question of the relation between 'religion and 'education' to arise—by means of the addition of a preposition or conjunctive that would mark some kind of relation between the two—a problematic might then arise as to *how* each side is connected. This would, in turn, not only enable questions to arise as to what form such a juxtaposition or amalgamation *might* take, but also, in the light of this, how each term in that relationship is changed or modified by its other. So what might be the implications of acknowledging these relations and of taking an approach that might, instead, foreground the ongoing, unsettled nature of their unfolding in partnership?

Michel Serres (Serres and MacArthur, 1995, 47) observes that whilst religion is typically linked to its Latin root *religare*, meaning 'to attach' (with this derivation leading to the popular view of religion as associated with 'binding', or constraint), there is another derivation, via Seneca, in which the term religion translates as 're-reading'. This derivation, which Serres regards as the more plausible, might suggest some affinity between the discourses of 'religion' and 'education' insofar as education (*ēducēre*) is concerned with 'leading out' (Masschelein, 2006; 2010a, b) and religion with an ongoing 're-reading' that is a consequence of this movement into the new. Such an etymology might indicate, from the outset, that 'education' and 'religion' could, in broad terms at least, be seen as complementary activities, with the exploratory and open-ended orientation of the former being complemented by the necessity to constantly re-appraise and re-articulate, in the latter. Furthermore, it is noteworthy that such a way of conceiving their relationship has close affinities with strands of thinking within more recent feminist philosophies that point to the significance of natality, with the birth and arrival of the new, over a concern with that which has already arrived or been achieved (e.g., Arendt, 1958; Jantzen, 1998; Irigaray, 2004; Jasper, 2012).[2] These productive links are picked up in more detail in Part Two, where we entertain different ways of thinking and practising that draw upon alternative philosophical traditions and imaginaries from those currently assumed. Having raised the question of the relationship between 'religion' and 'education', we now consider how the inter-relation of 'religion' and its study within 'education' has been conceived to date. In particular, we explore how the spaces of their interaction have been imagined and the implications of this for both theory and practice.

(iii) RE and the Spatialities of Knowledge Production

One starting point for considering how the discourses of 'religion and 'education' have been related in practice is to draw upon writings that focus upon the spaces of their intersection. Rather than focusing—as in Chapter one—upon analysis through time (a diachronic analysis), spatiality studies are primarily concerned with thinking across time (a synchronic analysis) so as to focus upon relations that obtain within a given assemblage of ideas,

Assembling RE—Spaces, Relations and Translations 33

people and things. The 'spatial turn', as it has become known, is a widely influential movement of ideas that has had a significant impact upon the academy, within multiple disciplines, perhaps most especially within geography. A key point of departure for this work was Lefebvre's (1974) *La production de l'espace* (first translated into English in 1991) that drew together thinking about the social, mental and physical conceptions of space (Knott, 2005). A broad range of theorists has contributed to this movement, with notable contributions from Foucault (1986; 1991), Harvey (1990; 1993), Massey (1994; 2005) and Soja (1996), to name but a few.

It is noteworthy that the spatial dimensions in regard to religious thematics have had particular prominence within this movement, with the writings of Certeau (1984; 1986) especially, but also theorists such as Bhabha (1994) and Spivak (1994), in their studies on the politics of location and marginality, also having direct links with a number of key RE issues. More recently, there have been some very productive links made between spatiality and the discourse of religion in the works of Knott (2005) and Tweed (2006), for example. Within educational thinking and practice, too, spatiality has exerted a significant impact on the kinds of analysis undertaken, with the identification of spatial, relational and socio-material dynamics becoming increasingly acknowledged (Edwards and Usher, 2000; Paechter and Edwards, 2001; Reeves, 2010; Reeves and I'Anson, 2014).

Closely linked with this spatial turn, the work that metaphors do within discourse has become foregrounded, both within multiple practices of everyday life (Lakoff and Johnson, 1981; 1999; 2003) and within the study of religious discourse, whether this is characterised as theology, RS or RE (Knott, 2005; Tweed, 2006). Here, it is recognised that metaphors do significant work in terms of associating ideas, valuing one thing over another and with orienting people within a given space. Thus, within education, for example, metaphorical tropes such as 'higher' level study, an attainment 'gap' and a 'spiral' curriculum routinely inform educational framings with significant consequences for practice (Paechter and Edwards, 2001; Paechter, 2004). It is therefore vital that the work that these metaphors do in constructing sense and in drawing attention to some facets of relations but not others is attended to in a critical manner. To take an example, one of the metaphors frequently used in relation to teaching is that of 'teaching as a craft'; such a metaphor draws attention to the long practice that is necessary to become proficient and references also the scene of educational formation that the teacher exercises over his or her students, that might have some equivalences with the ways in which a potter moulds the clay that will subsequently take on an independent form etc. However, in drawing attention to *these* dimensions of teaching, the craft metaphor may also fail to acknowledge or value other crucial differences—such as, for example, the social contingency that characterises pedagogical practice, which is different to the material contingencies present in the potter's relation to clay. Hence, the use of the craft metaphor within educational sites as a description of pedagogical practices

34 *Diagnostic*

needs to be used with caution; otherwise, significant aspects will be down-played or rendered invisible (Cope and I'Anson, 2003).

The way in which a particular gathering of people, ideas, materials and practices is conceived has sometimes been referred to as constituting a partic-ular 'plane' of sense-making (e.g., Abell and Lederman, 2007). Such a plane of sense-making will differ quite markedly depending on the kinds of relations that are in play and will have far-reaching effects in terms of what is fore-grounded—as a matter of concern—and, by the same token, what is rendered marginal or indeed invisible as regards lines of inquiry that can be legitimately pursued. Of course, to frame this in terms of a plane of sense-making is at once to draw upon a spatial image that orientates attention to the geographies of knowledge production. We have already seen (above, Chapter One) that there is a spatial dimension to the positioning of RE between, on the one hand, 'confessional approaches' and, on the other, approaches that explain or inter-pret 'religion' within their own discursive terms, whether this be psychology or sociology, for example (e.g., Stausberg, 2009; Dressler and Mandair, 2011; Pals, 2014). These are sometimes described in the literature (especially by advocates of methodological neutrality) as 'reductionistic' or 'extra-religious approaches' (e.g., Smart, 1973a,b), but the spatial implications of this way of conceiving subject identity extend much further in practice.

The approach taken to RE in schools by Ninian Smart was aligned with that promoted in regard to the new field of 'Religious Studies' that he had worked upon within the university sector (Smart, 1972). That is to say, it was positioned between, on the one hand, 'insider' accounts, such as the-ology and 'outsider' accounts, such as those offered by psychology and sociology, on the other. To this extent, the approach to RE has, since the time of Smart, framed making sense of 'religion' as a matter of concern in educational contexts, within spatial terms. More specifically, given the putative risks associated with religious discourse—with fears of conversion and recruitment to particular outlooks always haunting its presence in the classroom—a *spatial solution* was proposed through the establishment of a clearly demarcated *middle ground* for RS (see Figure 2.1).

The new approach to the study of religion, with its distinctive framing and methodology, was rhetorically positioned as an autonomous field of inquiry that was separate from what had gone before. As such, this new dispen-sation was neither informed by an 'insider's' closeness that would seek to align would-be inquirers within a particular tradition's epistemic commit-ments, seen as characteristic of theological approaches (the first column in Figure 2.1); nor, on the other hand, was this subject to 'outsider'/'reduction-istic' approaches (the third column in Figure 2.1). Under the 'reductionistic/extra-religious' heading, disciplines such as sociology and psychology were grouped together—where a translation of distinctively religious terms into another discipline's vocabulary was effected; from the standpoint of 'meth-odological neutrality' (the second column in Figure 2.1), this was regarded as thereby 'explaining away' the distinctiveness of religious discourse as such.

Assembling RE—Spaces, Relations and Translations   35

1. Confessional Approaches:	2. Methodological Neutrality:	3. Reductionistic/'Extra-Religious' Approaches:
The student is positioned as aligned/identified with the subject matter. To this extent (as viewed from a non-aligned standpoint), the inquirer is too close to the knowledge claims and a particular framing is assumed. This is regarded as educationally inappropriate since in a pluralistic society, no such committed perspective can be assumed of all. Furthermore, other religious traditions are translated within the terms of this particular standpoint.	A variety of strategies (such as the practice of 'bracketing' truth claims, where the aim is to leave behind personal identifications) position the student at a distance from the objects of inquiry. This produces a detachment that renders the process of inquiry sufficiently objective and appropriate to a pluralistic educational context. The 'new' approach is thus positioned between the two rival approaches and, as such, is to be preferred to either alternative.	Such approaches explain 'religious' aspects within other terms. Thus, 'religious' aspects are translated into (e.g.) sociological or psychological discourse. Here, the discourse of 'religion' is subsumed within another discourse with its own terminology and explanations. The case against such approaches is that they effectively do away with distinctively religious determinants and ontologies and the logics that inform particular religious discourses.

Figure 2.1 Methodological neutrality positioned between competing alternatives.

As Smart (1973a 36) himself put this, '[t]he existence of internal structural explanations, as well as dialectical ones, seems to show that a simple reductionism is ruled out'. It was argued, therefore, that under the sign of neutrality a third or middle way situated between the two alternatives of confessionalism and reductionism was conceivable and that this offered precisely the kind of interpretative space necessary to do justice to such 'intra-religious' logics (Heelas, 1978). Indeed, such was the simplicity and persuasiveness of this spatial delineation of different approaches to making sense of religion that henceforth it became necessary to construct and understand religious imaginaries within these logics. Through positioning the new approach spatially between its two rivals, a new disciplinary space was manufactured that effectively demarcated, delimited and thus defined its own legitimacy and procedures, in contrast with these rival approaches (McCutcheon, 1997).

   In this connection, it is noteworthy that Smart's intention was to constitute a *science* of religious understanding, as is made clear in the title: *The Science of Religion and the sociology of Knowledge* (1973a). This brings with it a set of assumptions both as to how an 'object' of inquiry is constituted (the strategies through which it is abstracted from the particularities of a situation so as to become a stable focus) and the relation of the subject of inquiry (the knower) to this. The project of constructing a 'science of religion' paralleled the need to construct the subject area as 'objective' and

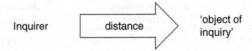

Figure 2.2 The scene of learning: objectification and the creation of distance between observer and observed.

hence as not having an influence upon, or affecting, the would-be student. In other words, once again, this required a *distancing* such that the object of inquiry could be considered in ways that did not presume, nor call forth, the implication of the subject inquiring (see Figure 2.2).

This spatial imaginary creates a necessary *gap* between a student's own commitments and identifications and the focus of their inquiry. The scene of education is therefore regarded as necessarily separate from the actual field of inquiry—which concerns interested participants in some *other* space 'out there'—at a safe enough distance to avoid exerting influence upon students.

According to Doreen Massey (2003, 75), the ideal of objectivity implies 'the possibility of a positionless objectivity'. To the extent that the ideal of neutrality hankers after the construction of such an objectivity as an ideal, the educational scene will involve students being positioned at a distance from their subject of inquiry (Gearon, 2013). Within such a framing, the classroom is necessarily set apart—and at some remove from—the worlds to which its practices of study refer. Re-reading the policy documents that launched the new approach to studying religion in schools (such as *Working Paper 36* (Schools Council, 1971) and *The Millar Report* in Scotland (SED, 1972)) from a perspective that takes seriously the spatial and material dimensions of knowledge production, it is surprising to see that the actual space of the classroom and the relational practices that inform sense-making are completely excluded from its consideration. Through practices such as the bracketing of truth claims (see below), the classroom space is constructed as an ideal knowledge space in which rational knowledge about complex and messy cultural situations is distilled into knowledge that is uncontaminated by affective considerations. To this extent, the classroom scene is conceived in a manner not unlike the position of the angels in Wim Wender's (1987) film *Wings of Desire*, where these beings—quite literally—fly above the conditions of material engagement and the affectivity that is its consequence. In such a scene, the knowledge that is privileged is not one that might emerge from material implication and enactment within these terms, but from a disengaged observation and representation.

(iv) 'Religion': Felicity Conditions

The foregoing analysis also raises the question as to whether the production of such a distance between a student and the focus of their inquiry is appropriate to making sense of 'religion' at all. This is because the kind of

Assembling RE—Spaces, Relations and Translations 37

objectivity produced through the gathering of practices, materials, theories and concepts around the metaphor of neutrality works towards a detachment and abstraction that may run counter to the dynamics in play within a particular religious imaginary. In this connection, Latour's more recent work (2013a) is concerned with articulating how distinct modes of existence have different associated ways of operating, since practice within, for example, scientific and legal modes is empirically found to differ. According to Latour (2013a), 'religion' is a distinct mode and the 'felicity conditions' of engaging religious speech involve the *overcoming of distance* in order to achieve closeness. Indeed, Latour (2013a, 112) goes so far as to state that: 'a religious tale . . . has never sought anything other than to convert the distant into the near'. Insofar as the present orientation in RE directs attention *away* from what is present to some putative 'out there' at some *distance* from the scene of inquiry and from the immediate interests of the inquirer, this may, at least within these terms, amount to a *misdirection* in that it fails to understand the performative requirements for approaching 'religion' conceived as a mode of existence as such. The direction of travel in the official account of RE, according to this line of argument, is precisely the *inverse* of that informing a specifically religious impetus and orientation. Latour (2013a, 46) illustrates this claim through a discussion of the 'utterly humdrum, utterly banal example of the lovers' dialogue', which he regards as emblematic of the kinds of closeness towards which religions work: '. . . you are not looking for access to the far distant but want to get closer to the person you are addressing, and then what you gather will never be information' (Latour, 2013b, 29; cf. Caputo, 2001, for a parallel approach). Consequently, according to Latour (2013b, 28),

> Nothing has made religious speech more inaudible, more unsayable than the ungodly habit of behaving as if it could follow the path of reference, just a bit less neatly, a bit less clearly, a bit less demonstrably [. . .]

Clearly, the current academic study of religion is usually distinguished from the felicity conditions that—in Latour's terms—inform the ongoing dynamics that produce what he regards as 'religious speech as such', and undoing such a separation would no doubt have quite radical consequences for the practice and self-understanding of RE within education. Nevertheless, posing the spatial question of nearness and distance in this way does serve to raise the issue of *how near* or indeed *how far* the would-be student of religion is positioned in relation to their inquiry. Approaching the relation of the student to their inquiry in this way foregrounds ways in which practices such as 'bracketing' severely limit the possibility of a text making some kind of claim upon its interlocutor (i.e., reducing this distance). Bracketing (*epochē*), in this connection, is a practice derived from phenomenology, where the aim is to suspend judgment in relation to the existence of putative realities, whose existence cannot easily be determined or agreed upon. The terms in question are therefore bracketed so that questions other than arguments for

38   *Diagnostic*

and against their existence and characterisation can be considered. As such, the practice of bracketing is a key practice in the construction of a rhetoric of neutrality insofar as the claim is made that all manner of discourse can be given a fair hearing without determining in advance its truth or otherwise. And this, moreover, is a key practice that renders 'religious' subject matter 'safe' for examination within RE classroom and seminar contexts. However, that safety is bought at the cost of creating a distance between the student and the very matters of concern that they study, for this is to *foreclose the possibility of an engaged reading* of a text (considered in the broadest of terms) that might issue in some kind of existential claim upon that reader. Adam Nicolson (2014, 6), for example, after reading Homer at school in Greek and finding little to enthuse him, suddenly encountered the power of the text in translation, as he re-read *The Odyssey* many years later on a sailing trip from Falmouth:

> . . . I suddenly felt that here was the unaffected truth, here was someone speaking about fate and the human condition in ways that other people only seem to approach obliquely; and that directness, that sense of nothing between me and the source, is what gripped me.

And yet, it is precisely the possibility of such an existential claim that for Rowan Williams (2014), in his 2013 Gifford Lectures, constitutes a key religious dynamic. This consists in the reader becoming in some way accountable to the text, rather than the text to the reader. In a context where distance is privileged, priority is accorded to the subject questioning the other, whereas a distinctively *religious* dynamic might imply precisely the reverse dynamic: the subject's interrogation *by the other*.[3] The recourse to bracketing creates a strategic reading where the reader remains in control of the text, rather than such an encounter being the occasion for challenge or indeed, the experience of disconcertment (Law and Lin, 2010; I'Anson and Jasper, 2011). Within such an economy, the possibility of transformation of the subject may be a necessary condition of understanding the other at all—and yet, this is explicitly ruled out at the outset (Latour, 2013a, 17).

As Latour (2015, 36) observes elsewhere:

> No matter how respectful we have all learned to be in our daily encounters with the others' agencies, bracketing all questions of ontology (for perfectly sound scientific reasons at first) has nevertheless failed to enlarge *our own* repertoire of legitimate agencies acting in *our* world. If they remain active, it is only in *theirs*. By bracketing *their* ontological claims, it is in effect *our* ontological claims that have been bracketed as well—or rather deep-frozen.

This failure to enlarge our own repertoire may not only be questionable on religious grounds, but might also be questioned on *educational* grounds, too

Assembling RE—Spaces, Relations and Translations 39

(Conroy *et al.*, 2013, 219ff.). The tactic of bracketing truth claims further distances the inquirer from the possibility of an *educational encounter* with the text and hence the possibility of change. As Santo and Standish (2012, 8) have observed, a minimal understanding of education would appear to involve precisely this possibility of being changed in relation to the texts encountered.

> Education leads not so much upward, toward some kind of ethereal transcendence, as downward and back to the rough ground, with each new step we take, each moment of crisis, affording a new *point d'appui*. And these steps on the way suggest, at each point, a potential turning of our efforts, where the turning of philosophy as education begins to suggest a 'secular version of conversion'—say, transcendentalism without the supernatural.

Reflection upon this 'turning of our efforts' in response to a text's (or a situation's) provocation, begins to draw out some of the implications of engaging with education as such. Furthermore, a closer analysis of what takes place on occasions of actual textual encounter, such as that provided by Judith Butler (2012) in relation to her own reading of Whitehead, begins to problematise many of the assumptions and distinctions that we routinely perform. As Butler (2012, 4) expressed this:

> . . . what I happen to remember is less important than how reading [Whitehead] came to affect me, which is to say, how the text acted upon me even if I was not fully aware of how it acted.

This begins to undo familiar and comfortable subject–object distinctions, as the reader is solicited by—as she in turn works upon—the text in question. At the very least, on such occasions, the distance implied by such distinctions appears to be undone, as is the assurance of mastery. The question of the felicity conditions for engaging with a particular matter of concern and the kinds of practice that are appropriate to this are thus raised with even greater urgency. So there are strong educational reasons, in other words, for questioning any subject rationale, methodology and framing that appears to close down and limit in advance the outcome of a particular encounter or engagement.

(v) Objectivity and Scientific Practice: Mapping Translations

Given that the warrant for creating a distance between subject and text derives at least in part from an appeal to the kinds of objectivity often associated with a perceived ideal of scientific methodology, it might be worth exploring whether, and to what extent, such an understanding actually informs the construction of scientific practice (e.g., Smart, 1973a). In recent

40   *Diagnostic*

years there have been a number of studies that aim to surface the diversity of social and material practices that take place within a range of different organisational contexts. Of particular interest have been studies that set out to articulate the practices, relations and technologies that are gathered under the name of 'science', such as in health care practice. The accounts produced by ethnographers working in these contexts are striking, not least because they often foreground activities that differ considerably from the kinds of narrative that practitioners themselves might give of what it is to 'do' science, for example.

One of the insights from Latour's early work with Woolgar (1986) at the Salk Institute in California, for example, was the extent to which scientists were actually engaged in acts of writing, situated away from the laboratory work that would usually figure large in scientist's own accounts of their practice. Latour's (1999) subsequent study, *Pandora's Hope*, accompanied scientists on a scientific trip to the edge of an Amazon rainforest and charted some of the routine practices that soil scientists and botanists deployed in the production of scientific theory. Here, Latour observed how distinct practices such as using quadrants for sampling, codings, diagrams and charts involved a series of transformations of raw material into different kinds of data, which in turn became transformed into the particular theories that were subsequently disseminated through text. According to Latour, each of these transformations amounted to a form of translation—since in the move from soil to numerical figure on a chart, for example, soil was translated into a numeral that could be related to other data. As a process extended through time, Latour (1999) noted that the scientific inquiry involved multiple, successive translations in which connection with raw material is gradually lost, while new insight through greater generality is gained.

Readings (1992, 183) has noted that translation derives from the Latin *trans-latio*, which means to lift across, move or transfer. This work of mediation (as raw material is translated into data that then becomes conceptualised and theorised) tends to become invisible once the successive stages involved have become established, once an 'end point' is reached the links in this complex chain of translation are no longer visible (Latour, 1999). A forgetfulness of all the translations that have to be performed as part of a given scientific inquiry creates the illusion that the conclusion is immediately given. What tends to follow from this is a belief in an unmediated word-world correspondence—that a particular word or concept directly maps onto reality, without all the intermediary chain of translations having to be performed for this to be the case.

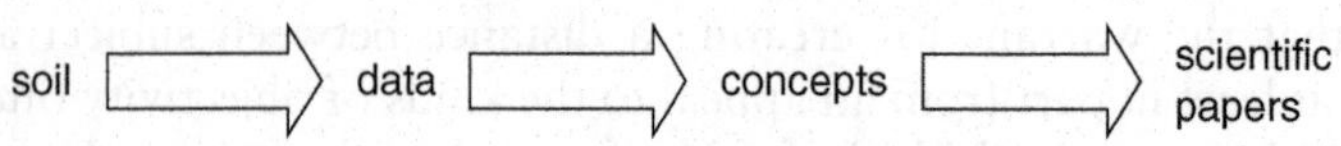

soil ⟹ data ⟹ concepts ⟹ scientific papers

Figure 2.3 Scientific process as translation.

Such work problematises a number of familiar assumptions that inform how scientific inquiry is carried out. A naïve objectivist account is only possible if each of the multiple translations from raw data to abstract concept are forgotten and rendered invisible. By the same token, the belief in a detached subject position in relation to the production of such knowledge is only possible if the complex and heterogeneous gathering of tools, materialities and practices that together make such an account possible are ignored in its subsequent description.

The importance of registering the practices and materialities involved in the making of sense is especially clear in Anne-Marie Mol's (2003) study of the workings of a hospital in the Netherlands. Mol's analysis suggested that a particular disease (in this case, *atherosclerosis*, a disease of the arteries) was performed differently according to the specific assemblage of specialists, equipment and practices enacted in each specialist area. It is only because we routinely forget about the different practices and instruments gathered to make sense in each case that these can be regarded as 'the same'. What becomes clear from Mol's (2003) analysis is that whilst there may be considerable overlap between how atherosclerosis is performed in a doctor's surgery, an X-ray centre and in a laboratory, there may nevertheless be significant differences that simply referring to this as a single entity—'atherosclerosis'—overlooks.

In pointing to the complexities of practice, equipment and translation in each of these cases, naïve assumptions concerning the objectivity and distance involved in the production of scientific knowledge are undone. A feature informing all of these studies is that of noticing practices and features in a situation that might otherwise be regarded as of little significance or indeed not even noticed. What is also significant about such studies is that they enact a kind of philosophical empiricism in which attention to relational practices and their continuance through time becomes the occasion for critical inquiry and reflection. Through attention to routine scientific practice, such studies call into question the goal of achieving a detached and autonomous subject position, which the trope of neutrality promotes; a key rationale that has justified practice under the sign of neutrality is therefore undone.

(vi) RE and the Work of Translation

In what ways might attention to this work of translation, practices of writing and attending to invisibilities be relevant to the practice of RE within educational spaces? If we attend to the work of translation involved in rendering a complex cultural situation present within a classroom, there are also far-reaching practices of translation involved that are a condition of the possibility for the knowledge/writing practices that habitually take place. It is noteworthy that, in relation to educational practice, many of these

42 *Diagnostic*

translations predate the actual activities that take place in the classroom; they are performed through the framings that subsequently inform lesson design, textbooks used, and pedagogical practice more generally within the classroom. Becoming mindful of this work of translation is educationally significant especially in relation to RE, since this:

(i) focuses on the relations involved in this process. Such an analysis is therefore dynamic and processual rather than static and bounded, since it is attentive to the actual gathering of people, materialities, concepts, tropes and theories that together constitute a particular way of making sense. Insofar as these elements are acknowledged, there is an opening towards greater relational and spatial complexity;

(ii) potentially problematises one particular way of linking a cultural context to a particular concept, category or phenomenon (which, if it remains unproblematised, is likely to involve the imposition of characteristically Western assumptions);

(iii) opens up new relational/transformational possibilities for sense-making.

Such an approach is constructivist in orientation, concerned, as it is, with identifying the kinds of relations and configurations that are actually in play. As such, it may help students who might otherwise find the work of translation problematic through making the steps involved in putting together a particular educational sense more explicit.

In his more recent work, Latour (2013a) has sought to problematise further the hiddenness of these translations, especially in relation to digital technologies and what he calls, as a short hand, 'double-click': the ways in which using a computer mouse, through the action of double-clicking on a link, appear to immediately take the user to particular information. None of the decisions taken along the way as to what to include, exclude and the manner of its presentation are made available in—what appears to be—an instantaneous response. In this case, the mediations also involve issues of digital encoding through, for example, algorithms, the effects and implications of which have been characteristically ignored (Edwards and Carmichael, 2012).

(vii) Forms of Translation: The Concept of Belief

In relation to RE, there are a series of concepts, orientations and practices that tend towards an erasure of the chain of translations and mediations that produce a particular kind of sense. Certain forms of transcendence with metaphors of height and altitude are especially associated with language identified as religious (Latour, 2013b, 35), and these can be seen as a product of such processes of translation. In particular, situations of practice tend to be described through abstract categories, and one way of illustrating this is to take a particular concept and examine how it is mobilised in practice. Here, we take a ubiquitous

Figure 2.4 Belief and the erasure of translations.

concept associated with RE—that of belief—so as to analyse the translations that it effects in the making of particular kinds of sense.

In the case of belief, the direction of travel is primarily *away* from the messiness of material practice towards a more abstract, cognitive production.

In place of attending to the specific practices, materialities and events that take place within a particular setting, sense-making in RE is often achieved through a translation into the form 'x believes y', and this is especially noticeable in the case of examination practices in RE (see below).

Of course, abstraction in and of itself is not necessarily problematic, since there are potential gains to be had through, for example, acts of comparison across sites, which only become possible through a focus on certain features to the exclusion of others. An abstract concept only becomes problematic if the specific ways in which it operates are no longer subject to critical scrutiny, giving the impression that a definitive conclusion has been reached. In this connection, Strhan (2010) has also registered concern that current approaches that make use of the concept of 'belief' uncritically can lead students within RE contexts mistakenly to think that they have a secure grasp and understanding of a particular 'religion or culture' once they have achieved a cognitive mastery of its 'core beliefs'. Such an educational framing leads to both closure and an ethically questionable stance *vis-à-vis* practices, materialities and events under investigation.

(viii) Examining RE

These ideals concerning the kinds of spaces, relations and translations that a specific form of RE might consist in are most clearly expressed in the requirements for its examination. Here, an analysis of an actual examination paper will serve a kind of case study, focused upon a specific artefact, that will enable us to identify how the orientations that we have been considering touch down in practice.

The culmination of RE within school contexts—and often, in universities, too—is the examination hall. Here, students are seated in rows at individual desks. They are not permitted to communicate, to move or to express themselves at all save for acts of writing upon a blank page. This ritual performance also says something important about the kind of knowledge and the kinds of practice that are most valued: the gathering of materials,

44 Diagnostic

concepts and practices that inform the qualification framework, examination practices and curriculum arrangements, although distinct, nevertheless work together to constitute certain kinds of truth and certain kinds of subject, which, in turn, produce certain kinds of others in relation to these. Three arrangements can be identified that simultaneously govern the behaviours of candidates taking examinations while together constituting a set of assumptions about knowledge, culture and representation. These are: the qualifications framework, examination regulations and curriculum arrangements. The *kinds of truths* produced in relation to RE through these various translations construct what it is to understand a particular 'religion' but also imply a particular standpoint from which sense is made and a particular subjectivity of the one engaging in such activity.

(a) The Qualifications Framework: Sameness and Equivalence

Whilst the end point of schooling for students is the examination hall, the scripts that are produced within the examination hall then have to be marked and graded. Candidates' responses to the questions set are translated into a numerical tally that in turn issues in the award of a final grade for the papers taken. The grades awarded to each candidate for the different subjects taken then become tokens in a broader qualifications framework that permits and denies access to other educational and work contexts. In other words, in sitting an examination, a student is—simultaneously and through time—part of multiple, distinct, yet intersecting processes that accord value, variously translate and constitute particular kinds of award. Within a Scottish context, the Scottish Qualifications Authority (SQA) exercises responsibility for warranting recognised kinds and levels of qualification within school contexts.

The SQA organises these awards into various levels, between one and twelve, with level twelve representing doctorate status and level one 'Access 1', and into the amount of credit achieved, which indicates the 'volume' of learning at each level (SQA, n.d.). The focus of this case study is specifically an analysis of the Religious, Moral and Philosophical Studies (RMPS) Higher Examination, which is a level six qualification within the Scottish Credit and Qualifications Framework (SCQF). However, the ways in which knowledge of RE is organised within that examination owes much to its setting within the broader SCQF and the set of expectations as regards structure and ordering that are seen to produce parity across both other subject areas and other national qualification frameworks. In this connection, the leaflet 'Qualifications can cross boundaries' (SQA, 2011a) provides an overview of how each level of award articulates with equivalent qualifications in England, Wales, Ireland, Northern Ireland and with other countries within the European Qualifications framework (EQF).[4]

The intention informing such processes is to produce equivalence between attainment in different subject areas within different national contexts. This presumes common understandings *apropos* what constitutes knowledge and associated educational practices such as analysis, comparison and evaluation. The advantages of such ordering are clear: a level of certainty in regard to educational attainment irrespective of context, based upon the authority of qualifications bodies, such as the SQA, and international frameworks, such as the EQF. However, this involves a collective effort to constitute 'sameness' and the alignment of practices across multiple spatial domains. This also instantiates a dominant epistemic culture (Knorr Cetina, 2007) as the arbiter of truth and, as such, raises a number of issues, especially as regards the position of marginal traditions of enquiry that may not fit quite so easily within this.

(b) Examination Practices: Acts of Writing

There are detailed codes of conduct that govern how candidates for examinations are to behave whilst sitting their examination. An example of this is the SQA (2012) booklet issued to candidates that explains what is expected and actions that are prohibited. The net effect of such stipulations is that candidates each inhabit their own individual island within an examination hall. Each becomes a Robinson Crusoe-like figure, cast away for their allotted time to their particular island[5] within the examination hall. What matters is the individualised act of writing upon a blank page; disembodied cognitive performance is the order of the day. Such an orientation to knowledge values stasis over movement and privileges vision over what are regarded as lesser senses, such as touch. It produces subjects who are detached from the world, who externalise their thoughts through acts of writing.

(c) Curriculum Arrangements: Ordering Practices

In terms of the actual content of the RMPS Higher Examination, our focus is upon a past SQA Second Paper, where students have 55 minutes to answer one question, in which they select one from a choice of six available 'world religions'. The questions for each religion are assigned a total of 40 marks, with these being equally divided between knowledge and understanding (KU) and analysis and evaluation (AE). In this analysis, we will chiefly consider the 'Arrangements' document produced by SQA (2010) that outlines the examination syllabus, but we will also illustrate points raised by drawing upon papers set in 2010 and 2011a, and the 'Finalised Marking Instructions', which are available via the SQA (2011a) website.

One of the first things noticeable is that each of the world religions is ordered according to the same 'organising principles' in a tripartite schema:

(a) The human condition;
(b) The goals of existence;
(c) The means to achieve these goals.

(SQA, 2010, 6)

46 Diagnostic

Set out diagrammatically, the relationship between the three aspects might be represented as follows:

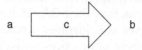

Figure 2.5 The relationship between the three organising principles.

Each of these organising principles is, in turn, associated with two specific questions:

(a) The human condition:

  (i) What is the human condition?
  (ii) What is the cause of the human condition?

(b) The goals of existence:

  (i) What are the goals during life?
  (ii) What is the final aim of existence?

(c) The means to achieve these goals:

  (i) How are the goals achieved?
  (ii) Which practices help to achieving the goals?

(SQA, 2010, 6)

A common overarching framework leads to similar questions being posed in respect of each tradition. This is especially so in the 2011 paper, where question 1(a) for each religion is 'How do x describe the human condition?' where x is one of the six world religions. One of the immediate effects of this particular ordering is a somewhat arbitrary gathering of concepts and practices in relation to each of these themes. It is, for example, highly questionable whether it makes sense to suggest that 'Hinduism' has a unified conception of the human condition at all (Caldwell and Smith, 2000).

Although the three organising principles are interrelated, there is, nevertheless, a distinct order in which these are set out. In practice, this means that the more abstract aspects in relation to the concept 'the human condition' are given primacy, with the more practice-oriented aspects ('the means') following on from this once 'the goals' have been set out. Thus, in the 2010 Paper 2 Section 1 on Buddhism, for example, candidates are asked '(a) Describe what Buddhists understand by Dukkha' and '(b) Explain the relationship between Dukkha and other aspects of the human condition'. It is not until question (f) (out of a total number of seven questions) that there is a question directly concerned with practice: 'In what ways do Buddhist meditate?' This is paralleled in the questions set for the other 'world religions'.[6]

Given the examination format and the need for a certainty of response, it is hardly surprising that beliefs have been privileged over the messiness of practice. Beliefs are amenable to clear statement and thus permit a positivity that is desirable within an examination context where marks have to be awarded for correct (and unambiguous) assertions. This has an impact upon the kinds of knowledge that are privileged, for as Strhan (2010, 31) has observed:

> . . . exam specifications, determining to a large extent the content of the curriculum, tend to present religion in too simplistic terms as assent to certain religious propositions.

Although often assumed to be a universal category, the concept of belief is more justly described as a Western category that is closely bound up with the history of Christianity (Lopez, 1998). One of the effects of this is to constitute objects of knowledge that are abstracted from social and material practices (I'Anson and Jasper, 2011). Furthermore, the concept of belief is tied up with an imaginary that presumes that the world remains much the same regardless of what actually happens to particular believers. There is, in other words, an assumption of a single, all-encompassing reality that is 'out there' and which is stable and amendable to easy description, over alternative accounts that acknowledge movement and dynamic interconnectedness (Law, 2011).[7]

In contrast to beliefs, to think about practices involves confronting their resistance to easy translation into thought (Certeau, 1984, 173). The difficulty attendant on engaging with socio-material practices is nicely caught in Crang's (2000, 141) reference to '[t]he mark of a perturbation or rupture [. . . that is] a necessary part of thinking about practices . . .' According to Certeau (1984, 22), reason allied to beliefs involves 'a logic of mastery and transparency', and one should be suspicious of too easy a transparency, intelligibility and visibility. It would appear that the authors of the curriculum '*Arrangements*' document are also aware of this danger. Concerns are expressed (SQA, 2010, 7, 30), lest an approach be taken that is completely disconnected from actual life worlds.

> . . . care must be taken to avoid a wholly abstract study of religious beliefs which makes no reference to the lives of members of religious communities.

However, given the orientation produced by the organising principles, coupled with the demands of the examination processes, such an abstraction towards an ideal content becomes a very real likelihood with the corollary that reference to practice merely supplements this. This tendency away from the specificities of practice and material engagements is further reinforced by the second ordering practice.

48 Diagnostic

The second ordering practice appears in the *'Arrangements'* (SQA, 2010, 6), where there is a clear statement of priority in regard to the direction of analysis:

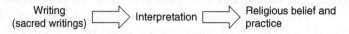

Figure 2.6 The Direction of Analysis.

A particular understanding of texts is therefore given pride of place over other potential ways of making sense, such as through empirical observation and description of practices, for example. In Certeau's (1984, 134) terms, this is to install a text-based 'scriptural economy' at the outset, and he saw such a move as characteristic of modern Western approaches, and

> ... one can read above the portals of modernity such inscriptions as 'Here, to work is to write', or 'Here only what is written is understood'. Such is the internal law of that which has constituted itself as 'Western'.

Certeau (1984, 134) draws out a number of significant elements within this Western economy of sense-making. One such element is the blank page, which 'delimits a place of production for the subject' whilst also assuming 'the withdrawal and the distance of the subject in relation to an area of activities. It is made available for a partial but regulatable operation'. Certeau (1984, 134) continues that

> [t]his is the Cartesian move of making a distinction that initiates, along with a *place* of writing, the mastery (and isolation) of a subject confronted by an *object*.
>
> (emphases in original)

The object of knowledge in this case is a textually produced concept that is the product of a series of framings and practices, some of which have been identified above. Since it is assumed that the object of knowledge refers to some situation 'out there', attention tends to be focused upon this rather than upon the relations and processes through which the object of knowledge is itself produced. Given the way in which the examination processes work to produce ideal objects of knowledge that are abstracted from actual situations of practice, there is a danger that this produces a limiting environment that, in Knorr Cetina's (2007, 364) words, turns in on itself, with 'a tendency to impose and expand [. . .] its own structures and concerns', notwithstanding pleas to the contrary in the *'Arrangements'* document.

The Course Aims within the *'Arrangements'* (SQA, 2010, 5) state that the intention is to 'develop a philosophical approach to the study of beliefs, values and issues which are of importance in the world today'. This is taken to mean the development of knowledge and understanding of religious beliefs, values and issues, together with development of skills of analysis, critical thinking and evaluation, both as regards the 'religions' encountered and in relation to pupils' own beliefs and values. Whilst the development of this critical and evaluative outlook is required of candidates for the RMPS Higher Examination, this does not extend to the theoretical framings that inform curriculum-making in RE as such.[8] The following two sentences suggest possible misgivings, were this framework to be followed through in a too deliberate way:

> . . . care must be taken to avoid *distorting candidates' understanding of the religion* by *over-concentration on this framework*. A *balanced understanding* of the chosen religion will only be achieved through a comprehensive study of all prescribed sources and all mandatory content.
> (SQA, 2010, 29 emphasis added)

How 'balance' is to be understood in this context is not made clear. Given that there are many ways in which the subject area might conceivably be organised, the particular choice of approach might, therefore, be regarded as somewhat arbitrary in the absence of some theoretical or pragmatic justification. Furthermore, this framework, as we have seen, orientates analysis away from the social and material specificities of the present day so there is a fundamental tension between the intention to enable young people to think critically about 'beliefs, values and issues which are of importance in the world today' (SQA, 2010, 5) and the methods and framings actually deployed. In this connection, it is noteworthy that none of the questions in the Higher RMPS Paper 2 ask candidates to comment upon, or make reference to, *any* contemporary event or situation. Moreover, none of the examples of marks awarded provided in the 'Finalised Marking Instructions' (SQA, 2011b) makes reference to any actual event or happening either; in short, abstract, disembodied and decontextualised understandings would seem to be the order of the day.

The reflexivity encouraged does not extend to a critical interrogation of the concepts and categories deployed within the field either. Given the lively debate around the appropriateness of the category 'religion' within the academic study of religion, (e.g., McCutcheon, 2003; Fitzgerald, 2007a, b; Stack *et al.*, 2015 etc.) during the past 15 or so years, for example, this might be seen as an appropriate dimension for inclusion, since this has material consequences for analysis and sense-making practices in RE at the present time. So what are the effects of this way of proceeding?

(d) Producing Religion, Subjectivity and Truth

The educational framing that informs the Higher RMPS approach would appear to install an instrumental rationality as being fundamental to religion as such: simply put, it is on the basis of the characterisation of the human condition that a particular means is necessary in order to attain the 'goals' of that tradition, which are diversely characterised. 'Religions', on this reading, each present a technology to achieve these different putative goals. Organising things this way puts centre stage the beliefs that constitute the human condition in each case. However, 'belief', as we have seen, is a distinctive Western concept that orientates analysis towards abstract, disembodied and positive statements. This knowledge is propositional in form and independent of specific contexts—thereby implying that there is an ideal set of beliefs and commitments, even if particular adherents may not share all of them.[9]

This commonality of framework together with the ordering practices suggest that all six 'world religions' are:

(i) indefinitely translatable
(ii) equivalent
(iii) fundamentally unified in being an instrumental technology for achieving salvific purposes
(iv) transparent insofar they are in principle translatable into a series of positive linguistic statements.

The subject produced through such processes is, moreover, positioned as detached from the objects of knowledge that are the immediate focus of concern; what it is to know a 'religion' is taken as primarily an epistemological and evaluative task that involves mastery of the objects of knowledge. To this extent, there are also strongly gendered assumptions informing the kinds of knowledge that are valued, and we will take up this issue in much more detail in Chapter Four. Thus, the qualifications framework, examinations practices and curriculum arrangements mutually reinforce one another in producing a gendered Cartesian subject and a particular approach to RE. And it is here, especially, that the three processes that we have analysed interlink to produce particular truths about 'religion' and subjectivity.

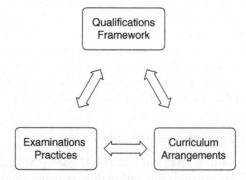

Figure 2.7 The relations between the three aspects.

Assembling RE—Spaces, Relations and Translations 51

In this connection, Laing (2008) has analysed how multiple processes that initially appear to be distinct come together to reinforce and 'animate' a set of assumptions, practices and material gatherings so as to constitute a particular assemblage of truth. Rose (1999, xii) has likewise drawn attention to the need for sensitivity to 'the kinds of connections and relations amongst diverse elements that have brought our contemporary ways of thinking, judging [and] acting into being'.[10]

Such an analysis as the foregoing suggests that the truths produced—in relation to RE and subjectivity—are the outcome of multiple relations and practices that intersect to reinforce a distinctive Western imaginary that is Cartesian in form. What emerges from our analysis of the curriculum arrangements is that this tradition of enquiry, in order to produce the kinds of truths that it does, necessarily excludes much from its framing. Tracing the contours of this particular approach, however, also permits its problematisation: opening up the question as to whether it is possible to think of RE in other terms.

(ix) Conclusion

In this chapter, we have explored how a dominant framing of RE was assembled through a variety of socio-material practices, tropes and concepts that were a considered response to a series of problematics faced in the early 1970s. Our focus has been upon the relationships and translations established across time that have enabled the formation of a distinctive spatial imaginary in RE—that has been remarkably resilient. A case study that used an examination paper as an artefact enabled us to identify—and problematise—how some of these key understandings touch down in practice within the context of a broader qualifications economy. Such socio-material practices rhetorically position—and hold in place—a particular approach to RE in contradistinction to other ways of doing on. They also, as we have seen, position the student in a detached and disengaged relation to its characteristic matters of concern, and we have questioned whether this can be regarded as educational in the light of the *indifference* this tends to produce. And so a critical analysis enables us to identify how these spaces, relations and translations have in turn led to a current crisis of plausibility in RE, since there have not been mechanisms in place that might enable the articulation of more engaged approaches that might respond to new theoretical, cultural and educational changes.

In Part Two we will explore a variety of different ways forward that might provide resources with which to reconceive the educational project of RE in ways that are more open to difference. Before we turn to that investigation however, it is worth noting that the dominant approach to RE—as a particular way of constituting a plane of sense-making—has had certain advantages. Such a framing has permitted a subject such as RE to take its place alongside other subject areas and thereby become part of a broader economy

52 Diagnostic

of knowledge where attainment within examinations produces tokens that permit entry to other educational spaces, such as universities. However, such achievements in terms of broader subject recognition—alongside attendant benefits associated with the stabilisation and consistency in regard to practice and terminology—are, we contend, bought at considerable cost. To be more specific, the objectification of knowledge that this produces also leads to the *non-affectingness* of the objects of inquiry, since these are presented in a positivistic mode that mimics a particular (although, as we have seen, highly questionable) understanding of a dispassionate ideal that is the mark of scientific inquiry properly so called. The ideal of distance, therefore, brings in its trail a number of difficulties; not the least of these is *indifference*—since RE is presented in a non-affecting and non-affective way. Moreover, through the various translations that are performed under the sign of neutrality, difference becomes *insufficiently different* to unsettle or to provoke interest. The net effect of this production of distance and non-affectingness is both disenchantment and indifference. This raises the question as to whether there are other traditions of inquiry that might be drawn upon to construct more engaged imaginaries that are open to difference. In the following chapter, we outline a very different style of reason that is to be found in the writings of Spinoza and which might in turn provide both the conceptual resources and orientation to enable the project of RE to be re-imagined afresh.

Notes

1. Here, we are referring to a broad range of curricular arrangements that draw upon, and are informed by, a settlement that was achieved in the 1970s, associated with the work of Ninian Smart. For a recent empirical research project that maps this terrain, see Conroy *et al.* (2013).
2. The implications of this concern with natality also extend to the kinds of topics that are privileged for study within educational sites. Jantzen (1998; 2004), in particular, has noted the tendency to focus upon issues regarding death over thinking through the implications of birth, emergence and the new as significant problematics. Such a critique raises critical questions as to the kinds of topic areas that tend to be privileged within RE moral issues courses, for example.
3. The point being raised here is the more general point, that the dynamics implied by the subject position in RE lead to the inquirer remaining effectively in control of the encounter with a text. One might wish to question whether such a dynamic is necessarily 'religious' as such—since this experience is a familiar one to readers of literary texts (which includes *The Odyssey*) and aesthetic experience when one is 'undone' through encounter with a work of art (such as the art critic Ian Fuller's (1981) encounter with Robert Natkin's work). Furthermore, one might also wish to raise the question as to whether the experience of 'becoming undone' is always a positive one. The experience of women registering unease because of 'the subject's interrogation by the other' is a case in point. Without further qualification, this could be uncomfortably close to the kind of 'religious' discourse that has rendered women peculiarly unsatisfactory/ sinful/problematic. Hence the otherness that interrogates needs to be seen as capable of overthrowing/challenging historically and culturally contextualised forms of *legitimated* interrogation.

Assembling RE—Spaces, Relations and Translations   53

4. This follows the recommendation by the Council and Parliament of the European Union in 2008 that such a framework be implemented so that appropriate qualifications can be referenced to the EQF by 2012.
5. The significance of Defoe's Crusoe myth for modernity is explored by Certeau (1984, 136).
6. For the Christianity option, for example, candidates are asked '(a) Describe what Christians understand by the term "sin"' and '(b) Explain the relationship between sin and other aspects of the human condition' and again, it is not until question (f) that there is a question directly linked to practice: 'In what ways do Christians put their faith into action?'
7. According to Law (2011, 2): 'Is it simply that people *believe* different things about reality? Or is it that there are *different realities* being done in different practices? If the first of these positions is right, then we're in the business of beliefs, perspectives and *epistemologies*. If it's the second then we're being backed into issues of *ontology*. Here's the analytically radical nature of this second position. We're in the business of treating reals as *effects of contingent and heterogeneous enactments, performances or sets of relations*'. (Italics in original)
8. It is simply stated that: 'The Organising Principles and Questions provide a *useful* framework for the study of each religion. This framework can also be used as an *effective learning and teaching tool* to help candidates organise and reflect on the main aspects of the religion they study'. (SQA 2010, 29 italics inserted).
9. In this connection, the exchange between Jackson (2008) and Wright (2008) is interesting.
10. Here, for reasons of space, we have only considered three such intersecting processes, but other processes, such as inspection regimes, might also be included. Were this to be the case, these lines of intersection would be multiplied.

Bibliography

Abell, S.K. and Lederman, N.G., 2007. *Handbook of Research on Science Education.* London and New York: Routledge.

Arendt, H., 1958. *The Human Condition.* London: University of Chicago Press.

Butler, J., 2012. 'On this occasion'. In: R. Faber, M. Halewood and D. Lin eds., *Butler on Whitehead: On the Occasion.* Lanham: Lexington Books, pp. 3–18.

Caldwell, S. and Smith, B.K., 2000. 'Introduction: Who speaks for Hinduism?'. *Journal of the American Academy of Religion*, vol. 68, no. 4, pp. 705–710.

Caputo, J.D., 2001. *On Religion.* New York: Routledge.

Certeau, M.d., 1984. *The Practice of Everyday Life.* Berkeley, Los Angeles and London: University of California Press.

Certeau, M. de. 1986. *Heterologies: Discourse on the Other.* Minneapolis: University of Minnesota Press.

Conroy, J.C., Lundie, D., Davis, R.A., Baumfield, V., Barnes, L.P., Gallagher, T., Lowden, K., Bourque, N. and Wenell, K., 2013. *Does RE Work? A Multi-dimensional Investigation.* London, New Delhi, New York and Sydney: Bloomsbury.

Cope, P. and I'Anson, J., 2003. 'Forms of exchange: Education, economics and the neglect of social contingency'. *British Journal of Educational Studies*, vol. 51, no. 3, pp. 219–232.

Crang, M., 2000. 'Relics, places and unwritten geographies in the work of Michel de Certeau (1925–86)'. In: M. Crang and N. Thrift eds., *Thinking Space.* London and New York: Routledge, pp. 136–153.

Dressler, M. and Mandair, A.-P.S., eds., 2011. *Secularism and Religion-Making.* Oxford and New York: Oxford University Press.

54 *Diagnostic*

Edwards, R. and Carmichael, P., 2012. 'Secret codes: The hidden curriculum of semantic web technologies'. *Discourse: Learning and Teaching in Philosophical and Religious Studies*, vol. 33, no. 4, pp. 575–590.

Edwards, R. and Usher, R., 2000. *Globalisation and Pedagogy: Space, Place and Identity*. London and New York: Routledge.

Fitzgerald, T., 2007a. *Discourse on Civility and Barbarity: A Critical History of Religion and Related Categories*. Oxford: Oxford University Press.

Fitzgerald, T., 2007b. 'Encompassing religion, privatized religions and the invention of modern politics'. In: T. Fitzgerald ed., *Religion and the Secular: Historical and Colonial Formations*. 2007 ed. London and Oakville, CT: Equinox, pp. 211–240.

Flood, G., 2012. *The Importance of Religion: Meaning and Action in Our Strange World*. Oxford: Blackwells.

Foucault, M., 1986. *The Care of the Self: The History of Sexuality 3*. New York: Pantheon Books.

Foucault, M., 1991. 'Space, power, knowledge'. In: P. Rabinow ed., *The Foucault Reader: An Introduction to Foucault's Thought*. London: Penguin, pp. 239–256.

Fuller, I. 1981. *Robert Natkin*. New York: Harry N. Abrams Inc.

Gearon, L., 2013. *On Holy Ground: The Theory and Practice of Religious Education*. London and New York: Routledge.

Harvey, D., 1990. *The Condition of Postmodernity*. Oxford: Blackwell.

Harvey, D., 1993. 'From space to place and back again: Reflections on the condition of postmodernity'. In: J. Bird, T. Curtis, G. Putnam and L. Tickner eds., *Mapping the Futures: Local Cultures, Global Change*. London and New York: Routledge, pp. 3–19.

Heelas, P., 1978. 'Some problems with religious studies'. *Religion*, vol. 8, no. 1, pp. 1–14.

I'Anson, J. and Jasper, A., 2011. '"Religion" in educational spaces: Knowing, knowing well, and knowing differently'. *Arts and Humanities in Higher Education*, vol. 10, no. 3, pp. 295–314.

Irigaray, L., 2004. *Key Writings*. London and New York: Continuum.

Jackson, R., 2008. *Religious Education: An Interpretive Approach*. London: Hodder Education.

Jantzen, G.M., 1998. *Becoming Divine: Towards a Feminist Philosophy of Religion*. Manchester: Manchester University Press.

Jantzen, G.M., 2004. *Foundations of Violence: Death and the Displacement of Beauty*, vol. 1. London and New York: Routledge.

Jasper, A., 2012. *Because of Beauvoir: Christianity and the Cultivation of Female Genius*. Waco, TX: Baylor University Press.

Knorr Cetina, K., 2007. 'Culture in global knowledge societies: Knowledge cultures and epistemic cultures'. *Interdisciplinary Science Reviews*, vol. 32, no. 4, pp. 361–375.

Knott, K., 2005. *The Location of Religion: A Spatial Analysis*. London: Equinox.

Laing, A., 2008 unpublished. *Changing Disabling Practices*. PhD ed. University of Stirling (Department of psychology).

Lakoff, G. and Johnson, M., 1981. *Metaphors We Live By*. Chicago, IL: University of Chicago Press.

Lakoff, G. and Johnson, M., 1999. *Philosophy in the Flesh: The Embodied Mind and Its Challenge to Western Thought*. New York: Basic Books.

Lakoff, G. and Johnson, M., 2003. *Metaphors We Live By*. Chicago and London: University of Chicago Press.

Latour, B., 1999. *Pandora's Hope: An Essay on the Reality of Science Studies*. Cambridge, MA: Harvard University Press.

Assembling RE—Spaces, Relations and Translations 55

Latour, B., 2013a. *An Inquiry Into Modes of Existence: An Anthropology of the Modern*. Cambridge, MA: Harvard University Press.

Latour, B., 2013b. *Rejoicing Or the Torments of Religious Speech*. Cambridge and Malden, MA: Polity.

Latour, B., 2015. 'Waking up from "Conjecture" as well as from "Dream": A presentation of AIME'. *Tsantsa*, vol. 20, pp. 34–40. Paper originally given as the GAD Distinguished Lecture, at the American Anthropology Association meeting Chicago, 21st November 2013.

Latour, B. and Woolgar, S., 1986. *Laboratory Life: The Social Construction of Scientific Facts*. Princeton, NJ: Princeton University Press.Law, J., 2011. 'What's wrong with a one-world world'. Paper presented to the Center for the Humanities, Wesleyan University, Middletown, Connecticut on 19th September, 2011. This version was published by heterogeneities.net on 25th September 2011. Available from www.heterogeneities.net/publications/Law2011WhatsWrongWithAOneWorldWorld.pdf.

Law, J. and Lin, W., 2010. 'Cultivating disconcertment'. *The Sociological Review*, vol. 58, no. S2, pp. 135–153.

Lefebvre, H., 1991. *The Production of Space*. Oxford, UK: Blackwell.

Lopez Jnr., D.S., 1998. 'Belief'. In: M.C. Taylor ed., *Critical Terms for Religious Studies*. Chicago and London: University of Chicago Press, pp. 21–35.

McCutcheon, R.T., 1997. *Manufacturing Religion: The Discourse on Sui Generis Religion and the Politics of Nostalgia*. Oxford and New York: Oxford University Press.

McCutcheon, R.T., 2003. *Manufacturing Religion: The Discourse on Sui Generis Religion and the Politics of Nostalgia*. Oxford: Oxford University Press.

Masschelein, J., 2006. 'Experience and the limits of governmentality'. *Educational Philosophy and Theory*, vol. 38, no. 4, pp. 561–576.

Masschelein, J., 2010a. 'The idea of critical e-ducational research: E-ducating the gaze and inviting to go walking'. In: I. Gurzeev ed., *The Possibility/Impossibility of a New Critical Language in Education*. Rotterdam: Sense, pp. 275–291.

Masschelein, J., 2010b. 'E-ducating the gaze: The idea of a poor pedagogy'. *Ethics and Education*, vol. 5, no. 1, pp. 43–53.

Massey, D., 1994. *Space, Place and Gender*. Malden, MA and Cambridge: Polity Press.

Massey, D., 2003. 'Imagining the field'. In: M. Pryke, G. Rose and S. Whatmore eds., *Using Social Theory: Thinking Through Research*. London: Sage Publications, pp. 71–88.

Massey, D., 2005. *For Space*. London, Thousand Oaks, CA and New Delhi: Sage.

Mol, A., 2003. *The Body Multiple: Ontology in Medical Practice*. Durham, NC: Duke University Press.

Nicolson, A., 2014. *The Mighty Dead: Why Homer Matters*. London: William Collins.

Paechter, C. and Edwards, R., 2001. *Learning, Space and Identity*. London: Sage (in association with The Open University).

Pals, D., 2014. *Nine Theories of Religion*. Oxford and New York: Oxford University Press.

Readings, B., 1992. 'Pagans, perverts or primitives?'. In: P. Dhillon and P. Standish eds., *Lyotard: Just Education*. London and New York: Routledge, pp. 168–191.

Reeves, J., 2010. *Professional Learning as Relational Practice*. Dordrecht, the Netherlands: Springer.

Reeves, J. and I'Anson, J., 2014. 'Rhetorics of professional change: Assembling the means to act differently?'. *Oxford Review of Education*, vol. 40, no. 5, pp. 649–666.

56 *Diagnostic*

Rose, N.S., 1999. *Governing the Soul: The Shaping of the Private Self*. London: Free Association Books.

Santo, B. and Standish, P., 2012. *Stanley Cavell and the Education of Grownups*. New York: Fordham University Press.

Schools Council, 1971. *Religious Education in Secondary Schools (Schools Council Working Paper 36)*. London: Methuen Educ. and Evans Bros.

Scottish Education Department (SED)., 1972. *Moral and Religious Education in Scottish Schools (The Millar Report)*. Edinburgh: HMSO.

Scottish Qualifications Authority (SQA), 2010. *Religious, Moral and Philosophical Studies, Higher Arrangements*. 2nd ed. n.p.: SQA.

Scottish Qualifications Authority (SQA)., 2011a. 'Qualifications can cross boundaries: A rough guide to comparing qualifications in the UK and Ireland'. n.p.: SQA.

Scottish Qualifications Authority (SQA)., 2011b. *RMPS Past Papers*. SQA.

Scottish Qualifications Authority (SQA). 2012. *Your Exam*.

Serres, M. and MacArthur, E., 1995. *The Natural Contract (Studies in Literature and Science)*. Ann Arbor: University of Michigan Press.

Smart, N., 1968. *Secular Education and the Logic of Religion*. London: Faber and Faber.

Smart, N., 1972. *The Concept of Worship*. London: Macmillan.

Smart, N., 1973a. *The Science of Religion and the sociology of Knowledge: Some Methodological Questions*. Princeton, NJ: Princeton University Press.

Smart, N., 1973b. *The Phenomenon of Religion*. London: Macmillan.

Soja, E.W., 1996. *Thirdspace: Journeys to Los Angeles and Other Real-and-imagined Places*. Malden, MA, Oxford and Carlton, Victoria: Blackwell Publishing.

Spivak, G. C. 1994. 'Can the Subaltern Speak?'. In: Williams, P. and Chrisman, L. *Colonial Discourse and Post-Colonial Theory: A Reader*. New York: Columbia University Press, pp. 66–111.

Stack, T., Goldenberg, N. and Fitzgerald, T., 2015. *Religion as a Category of Governance and Sovereignty*. Leiden and Boston: Brill.

Stausberg, M., ed., 2009. *Contemporary Theories of Religion: A Critical Companion*. London and New York: Routledge.

Strhan, A., 2010. 'A religious education otherwise? An examination and proposed interruption of current British practice'. *Journal of Philosophy of Education*, vol. 44, no. 1, pp. 23–44.

Strhan, A., 2015. PE SGB Keynote: 'Enchanting rationalities'. Available from www. philosophy-of-education.org/files/events/conference-papers-2015/PESGB%20 2015%20Keynote%20Panel%20-%20Strhan.pdf.

Tweed, T.A., 2006. *Crossing and Dwelling: A Theory of Religion*. Cambridge, MA and London: Harvard University Press.

Wenger, W., 1987. *Wings of Desire*. Axiom Films International Ltd.

Wildman, W.J., 2010. 'An introduction to relational ontology'. In: J. Polkinghorne and J. Zizioulas eds., *The Trinity and an Entangled World: Relationality in Physical Science and theology*. Grand Rapids: Eerdmans, pp. 55–73.

Williams, R., 2014. *The Edge of Words: God and the Habits of Language*. London, New Delhi, New York and Sydney: Bloomsbury.

Wright, A. 2008. 'Contextual religious education and the actuality of religions. *British Journal of Religious Education* 30, 1, 3–12.

Part 2

Thinking Otherwise— Resisting Indifference

Introduction to Part Two

Having, in Part One, diagnosed why current framings and practices within RE have led to indifference, the focus of Part Two is three chapters which, in very different ways, begin to think about and imagine RE 'otherwise'. Each chapter draws upon a different strand of theorising so as to think through different ways in which a rejuvenated understanding of RE might be conceived, as a prelude to the heuristic advanced in Part Three.

In the light of this, Chapter Three takes up some recent theorising that draws upon the writings of Benedict Spinoza as offering an alternative style of reasoning that privileges embodiment and relationality. This has been influential for a number of contemporary feminist theorists, and one of the ways into this style of reasoning is to consider how metaphor as such a focus displaces a number of tropes within the dominant tradition. This is taken up in Chapter Four more thoroughly in terms of *conceptual personae*, unsettling in particular the gendered metaphors that routinely inform our notions of 'common sense' and play out in our practice of RE, as in other, everyday sites of encounter. Having in previous chapters primarily focused on Western philosophical contexts, Chapter Five engages approaches to the study of Islam that challenge, quite radically, assumptions as to how it is understood, resisting the tendency to translate concepts into familiar Western categories and matters of concern. To this extent there is an opening to difference that invites a reconsideration of habitual assumptions and closures *vis-à-vis* the ways in which we engage in sense making activities within RE and other educational contexts. The scene is then set for Part Three, which, in the light of both our diagnosis and explorations of new approaches, takes forward the possibility of articulating a tradition of inquiry for RE between the academy and other educational spaces. In order to facilitate this, we propose an heuristic that might inform such ongoing dialogue between the various stakeholders.

3   Thinking Otherwise—Spinoza and Foucault

(i) Introduction

Chapter Three considers an alternative philosophical trajectory that might enable thinking and practice in other terms from those that inform dominant constructions of RE at the present time. The writings of Benedict Spinoza, it is suggested, enable the articulation of a series of new problematics for RE that, in being attentive to differing imaginaries and through acknowledging the work of transformation necessary if understanding is to be achieved, move decisively beyond the limitations associated with current framings. Here, we suggest an alternative trope to neutrality—that of diffraction—as being more appropriate to thinking through the implication of the would-be student within complex relational folds. Diffraction is a means of drawing out the differences in orientation between an approach predicated upon detachment and distance and one that can acknowledge relationality, implication and the changes that engaging difference might produce (Haraway, 1997; Barad, 2007). We argue that such an alternative trope to neutrality is desirable if the complexity of relations inherent in an educational scene is to be acknowledged.

Key elements in the alternative philosophical trajectory articulated through contemporary readings of Spinoza are taken up in the later writings of Michel Foucault, and we argue that these provide a number of productive ways forward for re-thinking RE as a series of encounters with difference in a more nuanced and ethical way.

(ii) The Rhetoric of Neutrality: A Metaphorical Critique

The chapter begins by taking up some of the key points of the critique offered in Part One. However, this critique, as a point of departure, is refracted through a metaphorical analysis. This is for two reasons. As was noted in Chapter Two, a focus upon metaphors is closely allied with a spatial analysis, and given that the focus of this chapter is upon ways of thinking differently, this rehearsal is refracted through a metaphorical analysis. Secondly, this metaphorical analysis is also important for drawing out ways in which

60 Thinking Otherwise—Resisting Indifference

Spinoza's style of philosophy departs from a number of key assumptions that have informed Western, post-Enlightenment thinking. So, for example, whereas for Kant, a metaphorical analysis enables us to see a fundamental ambivalence in regard to the passions and embodiment, an equivalent analysis in the case of Spinoza surfaces the extent to which his style of reasoning engages the passions through the imagination.

RE under the sign of neutrality might be considered ethical to the extent that it provides warrant for the representation of non-Western cultures within educational spaces that might not otherwise have been possible, and it encourages sympathetic attentiveness to the specific grammars of these cultures. But insofar as a rhetoric of neutrality appears to also stake a claim that *its* specific orderings and representations of these cultures do not materially make a difference—that, in other words, neutrality permits a kind of *unmediated access* to said cultures—there may be occasion for some disquiet. For as Caputo (1993, 220–1) has observed,

> To speak at all is to have recourse to a way of framing and phrasing, to fall back upon a way of dividing up an parceling out, to mark the world up (*archi-écriture*) and to stake it out in one ontocategorial way or another.

Neutrality, in other words, is simply one particular 'ontocategorial way' of making sense and of presenting and making visible certain features of one culture over others. The legitimations used in support of neutrality as an organising trope have in recent years become subject to critical scrutiny: it can no longer be assumed that frameworks that are premised upon neutrality have some sort of epistemological or ethical privilege (Chapter Two). In the light of this, claims to neutrality in a variety of disciplines have also been subject to far reaching theoretical critique in recent years.[1] As regards RE, the question of *whose* framings are deployed and their material and socio-political effects has been a particular focus of post-colonial critiques (Chakrabarty, 2000; Mandair, 2009) and in regards to male-normative framings; we will return to this in Chapter Four. So, for example, it is noticeable that the specific concepts that organise inquiry under the sign of neutrality— whether these be myth, ritual, rite of passage or experience (e.g., Smart, 1989)—are all terms of a distinctively Western provenance and, as such, quite different from a culture's own characteristic idioms and assumptions (Long, 1986). Moreover, as Fitzgerald (2007a, b) has argued, an organising category such as 'religion' is itself quite alien to most cultural traditions, and even within the West, its genealogy quickly reveals diverse meanings through time. Current understanding of 'religion' that assume that this consists of a set of beliefs and practices that can be found across all cultures is, moreover, a product of the modern period, at a time when Europe expanded trade and colonial interests throughout the world (Mandair, 2009). These critiques, along with related work in feminist and Science and Technology Studies

Thinking Otherwise—Spinoza and Foucault 61

(STS), lead to a questioning of the settled concepts, methods, practices and assumptions that together constitute sense within these terms. The presumption that a given approach is 'neutral' deflects critical attention away from the work that is performed in the making of sense within a particular milieu. The specific categories, framings and practices in and through which sense is constructed perform a series of translations that surreptitiously re-frame and re-produce 'religion' within recognisably Western terms. In short, 'religion', as Armour and St. Ville (2006, ix) observe, 'like gender and sexuality (and often with them), is a site where language, materiality, theory, and politics all come together in complex ways'.

Rather than taking neutrality at face value, therefore, it becomes necessary to enquire into the ways in which these different enactments are gathered together in the making of particular kinds of sense. One way of surfacing these assumptions is to attend to the images and metaphors that inform sense-making practices within these terms. This enables a surfacing of what Le Dœuff (1989) refers to as the philosophical imaginary, as this is implicated within a given context of inquiry. Gatens (1996, viii) has summarised the elements of such an imaginary as consisting in 'those images, symbols, metaphors and representations which help construct various forms of subjectivity'. Whilst philosophy is usually characterised through its break with myth, fable and imagery, philosophical texts are in practice populated with 'architects, foundations, dwellings, doors and windows . . . clocks, horses, donkeys . . . scenes of sea and storm', to name but a few (Le Dœuff, 1989, 1).[2] One illustration of the theoretical value of attending to metaphors[3] is Le Dœuff's (1989, 8ff.) exploration of the island metaphor as mobilised by Kant (1965) in *The Critique of Pure Reason*, which she regards as emblematic of the Kantian enterprise. Here, Kant uses the imagery associated with an island to differentiate truth (land) from the seductive illusions that are associated with 'the wide and stormy' sea. Considerable work is being achieved here in relation to Kant's project of justifying the role of philosophy in relation to the sciences, whilst simultaneously denying that metaphor and imagery are necessary for true knowledge. Through such means, a substantive position is both promoted through appeal to an imaginary, while, at the same time, that same imaginary is explicitly denied significance (Le Dœuff, 1989, 12). An act of division is therefore performed that separates off the imagination from true knowledge and understanding as such, which can only be attained through a conception of rationality that is abstracted from the passions.

A second illustration is the significance of the clock for Locke's philosophical imaginary as analysed by Jantzen (2001). Whilst Locke was by no means the first or only writer to deploy the image of the clock, he nevertheless played a significant role in inaugurating an imaginary that became characteristic of a particular approach to knowledge. And this approach, as Jantzen (2001, 7–8) argues, was to see nature as being essentially as lifeless and mechanical as the Strasbourg clock.

62   *Thinking Otherwise—Resisting Indifference*

The things of this world, plants, animals and people as well as minerals and stones, are like the Cathedral clock: they move, there is action and apparent life, but behind the scenes what we have is mechanism, matter in motion.

The consequence of this is an imaginary in which anything material is regarded as lifeless, and this includes human bodies, which henceforth become knowable as a mechanism, through mechanical means.

Mechanism continues to exercise a powerful hold upon medical practice—so much so that the metaphorical roots of this way of making sense have tended to become all but invisible and thus unavailable for critical scrutiny. These assumptions now inform everyday Western notions of 'common sense' and hence how this philosophical imaginary is played out in everyday life. Le Dœuff's particular interest is in the ways in which such a denial of material implication impacts upon the position of women; however, the concept of imaginary can also facilitate analysis of other collective productions that inform sociality. And, as Taylor (2004) has observed, one of the benefits of focusing on social imaginaries is that this enables us to focus on that which might otherwise remain as background, or out of field.[4] The focus on social imaginaries is to be distinguished from social theory to the extent that the latter tends to be the preserve of a minority, whereas the focus upon imaginaries affords analysis of more everyday formations that include 'common sense' notions (Taylor, 2004, 23). Thus, for example, Benedict Anderson (1991) in his *Imagined Communities* explores how 'the nation' in modernity weaves a collective through an assortment of material practices and objects.

How might such a metaphorical analysis inform a project concerned with re-thinking the style of reasoning in RE? If such a metaphorical analysis is performed in relation to the educational framing of RE, what is immediately noticeable is the extent to which visual modalities are privileged. It is commonplace, for example, to refer to 'world views' and 'ways of seeing', and this brings in its trail a number of characteristically Western epistemological assumptions, which—even though mobilised under the sign of neutrality—are far from neutral in their effects.

(iii) Privileging the Visual: Some Consequences

The Scottish philosopher John MacMurray (1969), in particular, was concerned with surfacing some of the relational and ethical consequences of this visual orientation in Western approaches to sense-making. In his *Gifford Lectures*, he critiqued fixed standpoints that privilege a detached standpoint of observation over one based on implication within a relational nexus, and parallels have been drawn between MacMurray's project and Fanon's post-colonial writings (Gardiner, 2004). According to MacMurray (1969, 16),

In reflection we isolate ourselves from dynamic relations with the Other; we withdraw into ourselves, adopting the attitude of spectators, not of

Thinking Otherwise—Spinoza and Foucault 63

participants. We are then out of touch with the world, and for touch we must substitute vision . . .

Within such an economy of sense-making,

> We behave as though we were 'pure subjects', observers only, unimplicated in the dynamic relatedness of real existence. Our activity, we assume, makes no difference to the things we think about, but only to our ideas of them, upon which alone we are operative.
>
> (MacMurray, 1969, 20)

The founding gesture of reflective practice is therefore premised upon a performative refusal to 'participat[e] in what it contemplates' (MacMurray, 1969, 17). This has far-reaching consequences: in the first place, it denies from the outset that the self is constituted in and through action, and secondly, it installs a seer-seen binary at the beginning of the reflective process, with the primary term of that binary always the one that is privileged. This leads to the 'traditional polarities of intelligibility' in which one side of a whole series of binaries is preferred over its inverse relation (Foucault, 2003, 54). The point of departure for knowing another is therefore both gendered and colonial, in that a fixed, disengaged standpoint is created from which judgment is given. Within such a framing, as Ménil (2003, 103) has put it, 'to explicate is to dis-implicate' since the enquirer is detached from their object and its relational nexus.

Visual metaphors can be a hindrance to understanding cultures that foreground embodied forms of knowing, such as touch and hearing. Ingold and Kurttila's (2000) work amongst the Sámi people in northernmost Finland, for example, is a case in point, where indigenous ways of inhabiting the land are more likely to acknowledge the feel of snow underfoot or the sound of reindeer bells and ice cracking. Nor is it accidental that visual metaphors proliferate in Western approaches to cultural difference, as these derive from a dominant Cartesian philosophical imaginary, the contours of which will be discussed below. This generates particular forms of 'common sense' that tend towards ahistorical forms of rationality that produce detachment and abstraction (Law and Mol, 2002). Within RE, as we have seen already, the concept of belief plays a significant part in identifying an object of enquiry over which detached analysis is exercised. Although often assumed to be a universal category, the concept of belief is a distinctively Western term that is especially associated with Christianity (Lopez, 1998). According to Keller (2002, 7), this

> . . . strong association, that religiousness is a matter of belief that transpires in the psychic space of an individual, is extremely limiting if one is trying to make sense of religiousness in the contemporary world.

The focus upon beliefs similarly has the effect of orienting analysis to disembodied cognitive performances as the way to 'see' and understand the

64 Thinking Otherwise—Resisting Indifference

other, over a concern with social and material practices. Beliefs become the privileged mode of access to another culture over a concern with material, affective and political dimensions in and through which any responsibility might be exercised (Chapter Two; I'Anson and Jasper, 2011).

A striking instance of this has been Western understandings of Buddhism, which have tended to privilege idealist interpretations over a concern with material dimensions. As Young (2010, 109) has observed, such an orientation

> . . . is more representative of Euro-American agendas than it is of pre-modern Asian Buddhist priorities. One of the many legacies of Protestant iconoclast and Enlightenment rationalist traditions, Buddhist studies in the modern West has not only fixed its gaze on doctrinal ideals, spiritual goals and mental disciplines, but it has also expressly denounced any form of Buddhism that valorizes the use of material objects.

Even though a minority of Western scholars have attempted to move beyond the privileging of beliefs over the significance of material dimensions in their analysis of Buddhism (especially after Schopen's (1991) critique of this tendency), this binary is still played out insofar as the focus of enquiry has simply flipped over to material concerns, to the neglect of the Buddhist philosophical discourse that is associated with this material practice (Rambelli, 2007). Feminist critiques such as Jantzen (1998) and Irigaray (2004) link this focus upon beliefs and truth conditions with a masculinist symbolic that performatively denies material implication. *A priori* categories and beliefs, coupled with overarching categories such as 'world views', all tend towards a two-dimensional plane of sense-making that empties events of their material, political and affective specificity.

(iv) Imaginaries

An analysis of some of the metaphors and terms that are routinely deployed suggests, therefore, that Western 'common sense'—that is to say, the assumptions that inform perception, understanding and judgment that tend to remain taken for granted—is characterised by a visual orientation that privileges detached judgment together with abstract and disembodied forms of sense-making. A rhetoric of neutrality does not problematise these orientations; rather, it is itself a product of this particular philosophical imaginary, drawing upon a range of visual tropes, and this has far-reaching implications for how other cultural traditions are understood.

The foregoing analysis would suggest that a rhetoric of neutrality, as a particular assemblage of assumptions, concepts, metaphors and practices, is itself a manifestation of a distinctive Western imaginary, rather than being neutral in its effects. And if that is so, all acts of sense-making—even under the sign of neutrality—will be materially refracted through the various tropes, concepts and practices that are gathered together in the making of

Thinking Otherwise—Spinoza and Foucault 65

a particular sense. There is, in other words, a politics involved as regards whose conception of reality prevails (Mol, 1999). A refusal to acknowledge this leads to the translation, and silencing, of one culture within the terms of another.[5] A more equitable way of proceeding, therefore, demands that the specific terms of *each* partner's imaginary be acknowledged in any encounter. It is therefore desirable, in other words, to attend to *how each party does the real*; 'doing ontics', in anthropologist Helen Verran's (2007) terms, then becomes a necessary dimension in practices of making sense if these make a claim to be ethical. But for this to be possible, it is necessary to engage traditions of thought that can in fact acknowledge the significance of different imaginaries and how these choreograph experience in ways that acknowledge relational and material implication (Verran, in Law and Lin, 2011). But such an orientation also involves the relinquishment of approaches that assume the possibility of detached and unimplicated ways of knowing, such as the visual orientation and tendency towards abstraction that informs dominant framings of RE at the present time.

(v) Re-Imagining Cultural Difference: Spinoza

One response to the limitations inherent in the Cartesian tradition and its associated forms of common sense is to draw instead upon alternative traditions of enquiry that afford different imaginative and conceptual possibilities. Spinoza's (1985) writings, in particular, offer a rich resource for thinking and practising differently and have been engaged by a variety of contemporary theorists keen to explore other patterns of sense-making.[6]

So what is characteristic of Spinoza's approach, and how might this offer resources for thinking RE otherwise? According to Deleuze (1988, 130), what is unique about Spinoza is that while 'the most philosophic of philosophers', he nevertheless 'teaches the philosopher how to become a non-philosopher'. Part of Spinoza's attractiveness, according to this reading, stems from a style of philosophising that foregrounds power, desire and imagination. And this concern with the imagination is, moreover, social, material and political in its implications. In providing an alternative philosophical lineage (Duffy, 2004; 2006), Spinoza's writings offer new means of expression for articulating a philosophy of difference (Deleuze, 1990; 1994) and provide resources for educational approaches that are more attuned to the political and socio-material orientations characteristic of more recent post-colonial, feminist and STS (Law, 2004). Taking Spinoza's texts together enables a complex reading, in which, according to Gatens and Lloyd (1999, 1),

> Politics, ethics, epistemology, metaphysics and philosophy of mind are interwoven . . . and their interconnections raise possibilities of alternative and richer ways of conceptualising contemporary political and social issues.

66   Thinking Otherwise—Resisting Indifference

Spinoza is concerned with both the ontological and epistemological dimensions of the imagination, and this has a number of consequences. As Gatens and Lloyd (1999, 35) succinctly put this,

> Imagination, rather than being just the ally of investigative reason, becomes itself the object of rational investigation.

In place of the passions being an unwelcome distraction from the philosopher's proper task, the imaginary and its associated affective domain become central to making sense at all. This is because Spinoza refuses a dualistic understanding of mind in relation to the body: *both* are of the same substance, although different modes of that same substance. For Spinoza, the mind 'is the idea of the body' (*Ethics*, II, 13, proof), and so whilst the mind and its powers and the body and its powers of action are distinct (*Ethics*, III, 2), their development is nevertheless in parallel (*Ethics*, II, 13, Schol). Affects mediate between these two, and, in referring to both mind and body, reason and the passions bring about new syntheses between entities that are usually kept distinct (Hardt, 2007). Since affects belong to both sides, they are necessarily implicated in our powers to affect the world and be affected by it. According to Spinoza, the greater the power to be affected, the greater our power to act (*Ethics*, IV, 38).

Whilst there are dangers associated with the imagination, it does not stand in a simple hierarchical relation to reason to be overcome in some Platonic ascent from the world of appearances to that of forms; it is instead a powerful ally of reason (Lloyd, 1998, 163). What becomes clear is that fictions are not to be regarded simply as illusions over against reality, but are rather 'constitutive of our collective construction of a social world' (Lloyd, 2000, 32). Indeed, it may be more appropriate to regard these figments of imaginaries as *ficciones*—a term coined by the Argentinian writer Jorge Luis Borges that refuses the binary truth *or* fiction and instead acknowledges that in practice, most of our understandings partake in *both* 'truth' and 'fiction' properly so called. An acceptance that our coinage is *ficciones*, rather than neatly divisible into either category can instead, encourage us to 'take up . . . the story of . . . [our] own ontological errancy' (Wyschogrod, 1998, 32). Be that as it may, while the task of reason is to critique the inadequacies of certain fictions, the imagination is never left behind on this reading: '[w]e do not cease to imagine, just because we begin to know' (Lloyd, 1998, 164, summarising Bertrand, 1985, 67–8). So the purpose is to understand the operations of a given imaginary, rather than to overcome them, for human knowledge is always embodied. This enables a style of reasoning that can think implication (*in media res*) and acknowledge that traditions draw their power from the imagination and the passions rather than from some more restricted rationalistic approach (Gatens and Lloyd, 1999, 88). The consequence of this is that some kind of opacity will always accompany thinking,

Thinking Otherwise—Spinoza and Foucault 67

and, according to Butler (2005), far from being just a limitation, this may in turn provide a susceptibility for understanding another.[7]

Imagination also provides a bridge to the social world and is constitutive of shared and collective imaginaries that are institutionally mediated (Negri, 1991). It is thus indispensable for an awareness of both how our own—and other's—bodies are affected collectively, in multiple ways. In all this, the emphasis is upon the constructive and productive nature of the imagination: our imaginaries are intrinsically bound up with how we enact 'the real' and the socio-material gatherings that this entails.

(vi) Spinoza's Contribution

There are three further distinctive aspects of Spinoza's approach to the imaginary that are of particular relevance to making sense within educational spaces. These concern: (a) orientation to analysis, (b) mode of analysis and (c) access to truth; each of these will be considered in turn, although in practice, each is interrelated.

(a) Orientation to Analysis: Conatus

One of Spinoza's best known concepts is that of *conatus*, which he characterises as the 'striving by which each thing strives to persevere in its being' (*Ethics*, III, 7). However, the self that strives to preserve itself is not necessarily a singular being, for it is in the complex interplay of relationships with others that life is augmented or diminished. According to Butler (2006, 113)

> . . . life means to participate in life, and life itself will be a term that equivocates between the 'me' and the 'you', taking up both of us in its sweep and dispersion. Desiring life produces an *ek-stasis* in the midst of desire, a dependence on an externalization, something that is palpably not-me, without which no perseverance is possible.

And so *conatus* is concerned with both individual and collective becomings, and as such, it is fundamentally relational and affirmative. As Deleuze (1988, 28) has commented

> [t]he ethics is necessarily an ethics of joy: only joy is worthwhile, joy remains, bringing us near to action, to the bliss of action.

To this extent, as Anderson (2009) observes, there are affinities here with the work of Jantzen (2004), who critiqued Western imaginaries as being primarily oriented to violence and death over a concern with life and natality. A concern with life itself and its present and future relational unfoldings is, therefore, one of the consequences of such a Spinozist orientation. This

68   *Thinking Otherwise—Resisting Indifference*

marks a fundamental difference in orientation as regards the kinds of meta-phors that properly inform analysis, away from the machinic metaphors that have informed dominant Western medical approaches, as described above, and away from the tendency to privilege detachment and abstraction within RE, too.

(b) Mode of Analysis: Ethology

The second contribution to imagining otherwise is Spinoza's *ethology*, which is an approach to analysis that is radically open: the emphasis here is upon trying not to foreclose in advance what may happen. In Deleuze's (1988, 125) words, '. . . you do not know beforehand what a mind or body can do, in a given encounter, a given arrangement, a given combination' (cf. *Ethics*, III, 2). Since it is not known what kinds of sense-making will issue in relation to a specific encounter within RE, this represents a fundamental departure from approaches where the terms of understanding are given *a priori*. In place of a grid of intelligibility that attempts effectively to pre-order a given encounter, an ethological approach tries to be open to what actually hap-pens. So, for example, rather than a lesson or seminar being exhaustively planned in advance, an ethological approach will be concerned with the emergence of opportunities for new insight and innovative production that exceed what the educator might have anticipated. In this connection, assem-blages that include technologies, such as digital cameras, can lead to new relational configurations—new collective bodies, in Spinoza's terms—that issue in projects that appear to act back upon participants in ways that lead to accomplishments that can surprise all those concerned (I'Anson, 2011). As such, ethology is concerned with the relative speeds and intensities of events that take place: '[t]he speed or slowness of metabolisms, perceptions, actions, and reactions [that in turn] link together to constitute a particular individual in the world' (Deleuze, 1988, 125).

What this illustration also suggests is that what a 'body' consists of cannot be foreclosed in advance of a particular relational gathering taking place. The 'body' in question may well exceed a singular individual; in other words, how a given 'body' is composed is also open to question and could just as easily be 'a linguistic corpus, a social body, a collectivity' (Deleuze, 1988, 127). And so questions of scale are not foreclosed, but neither in this account is the 'human' privileged either. If a body and its possibilities cannot be determined in advance, it becomes necessary to inquire into how a given practice or entity is composed: what is the nature of a given assemblage, and in what ways does this augment or diminish its capacities? The upshot of such a socio-material approach is that sense-making becomes empirical and experimental. Rather than events becoming emptied out (or 'de-eventualised' as Harrison (2002) puts this), there is, instead, a radical attention to how realities are assembled in and through material-semiotic relations in a spe-cific moment, occasion and place. So there are some interesting affinities

Thinking Otherwise—Spinoza and Foucault   69

between Spinoza's way of thinking and more recent socio-material orientations (Law, 2009).[8]

This attention to specific sites means that sense-making has to proceed on a case-by-case basis, since there is no 'reality in general', but only the ways in which realities are composed and made sense of in *this* place, at *this* time and with *these* effects. Here, there is a shift in emphasis away from 'world views' to practices of world-making: to the new framings and productions that become possible, if different repertoires are engaged (Henare *et al.*, 2007). Making sense, therefore, involves exploring how people, practices, artefacts and concepts are gathered together and ordered as a 'body' within a particular locale, including that of a school or seminar room. Such an exploration of cultural difference—as world-making—will also involve taking up different aspects (in this instance, a concept, in that, a material artefact) to see what difference this might make. This might, for example, involve exploring how a different concept re-frames an existing way of approaching a matter of concern through placing this in a different temporal or spatial context or through undoing familiar distinctions and orderings and mapping the consequences of this. In each such instance, the focus of attention is on the differentiating effects of engaging this difference: how, that is, reality is diffracted otherwise. To this extent, making sense is not from a detached and neutral vantage point but from an engaged position in the midst of multiple relations, where engaging in practice will simultaneously lead to action—and being acted upon.[9]

Given the difficulties that are attendant with the trope of neutrality, insofar as this privileges a disengaged and a non-affected subject position, it might be worth considering a different orienting trope with which to think through some of the implications of engaging with matters of concern within RE. One such trope is that of 'diffraction', which has been especially associated with the work of Haraway (1997) and Barad (2007). Diffraction as a concept derives from science studies into the effects of waves. As such, it is concerned with the complexities of relations that obtain in a given field and the difference that being implicated within that field makes. As Barad (2007, 185) has put this,

> [w]e don't obtain knowledge by standing outside the world; we know because we are of the world. We are part of the world and its differential becoming.

As a trope, diffraction is empirically oriented and attentive to the interruptions brought about by difference within a scene. Hultman and Taguchi (2010, 529) express this well when they observe that such difference is

> . . . caused by connections and relations within and between different bodies, affecting each other and being affected, whether it is viruses, humans or sand. This makes each of these bodies differentiate *in themselves*, continuously—one singular event after the other.

70 Thinking Otherwise—Resisting Indifference

By the same token, the trope of diffraction is also associated with the complexities involved in *giving an account* of these complex processes in ways that register the effects that such implication within a field makes. In other words, with the trope of diffraction, it is no longer possible to simply erase from view the complexity of relations that are present. Not the least reasons for this is that—as John Law (2009) once observed—to the extent that an entity or practice is invisible, it is probably doing considerable work in holding together a given state of affairs.

In place of sense-making predicated upon a detachment and practices of abstraction, there is a focus on the specific socio-material orderings that together constitute a given ordering of the real. Such an approach tries to avoid the twin dangers of 'romanticizing materiality' on the one hand, or 'occluding humanity', on the other (Fenwick *et al.*, 2011, 180). But the specific ways in which humanity is acknowledged, within a Spinozean account, also departs from a series of conventional assumptions, especially as regards what is involved in coming to know the truth of oneself and another.

(c) Access to Truth: Philosophy and Spiritual Exercise (Askêsis)

A further way in which Spinoza's thought moves beyond the limitations of present framings concerns the practices involved in accessing truth. In his 1981–2 lectures given at the Collège de France, Foucault (2005) offers an original reading of the ways in which pre-modern philosophy differs from the style of philosophy characteristic of that produced after 'the Cartesian moment'.[10] Spinoza's project predates the modern period and has a distinctive orientation to knowledge: access to truth is not simply about a detached acquisition of knowledge through method, but derives from an approach where philosophy and spirituality are intrinsically linked. If philosophy is concerned with the conditions and limitations under which a subject might have access to truth, spirituality here concerns 'the search, practice, and experience through which the subject carries out the necessary transformations on himself [sic] in order to have access to the truth' (Foucault, 2005, 15). Such a transformation, achieved through various practices of reflexivity, is the price to be paid for access to 'truth'. So the subject, in this reading, is not capable of access to truth *without* such work, and, moreover, the 'truth' in question exceeds a simple act of knowledge as such.

Foucault (2005) argues that if the post-Cartesian approach can be seen as operating under the sign of 'know yourself' (*gnōthi seauton*), the more traditional orientation characteristic of Spinoza is under the sign of 'care of the self' (*epimeleia heautou*), which subsumes 'know thyself' within a much broader framing. In relation to Spinoza, Foucault (2005, 28) describes this in the following terms,

> . . . a certain structure of spirituality tries to link knowledge, the activity of knowing, and the conditions and effects of this activity, to a transformation of the subject's being.

Thinking Otherwise—Spinoza and Foucault 71

A clear instance of this can be found in Spinoza's (1985, 16) *Treatise on the Correction of the Understanding*, where he writes,

> . . . before all things, a means must be devised for improving the understanding and purifying it, as far as may be at the outset, so that it may apprehend things without error, and in the best possible way.

Here, the metaphor of purification points to a set of practices that exceed what would be taken as proper to the philosopher's task. As Foucault (2005, 27) comments,

> [y]ou can see quite clearly there [. . .] how in formulating the problem of access to the truth Spinoza linked the problem to a series of requirements concerning the subject's very being: In what aspects and how must I transform my being as subject? What conditions must I impose on my being as subject so as to have access to the truth, and to what extent will this access to the truth give me what I seek, that is to say the highest good, the sovereign good?

Foucault (2005, 28) observes that this is a 'properly spiritual question' and the concern with reforming the understanding is

> . . . entirely typical of the still very strict, close, and tight links between [. . .] a philosophy of knowledge and a spirituality of the subject's transformation of his own being.

This is to move in a very different direction from the practices associated with the visual tropes that are characteristic of approaches predicated on a rhetoric of neutrality. This potentially opens up a different problematisation where questions as to the kinds of attention, social and material relations and practices, together with the forms of reflexivity necessary for considered practice, become necessary, if one is to make sense in ways that can acknowledge such complexity.

Spinoza's conception involves what might be termed a 'dramatics of truth' in and through which both the truth of oneself and that of the other can emerge. To this extent, Spinoza's writings offer an approach that McGushin (2007) has characterised as an etho-poetics. This takes the specific terms of a given imaginary seriously without translating these within the terms of a pre-existing interpretive grid. It is concerned with the work upon the self necessary to make sense of differences in RE spaces and is therefore open to questions as to the kinds of reflexivity and change that are appropriate in a given case.

With such a framing, making sense of difference can no longer be conceived as a primarily decontextualised epistemological concern, but instead foregrounds the ethical responsibilities that such work entails. In doing so, this also broadens the focus to encompass the relational context and the social and material performances that take place. Whilst writing practices

72 Thinking Otherwise—Resisting Indifference

still have a part to play, they become part of a broader ensemble of practices and materialities that work to acknowledge intractability, uncertainty and the limits associated with the production of truth. According to McGushin (2007, 286), with such an orientation,

> . . . philosophy is both a *poiesis*—a work we perform on ourselves— and a *technē*—a form of reflective awareness about how to work on ourselves.

Making sense within RE then becomes part of a broader project that enquires into precisely *which* practices are called for and *how* such practices are to be taken up in a particular case. Such a framing, therefore, installs ethical practice at the heart of becoming educated in RE. This is to orient attention to the very practices that produce knowledge and insight together with the kinds of reflexivity necessary to take up responsibility to others, where that consists in responsibility to a particular 'body', or a more general orientation conceived within an ecological horizon.

(vii) Conclusion: Towards Uncommon Sense?

This chapter has argued that Spinoza provides resources for thinking and practising differently beyond the limitations of current framings that inform RE that are predicated on a detached knowing within a pre-given—and pre-determining—framework. Since the inauguration of current approaches to RE some 40 or so years ago, there have been a series of developments within the academy associated with post-colonial, feminist and STS that have raised powerful political and ethical challenges to this way of framing an educational response. A metaphorical analysis suggests that, far from being 'neutral', current approaches in RE inscribe a characteristically modern, post-Cartesian reading. The upshot of this is that a dominant Western imaginary remains uncontested, while translating different and potentially rival approaches within its own characteristic terms. An alternative philosophical lineage inaugurated by Spinoza has been traced in which different imaginaries are potentially accorded their due significance in both individual and collective forms of sociality. Some of the educational challenges and opportunities that are afforded through engaging this broader and more capacious style of reasoning were then considered, especially in regard to Foucault's work—indexed under the sign of 'spirituality'—that foregrounds the ethical and transformational implications of such work. Of course, this is to leave behind the restricted educational horizon associated with neutrality: in moving beyond this limited and limiting account, there opens up the possibility of re-engaging educationally with difference through imaginaries that welcome the in-coming of the new.

An orientation that engages imaginaries, in other words, gestures towards new pedagogies and forms of experimentation. In Thrift's (2004) terms,

Thinking Otherwise—Spinoza and Foucault 73

this offers resources for a 'politics of imaginative generosity' within educational sites where difference is in play. Such an approach lays claim to being educational insofar as this 'leads out' from what is known already rather than inadvertently re-inscribing existing assumptions about the real and its possibilities.[11]

Notes

1. Claims to neutrality have become subject to sustained critique in a variety of different fields, whether in law (Spencer and Brogan, 2006), science studies (Harding, 1998), education (Weiss, 2006) or philosophy (Scolnicov, 1988), insofar as these claim 'neutrality as a value while espousing a substantive position' (Church, 1998, 238).
2. Much the same, *mutandis mutatis*, might be said in relation to metaphor and the social sciences. As Richardson (2000, 927) has summarised: 'Metaphors organize social scientific work and affect the interpretations of the "facts"; indeed, facts are interpretable ("make sense") only in terms of their place within a metaphoric structure'.
3. This is explored much further in Chapter 4.
4. In a recent paper, Law (2009) has hazarded that it is precisely in proportion to the hiddenness of such assumptions that work is performed in holding together a given social formation. If Law's contention as to the significance of 'collateral realities' is at all correct, this provides another powerful argument for the work of excavating and attempting to surface background assumptions, practices and materialities.
5. There are parallels here with Lyotard's (1988) work on the *differend*.
6. Examples include: Gatens (1996; 2009) (ed.), Deleuze (1990, 1988), Gatens and Lloyd (1999), Butler (2006) etc.
7. Acknowledging imagination and the passions, rather than a focus upon a more restricted, rationalistic approach, has implications for how educational policy is evaluated—and for how a rhetoric for educational change might be articulated. On this, see Reeves and I'Anson, 2014.
8. In a number of respects Spinoza's theorising might be seen as anticipating more recent theoretical developments within STS such as Actor-Network Theory, where, for example, the concept of 'symmetry' is a way of refusing to privilege 'the human' in the midst of complex heterogeneous networks.
9. There are parallels here with the 'middle voice' that Llewelyn (1991) describes, which is grammatical form that registers both the subject acting and being acted upon; in recent times, this has tended to be eclipsed through an exclusive focus on individual agency.
10. Foucault (2005, 14) is careful to place 'scare quotes' around 'Cartesian moment' so as to acknowledge the difficulties associated with the identification of the beginnings of this movement of thought.
11. This chapter develops some themes initially outlined in an earlier chapter (I'Anson, 2010).

Bibliography

Anderson, B., 1991. *Imagined Communities: Reflections on the Origin and Spread of Nationalism*. London: Verso.
Anderson, P.S., 2009. 'The urgent wish . . . to be more life-giving'. In: E.L. Graham ed., *Grace Jantzen: Redeeming the Presence*. Farnham and Burlington: Ashgate, pp. 41–53.

74 *Thinking Otherwise—Resisting Indifference*

Armour, E.T. and St.Ville, S.M., 2006. *Bodily Citations: Religion and Judith Butler*. New York: Columbia University Press.

Barad, K., 2007. *Meeting the Universe Halfway: Quantum Physics and the Entanglement of Matter and Meaning*. Durham, NC and London: Duke University Press.

Bertrand, M., 1985. *Spinoza et l'imaginaire*. Paris: Presses Universitaire de France.

Butler, J., 2005. *Giving an Account of Oneself*. New York: Fordham University Press.

Butler, J., 2006. 'The desire to live: Spinoza's Ethics under pressure'. In: V. Kahn, N. Saccamano and D. Coli eds., *Politics and the Passions, 1500–1850*. Princeton and Oxford: Princeton University Press, pp. 111–130.

Caputo, J.D., 1993. *Against Ethics: Contributions to a Poetics of Obligation With Constant Reference to Deconstruction*. Bloomington and Indianapolis: Indiana University Press.

Chakrabarty, D., 2000. *Provincializing Europe: Postcolonial Thought and Historical Difference*. Princeton and Oxford: Princeton University Press.

Church, R., 1998. The rhetoric of neutrality and the philosophers' brief: A critique of the *Amicus* brief of six moral philosophers. *Law and Contemporary Problems, Washington v. Glucksberg and Vacco v. Quill*, vol. 61, no. 4, pp. 233–247.

Deleuze, G., 1988. *Spinoza: Practical Philosophy*. San Francisco: City Lights.

Deleuze, G., 1990. *Expressionism in Philosophy: Spinoza*. New York: Zone Books.

Deleuze, G. 1994. *Difference and Repetition*. P. Patton trans., London and New York: Continuum.

Duffy, S., 2004. 'The logic of expression in Deleuze's *Expressionism in Philosophy: Spinoza:* A strategy of engagement'. *International Journal of Philosophical Studies*, vol. 12, no. 1, pp. 47–80.

Duffy, S., 2006. *The Logic of Expression: Quality, Quantity and Intensity in Spinoza, Hegel and Deleuze*. Aldershot and Burlington, VT: Ashgate.

Fenwick, T., Edwards, R. and Sawchuk, P., 2011. *Emerging Approaches to Educational Research: Tracing the Sociomaterial*. London and New York: Routledge.

Fitzgerald, T., 2007a. *Discourse on Civility and Barbarity: A Critical History of Religion and Related Categories*. Oxford: Oxford University Press.

Fitzgerald, T., 2007b. *Religion and the Secular: Historical and Colonial Formations*. London and Oakville, CT: Equinox.

Foucault, M., 2003. *Society Must Be Defended*. London: Penguin.

Foucault, M., 2005. *The Hermeneutics of the Subject: Lectures at the College de France, 1981–1982*. New York: Palgrave Macmillan.

Gardiner, M., 2004. '"A light to the world": British devolution and colonial vision'. *Interventions*, vol. 6, no. 2, pp. 264–281.

Gatens, M., 1996. *Imaginary Bodies: Ethics, Power and Corporeality*. London and New York: Routledge.

Gatens, M., 2009. *Feminist Interpretations of Benedict Spinoza*. Pennsylvania: Penn State Press.

Gatens, M. and Lloyd, G., 1999. *Collective Imaginings: Spinoza, Past and Present*. London and New York: Routledge.

Haraway, D., 1997. *Modest_Witness@Second_Millenium: FemaleMan_Meets_Onco-Mouse: Feminism and Tehnoscience*. New York: Routledge.

Harding, S., 1998. 'After the neutrality ideal: Science, politics, and "strong objectivity"'. *Social Research*, vol. 59, no. 3, pp. 567–587.

Hardt, M., 2007. 'Forward: What affects are good for'. In: P.T. Clough and J. Halley eds., *The Affective Turn: Theorizing the Social*. Durham, NC and London: Duke University Press, pp. ix–xiii.

Harrison, P., 2002. 'The caesura: Remarks on Wittgenstein's interruption of theory, or, why practices elude explanation'. *Geoforum*, vol. 33, no. 4, pp. 487–503.

Henare, A., Holbraad, M. and Wastell, S., 2007. 'Introduction: Thinking through things'. In: A. Henare, M. Holbraad and S. Wastell eds., *Thinking Through Things: Theorising Artefacts Ethnographically*. Abingdon and New York: Routledge, pp. 1–31.

Hultman, K. and Taguchi, H.L., 2010. 'Challenging anthropocentric analysis of visual data: A relational materialist methodological approach to educational research'. *Qualitative Studies in Education*, vol. 23, no. 5, pp. 525–542.

I'Anson, J., 2010. 'Re-imagining cultural difference'. In: T.L.K. Wisely, I.M. Barr, A. Britton and B. King eds., *Education in a Global Space: Emerging Research and Practice in Initial Teacher Education*. Edinburgh: IDEAS/SCOTDEC, pp. 223–230.

I'Anson, J., 2011. 'Childhood, complexity orientation and children's rights: Enlarging the space of the possible?'. *Education Inquiry*, vol. 2, no. 3, pp. 373–384.

I'Anson, J. and Jasper, A., 2011. '"Religion" in educational spaces: Knowing, knowing well, and knowing differently'. *Arts and Humanities in Higher Education*, vol. 10, no. 3, pp. 295–314.

Ingold, T. and Kurttila, T., 2000. 'Perceiving the environment in Finnish Lapland'. *Body and Society*, vol. 6, no. 3–4, pp. 183–196.

Irigaray, L., 2004. *Key Writings*. London and New York: Continuum.

Jantzen, G. M. 1998. *Becoming Divine: Towards a Feminist Philosophy of Religion*. Manchester: Manchester University Press.

Jantzen, G.M., 2001. 'Before the rooster crows: The betrayal of knowledge in modernity'. *Literature and theology*, vol. 15, no. 1, pp. 1–24.

Jantzen, G.M., 2004. *Foundations of Violence: Death and the Displacement of Beauty*, vol. 1. London and New York: Routledge.

Kant, I. 1965. *The Critique of Pure Reason*. N. Kemp Smith, trans. New York: St. Martin's Press.

Keller, M., 2002. *The Hammer and the Flute: Women, Power, and Spirit Possession*. Baltimore and London: Johns Hopkins University Press.

Law, J., 2004. *After Method: Mess in Social Science Research*. Abingdon, Oxford and New York: Routledge.

Law, J., 2009. 'Collateral realities'. Version of 29 December 2009. Available from www.heterogeneities.net/publications/Law2009CollateralRealities.pdf.

Law, J. and Lin, W.-Y., 2011. 'Cultivating disconcertment'. In: M. Benson and Re Munro eds., *Sociological Routes and Political Roots*. Oxford: Wiley-Blackwell, pp. 135–153.

Law, J. and Mol, A., 2002. *Complexities: Social Studies of Knowledge Practices*. Durham, NC: Duke University Press.

Le Dœuff, M., 1980. Editions Payot. *The Philosophical Imaginary, L'Imaginaire Philosophique*. 1989 ed. London and Stanford, CA: Athlone Press and Stanford University Press.

Llewelyn, J. 1991. *The Middle Voice of Ecological Conscience: A Chiasmic Reading of Responsibility in the Neighbourhood of Levinas, Heidegger and Others*, London: Macmillan.

Lloyd, G., 1998. 'Spinoza and the education of the imagination'. In: A.O. Rorty ed., *Philosophers on Education: New Historical Perspectives*. London and New York: Routledge, pp. 156–171.

Lloyd, G., 2000. 'No one's land: Australia and the philosophical imagination'. *Hypatia*, vol. 15, no. 2, pp. 26–39.

76 Thinking Otherwise—Resisting Indifference

Long, C.H., 1986. *Significations: Signs, Symbols and Images in the Interpretation of Religion*. Philadelphia: Fortress Press.

Lopez Jnr., D.S., 1998. 'Belief'. In: M.C. Taylor ed., *Critical Terms for Religious Studies*. Chicago and London: University of Chicago Press, pp. 21–35.

Lyotard, J., 1988. *The Differend: Phrases in Dispute*. Manchester, UK: Manchester University Press.

McGushin, E.F., 2007. *Foucault's Askêsis: An Introduction to the Philosophical Life*. Evanston, IL: Northwestern University Press.

MacMurray, J., 1969. *Persons in Relation*. London: Faber and Faber.

Mandair, A.-S., 2009. *Religion and the Specter of the West: Sikhism, India, Postcoloniality, and the Politics of Translation*. New York: Columbia University Press.

Ménil, A., 2003. 'The time(s) of the cinema'. In: J. Khalfa ed., *An Introduction to the Philosophy of Gilles Deleuze*, London and New York: Continuum, pp. 85–104.

Mol, A.-M., 1999. 'A word and some questions'. In: J. Law and J. Hassard eds., *Actor Network Theory and After*. Oxford: Blackwell, pp. 74–89.

Negri, A., 1991. *The Savage Anomaly: The Power of Spinoza's Metaphysics and Politics*. Minneapolis: University of Minnesota Press.

Rambelli, F., 2007. *Buddhist Materiality: A Cultural History of Objects in Japanese Buddhism*. Stanford, CA: Stanford University Press.

Reeves, J. and I'Anson, J., 2014. 'Rhetorics of professional change: Assembling the means to act differently?'. *Oxford Review of Education*, vol. 40, no. 5, pp. 649–666.

Richardson, L. 2000. 'Writing: A Method of Inquiry'. In: N. K. Denzin and Y.S. Lincoln, *The Sage Handbook of Qualitative Research*. Thousand Oaks, California, London and New York: Sage, pp. 923–948.

Schopen, G., 1991. 'Archaeology and protestant presuppositions in the study of Indian Buddhism'. *History of Religions*, vol. 31, no. 1, pp. 1–23.

Scolnicov, S., 1988. *Plato's Metaphysics of Education*. London: Routledge.

Smart, N., 1989. *The World's Religions: Old Traditions and Modern Transformations*. Cambridge and Victoria: Cambridge University Press.

Spencer, D. and Brogan, M., 2006. *Mediation Law and Practice*. Cambridge: Cambridge University Press.

Spinoza, B., 1985. *Complete Works*. Princeton, NJ: Princeton University Press.

Taylor, C., 2004. *Modern Social Imaginaries*. North Carolina: Duke University Press.

Thrift, N., 2004. 'Summoning life'. In: P. Cloke, P. Crang and M. Goodwin eds., *Envisioning Human Geographies*. London: Arnold, pp. 81–103.

Verran, H., 2007. 'Software for educating aboriginal children about place'. In: D.W. Kritt and L.T. Winegar eds., *Education and Technology: Critical Perspectives and Possible Futures*. Lanham, MD: Lexington Books, pp. 101–124.

Weiss, J., 2006. 'Critical theory, voice, and urban education'. In: J.L. Kincheloe, K. Hayes, K. Rose and P.M. Anderson eds., *The Praeger Handbook of Urban Education*, Westport, Conn: Greenwood Press, pp. 289–302.

Wyschogrod, E., 1998. *An Ethics of Remembering: History, Heterology, and the Nameless Others*. Chicago: Chicago University Press.

Young, S.H., 2010. 'The ideology of Buddhist materialism'. *Religious Studies Review*, vol. 36, no. 2, pp. 109–114.

4 Thinking Otherwise—Gender in the Mix[1]

(i) Introduction

An important theme introduced in the previous chapter and significant for the project of the whole book is how metaphors inform sense-making practices. Thus, Le Dœuff (1989) offers us a way of surfacing patterns of imagination in any given context of inquiry through the identification of a network of highly determinative metaphors working quietly and generally unnoticed within texts, relationships and institutions to sustain a particular philosophical imagination. In this chapter, once again taking the dominant Western Cartesian framework or style of reasoning as a point of reference, we will look in more detail at the sorts of 'common sense' its metaphorically inflected features produce in relation particularly to ahistorical, gendered and hierarchical understandings of rationality, detachment and abstraction (Lloyd, 1984; Law and Mol, 2002). The previous chapter noted how visual orientations leading to an understanding of detached judgment and the privileging of abstract and disembodied forms of sense-making contribute to a particular 'rhetoric of neutrality'. In this chapter, we explore how that rhetoric draws on gender and sexuality. Reference to Spinoza served to highlight how a different imagination opens up different conceptual possibilities. Reference to Spinoza provides other continuities at this point, too. Firstly, his concerns are social and material in their implications providing resources for educational approaches that are attuned to the relational and socio-material orientations emerging in more recent feminist and gender studies within the academy (Daly Goggin and Fowkes Tobin, 2009a; Anderson, 2013; Thatcher Ulrich and Carter, 2015). Spinoza also challenges the hierarchical binaries typical of the mind/body distinction within Western main/malestream thinking (Monro, 2005; Chanter, 2006).

The purpose of this chapter is to suggest ways of thinking differently, the better to address the indifference (detachment, abstraction and lack of connection to people's actual lived and gendered experiences) of the current account of RE. To this end, relational and contextual factors relating to gender and sexuality and to students' capacity and need for sense-making and negotiation in these areas have to be brought much more clearly into view. It

78 *Thinking Otherwise—Resisting Indifference*

is true that the present settlement advocates critical approaches. It is careful to avoid anything that could be regarded as unwarranted 'religious' interference in the provision of universal education, 'religious' being understood within an exclusive and exhaustive religion/secular dichotomy (Fitzgerald, 2007). But in its continued mobilisation of the rhetoric of neutrality, the ongoing account of RE is arguably still contained within a dominant and gendered way of viewing and experiencing the world. So firstly, we need to 'up the ante' on our critical thinking, resisting any temptation to give up on the struggle to engage critically with difference or to reduce it to simplistic relativism (Latour, 2004; Brown, 2005). One way to address the difficulties is, as part of our critical practice, to expand the range of what Rosi Braidotti calls *conceptual personae* (Braidotti, 2011, 12). Braidotti introduces this concept in *Nomadic Subjects* (2011) within a section headed 'against metaphors' (10) but rather than being against metaphors which are pervasive, she is against any understanding or use of metaphors that makes them out to be points of reference within a world of unitary subjects and stable meanings. Instead, 'the point is finding adequate representation for the sort of subjects we are in the process of becoming' (11). *Conceptual personae* are thus metaphorically inflected tools needed to help us grow a new framework of the imagination that allows for this becoming and supports the skills of students and teachers in mapping the unknown in gender terms. There is plenty of interesting feminist theory to draw on. Braidotti, for instance, gives us her understanding of the subjectivity of women in terms of 'becoming woman', where the term of 'woman' is not regarded as a limitation, but as a space of experimentation (Braidotti, 2002, 27) and an escape from 'phallicity' (Braidotti, 2002, 28). Other notable feminist approaches referenced in this section are Pamela Anderson's (2010) experiments with transcendence incarnate, endeavouring to bring about a feminist transformation of the Christian and Cartesian binaries, Carol Christ's (1979) feminist re-visioning of male-indexed spirituality and Judith Butler's (2004) deconstruction of gender essentialisms. In this section, we will consider just a small selection of feminist theory but want to encourage the widest possible exploration of feminist and intersectional action and thought.

It is indisputable, however, that traditional patterns of gender still shape the origins and spaces of RE. One example of this is the way in which essentialised notions of 'religion' or 'world religions' in popular discourses can take on characteristics that are strikingly similar to those associated with women or the feminine (Jasper, 2015b). Thus, 'religion' is described as being irrationally fixated on unjustifiable beliefs, just as untrustworthy (female) emotive irrationality (Lippy, 2009) is a strong thread in historical stereotypes of Western women, from the disobedience of Eve to the wandering womb of the 19th century (Thompson, 1999). In consequence, it is easy to make the case that this irrationality identified with the feminine needs to be dominated or controlled by the forces of normative and rational masculinity associated with the so-called 'secular'. In other words, it is a

Thinking Otherwise—Gender in the Mix 79

given that metaphor is not simply a characteristic of language or a matter of extraordinary rather than ordinary usage. Rather, it is seen everywhere, shaping life, thought and action and constructing our lives and work as educators and students in ways that are woven too deeply into the fabric of our lives to be identified without a conscious effort and some sort of active prompting. Since the European enlightenment, a gendered rhetoric of neutrality, disinterestedness and objectivity has flourished, proving enormously productive and profitable for some kinds of endeavour and sectors of society. And, of course, endeavouring to provide that active prompting, feminist, intersectional (Crenshaw, 1991; Hill Collins and Bilge, 2016) and post-colonial theory (Spivak, 1984; Mohanty, 1991; 2003) has been at pains to point out in the last few decades that these normative styles of reasoning have subordinated other sectors of society and excluded a rich variety of different imaginative sense-making possibilities. Here too, perhaps, is a context within which greater engagement and exchange across the different sectors or levels of education could be fruitful.

Thus, a distinctive aspect of Western metaphysics in the past has been its reliance on hierarchical binaries derived from metaphorical constructions of gender subordination in human relations. From these we have derived the idea, for example, of the isolated male or masculine genius with god-like creative power who is defined by his difference from the female. Raised above or required to control the female or feminine-identified world of material, emotion and bodily entanglement (Battersby, 1989; Kristeva, 1999–2002; Jasper, 2012), this is a style of reasoning that draws on aspects of a pre-modern Christianity whilst developing new applications within modernity. Casting the masculine into relief, the female or feminine is the reverse, the negative or 'the other' in the binary (Beauvoir, 1949). Even when she possesses determinative form and agency and is not simply reduced to terrifying watery chaos as ancient mythology, influencing more contemporary thought, has sometimes conceived her (Keller, 2003), she lacks intellectual capacity and, as essentially corporeal, is incapable of seeing beyond her own disordered desires (Jasper, 2007; 2012). At the most extreme, she is abject, contaminating or demonic, and any degree of violence against her is justifiable (Kristeva,1982; 2012; Trible, 1984). This is a legacy that sustains currents of violence and control that are still disproportionately directed against women as has been shown, for example, in Michael Johnson's electrifying work on typologies of 'intimate terrorism' (2008) that reflects precisely how controlling behaviours are sustained by the sense of masculine entitlement embedded within these framing metaphors. In her study of the philosophical imaginary, Michèle Le Dœuff (1989) identifies not only the unaccounted-for gaps and silences about women and the feminine within the ostensibly neutral discourse of male philosophers, but a wealth of such gendered metaphors and constructions: 'stories about men and women, myths about divine and human, imagery and asides about male omniscience and female humility' (Anderson, 2012, 205).

80 Thinking Otherwise—Resisting Indifference

Yet there can be different ways of imagining once we begin to recognise these problematic orientations. In the field of feminist theology, for instance, work has been done over several decades to try to challenge and re-vision the gendered metaphors for divine/human relationships inherited from the past (Christ, 1979; McFague, 1987; Althaus-Reid, 2000; 2004), making reference to different kinds of motherhood, to the Goddess or by radically challenging normative metaphors of cleanliness and decency as applied to women and the feminine-identified body. In the field of the feminist philosophy of science, Karen Barad's (2007) agential realist account of truth suggests that, contrary to a reductive view of science, observations do not occur to objects of an independent reality from which the observer is completely separated and in relation to which she or he can maintain the distance of perfect neutrality. Instead, these observations are a product of the intra-actions of humans, non-humans and things. New metaphors, styles of reasoning and the work of the imagination are needed to articulate and explore the findings of this still genuinely empirical methodology. This reveals us to be intersubjectivities, moving, interdependent parts of a kind of 'becoming subject' rather than a prefixed or motionless object to be seen from outside at a safe distance. In Barad's (2007, 207) words,

> If the discursive practices by which we seek to describe phenomena do not refer to properties of abstract objects or observation-independent beings but rather actively reconfigure the world in its becoming, then what is being described by our epistemic practices is not nature itself but *our intra-activity as part of nature*. That is, realism is reformulated in terms of the goal of providing accurate descriptions of that reality of which we are a part and with which we intra-act, rather than some imagined and idealised human-independent reality.
>
> (Emphasis in original text)

This new account represents in itself, a different understanding of truth that recognises the importance of interested, affective connections and relationships. In this connection, Barad draws upon the metaphor of diffraction. In relation to her understanding of the physics of light, she observes that it 'does not reflect an image of what is already there, but is actually involved in its ongoing production' (Davies, 2014, 2). In other words, as already discussed in Chapter Three, the metaphor of diffraction takes us further than reflection or even reflexivity (Hultman and Taguchi, 2010); knowledge is, as Davies (2014, 2) puts this, always changing in interrelationship with

> the reality that is observed and experimented with . . .Whereas reflection and reflexivity might document *difference*, diffraction is itself the process whereby *a difference is made*.
>
> (Emphasis in original text)

Thinking Otherwise—Gender in the Mix 81

What follows is a series of readings that attempt to frame RE under the sign of neutrality, in terms of different metaphors or conceptual assemblages that are perhaps better designed to allow for an understanding of this diffraction— that is, the idea that the incoming of the new is always changing our perceptions as a result of our interactions. To take one example, the concept of 'Christianity' in RE cannot be regarded as a discrete entity apart from the work of students, educators and researchers in these spaces who, through that work, themselves change through their participation in intersubjective interactions. The following readings will then draw on locational feminist terms of reference, intersectional or post-colonial feminist understandings that try to avoid the translation of distinctive, uniquely and fluidly contextualised experiences into fixed universal terms, acknowledging the 'historically and geographically specific forms in which, in this case, feminism emerges, takes root, changes, travels, translates and transplants in different space/ temporal contexts' (Friedman, 2001, 15). In sum, these readings explore four metaphors drawn from traditions, texts and less discursive imaginative frameworks, both historical and contemporary, that we hope have a capacity to engender a sense of the affective and transformative impact of difference particularly in relation to gender: transcendence incarnate, neighbourliness, spirituality and becoming undone.

(ii) Transcendence Incarnate

Hierarchical gender binaries as metaphors for all kinds of social, cultural and material inequalities remain as pervasive as they are problematic. They have colonised our epistemic spaces, including the official settlement of RE, and in relation to the issue of 'Christianity', for example, we would argue that we cannot even begin to frame it as a subject unless we recognise the limitations of previous views. Within this settlement or account at the moment, 'Christianity' is an object produced by a relatively small community of educationalists. At the same time, patterns of inequality still characterise the metaphorical landscapes of the mind in spite of legal frameworks regulating 'equality and diversity' in educational spaces.

Pamela Sue Anderson's notion of 'transcendence incarnate' as described in an essay on the lived body (Anderson, 2010) could be employed as a starting point for something different. She uses the terms 'transcendence' and 'incarnate' to help identify and unpack the Western metaphors of binary hierarchies invoking body and embodiment as inferior to the work of the rational mind, something that, in Chapter Three, we saw was not characteristic of the philosophical presumptions of Spinoza, for example. Anderson is committed to realigning these divisive gendered concepts on more terms that allow for a different, less binary and less hierarchical framework of understanding. She does this within a primarily philosophical context, though her work is obviously informed by an understanding of the Christian doctrine

82 Thinking Otherwise—Resisting Indifference

whereby transcendence as (masculine) divinity becomes incarnate within the historically contingent, vulnerable (female) body of an individual human being (the man, Jesus of Nazareth) as key to human salvation. An interest in body and embodiment is not exclusive to feminist scholarship of course; during the 20th century, these categories or concepts gained in intellectual significance through developments in psychoanalysis and other forms of philosophy that bucked the Cartesian trend of placing consciousness at a safe distance from material and bodily vulnerabilities. But it is certainly the case that feminists have recently been at the forefront of efforts to challenge existing styles of reasoning through a critical recognition of how the body has been associated with metaphorical female gender becoming the primary 'site of female oppression' (Isherwood and Stuart, 1998, 15) as a result. And whilst it would be contentious to charge the epistemic culture of RE as understood officially in the 21st century with being openly heterosexist, it remains the case that the body continues to be treated in these contexts as if it were mainly an irrelevant or inconvenient interloper—better suited to the limited and often devalued educational spaces of physical education or dance and drama. In the class/lecture room, bodies are required to make themselves as inconspicuous as possible, and their claims are eclipsed by the normative privileges of abstraction and distance. This is perfectly illustrated in what is currently the most significant act of schooling within the examination hall, in which the body must remain silent and practically motionless (see Chapter Two above).

In her essay, Anderson (2010) seeks to endorse the capabilities of the lived body because denial and rejection of such capabilities, undermine the processes of approval without which any capability a human being may have will be still born. Although Anderson is not writing exclusively about women's embodied capabilities, in a more specific reference to this question, she invokes Iris Marion Young's (2005) treatment of the ways in which the development of little girls is constricted under the sign of a devalued embodiment, expressed through metaphors of hierarchical gender. In normatively gendered spaces ruled by these metaphors, Young argues, girls quickly learn to hold back and lose even the approved bodily capability to throw or move like boys, who, conversely, are encouraged to launch themselves into the activity of mastering the physical, material world with no holds barred. Contributing to the same argument, it can be said that the female-identified bodies of women also draw down disapproval on themselves if they appear too 'masculine' in capacity (Newman, 2015; Spice, 2016). And of course, the body, which is already sidelined and disciplined because of gender-related styles of reasoning, is also marked by assumptions about race and class (Eddo-Lodge, 2014). Thus, bell hooks (1994) refers to the frustrations of African-American college students who experience stress when trying to 'conform to acceptable white, middle-class behaviours in university settings' (1994, 182). She observes how students from non-materially privileged backgrounds respond to disapproval by internalising normative

Thinking Otherwise—Gender in the Mix 83

values, changing and disciplining their bodily behaviours to become quieter and seeking to minimise their presence in educational spaces. This internalisation of discouraging and constricting disapproval is also picked up in Kelly and Radford's foundational paper on sexual violence (1990). They draw attention to the ways in which sexist behaviour is tolerated because of the internalised sense that disagreeable or harmful assaults on women are merely the consequence of the way they dress or behave; it is their own fault. The effects of disgust, fear or the sense of betrayal relating to the body are discounted. There, capability for keeping themselves safe is discounted, if not discouraged. In consequence, when they are assaulted, they maintain that 'nothing really happened'. As Kelly and Radford (42) put it

> . . . [w]hen women say 'nothing really happened' a frequent remark which prefaces accounts of things which did indeed happen—they are minimising or denying experiences. Very real things happen when we are followed or chased on the street, when . . . partners insist on sex or engage in systematic emotional abuse—we do not feel safe, our trust is betrayed.

In respect of gender equality in the 21st-century UK, there is now a legal framework that outlaws inequalities (Equalities Act, National Archives, 2010). And yet, women may still not have the confidence actually to invoke this law by, for example, raising their voices in public spaces. Their embodied capabilities having been regularly checked and frustrated, any expectation that these voices will, in Nelle Morten's phrase, be 'heard into speech' (1986) is undermined. As a result, it stands to reason that the official account of RE as a constituent part of our wider culture, risks remaining a site of body-schooling. In Latour's (1999) terms, people continually fail to recognise the series of translations through which connection with the materiality of bodily relations has been gradually lost to a word-world settlement that informs conventional, male-normative understandings of how language maps onto reality in terms of abstraction and distance. It so often appears to women in educational—as in other—spaces that actually 'nothing really happened'.

In the late 20th century, feminist theologian Mary Daly tried, in a pragmatic experiment, to separate some male and female educational spaces to allow for the specific affirmation of women and their embodied capabilities. This put her at odds with her employers at Boston College, Massachusetts, and eventually forced her into retirement, when action was brought against her on the grounds that she had infringed on equality legislation and was acting in a discriminatory way. Of course, Daly—in Anderson's terms—believed women were being restricted by normatively gendered styles of reasoning, intensified by the physical presence of men. Segregation was an attempt, in a limited way, to forestall a negative impact on their capabilities (Anderson, 2012, 54). Ussher explains these expressions of male or masculine hegemony

84 Thinking Otherwise—Resisting Indifference

in relation to the idea that women evoke in men a disturbing consciousness of their own embodied vulnerability, or, to put it otherwise, women and men continue to live out the consequences of an overarching metaphorical construction based on hierarchical gender in their relationships with each other on a daily basis. Women identified with embodiment remind men of their own susceptibility to desire, impairment and death, and their corresponding failure to live up to the impossible ideal of disembodied masculinity that our Western culture has preserved within modernity, relatively intact from its Christian and pre-Christian origins (Ussher, 2006, 1).

> Throughout history, and across cultures, the reproductive body of woman has provoked fascination and fear. It is a body deemed dangerous and defiled, the myth of the monstrous feminine made flesh, yet also a body which provokes adoration and desire, enthralment with the mysteries within. We see this ambivalent relationship played out in mythological, literary and artistic representations of the feminine, where woman is positioned as powerful, impure and corrupt, source of moral and physical contamination; or as sacred, asexual and nourishing, a phantasmic signifier of threat extinguished. Central to this positioning of the female body as monstrous or beneficent is ambivalence associated with the power and danger perceived to be inherent in woman's fecund flesh, her seeping, leaking, bleeding womb standing as site of pollution and source of dread.

In relation to the needs and negotiations of actual students, the experiences of women continue to resonate with Daly's analysis. Miranda Fricker (2003, 217–18) suggests that having to address a level of hostile male entitlement is still part of the experience of many female students, including those of the authors.

> What female philosophy student has not had that discursive experience with some clever young man ready to be one's superior if one gives him the least encouragement? One finds oneself audience to a dress-rehearsal of another's emerging intellectual authority, and this experience typically involves being on the receiving end of a . . . barrage of competitive energy still so automatic in many young men and so alien to so many young women . . .

Central to Anderson's essay is a challenge to the way in which embodied individuals understand themselves as either condemned or over-entitled simply through birth into gendered circumstances, evincing the fixed marks of gender which, in the case of those born female (or not male), 'inhibit and debilitate the capable body' (Anderson, 2010, 168). Elsewhere, she also seeks to legitimise forms of autonomy that allow for differently gendered people to realise capabilities at the same time for both love and reason (2012, 179), and this, too, is a fundamental and important part of the work. She is attempting not simply to reverse the polarity of reason and love—where the concerns of body and affect are located in the normative scheme—but also to help us recognise the full value of both. 'Love and reason' are, of course, capabilities traditionally caught up in—and in a post-Cartesian world, aligned with—the pattern or metaphorical style of hierarchical, binary gender. Woman is associated with love, with desire, vulnerability and affectivity and man with reason that, as we have seen within contexts influenced primarily by Christian and Enlightenment epistemic cultures, is generally associated with abstraction, distance and control of the material and physical world. Woman and the feminine thus become linked to the absence of a privileged capability for rational thought and to the lack of (self) control. At the same time, this privileged capability forcibly sets men and the masculine apart from considerations of desire, affectivity and vulnerability. In her essay, Anderson gives us two illustrations of how this metaphor of transcendence incarnate might be invoked to open up the possibility of conceptualising an equality that, at the same time, does not lose sight of difference.

One image or picture—a sculpture of Eve by a 12th-century artist, Gislebert (Anderson, 2010, 164)—evinces in a gesture of touching her own cheek, a kind of coming to or dawning of consciousness that allows for a lived experience besides or apart from the mythic story of Eve's fall from grace in the first book of the Christian Bible (Genesis 2:4–3:23). In terms of that gendered myth in the sculpture—giving colour and shape to gendered metaphors experienced more widely—the other hand reaches for the forbidden fruit. In other words, she gives in to temptation and establishes her identity as the paradigmatic sinner and mother of all sinners. Yet Anderson, drawing on Gislebert's sculpture and its appropriation by both Jeanne Hersch (1985) and Michèle Le Dœuff (2003), encourages us to read against this view. She suggests that the very fact that we can 'elucidate'—utilising, for example, the resources of Maurice Merleau-Ponty's idea of the body-subject who becomes aware of its own 'prereflective incarnation in the world' whilst remaining incarnate (Anderson, 2010, 164)—indicates a kind of pre-personal capable life before we become subject to these debilitating 'marks of gender'. This can be seen as 'the key to self-confidence; *both self-affirmation and other approbation*' (Anderson, 2010, 179, our emphasis). Of course, Anderson doesn't deny that the reading of Eve as a sinner contributes to our cultural and historical understanding of women, but in her understanding of the 'capable body', she bears witness to the philosophical potential for evading normative limitations through the affirmation (by the artist, the viewer, the woman herself) of these embodied capabilities.

Anderson's second example—Simone de Beauvoir's troubling encounter with Jean Paul Sartre in the Luxembourg Gardens in Paris that is described in the first volume of her autobiography, *Memoirs of a Dutiful Daughter* (1958)—serves, similarly, to illustrate a doubled legacy. As a young woman she argues with Sartre for three hours on a point of real concern; yet, 20 years

86 *Thinking Otherwise—Resisting Indifference*

later (344), she still sees his ability to win the argument as a justification of his privileged (male) status as Philosopher.

> I was simply not in his class . . . In the end I had to admit I was beaten: besides, I had realized, in the course of our discussion, that many of my opinions were based only on prejudice, dishonesty, or hastily formed concepts, that my reasoning was at fault and that my ideas were in a muddle . . .

Beauvoir defines women in her own philosophical work as 'the second sex'; she understands how and why she is bound up with assumptions about gender—signified in the previous example by Eve's hand reaching for the apple. She perceives the gap between this and her embodiment as a woman—metaphorically touching her own cheek—and yet she continues to conform to or perform her gendered role. Thus, Beauvoir's affections for Sartre—who becomes her lover shortly after this meeting—are already compromised by assumptions about her gendered embodiment even before she begins, intellectually, to evaluate herself in comparison with him. Miranda Fricker suggests that this structure has implications for both men and women; in this example, Sartre too had something to lose by not producing 'the discursive performance of a self-styled superior'. He might have lost Beauvoir's attention altogether (Anderson, 2010, 177).

However, what Anderson's reflections on the lived body and on transcendence incarnate enable us to do is to begin critically to dismantle these expectations and assumptions, not abandoning a commitment to transcendent thought as the powerful and enabling capacity to choose to think universally—to move beyond the limitations of the body as an object in the empirical world—but nevertheless keeping in mind the vision of Gislebert's Eve who, indicating her pre-reflective capacity through the gesture of touching her own cheek, shows that there is room to choose also to be fully aware of being incarnate. In other words, Anderson begins to mend the traditional split, hugely expanding what women can be seen to do and be and resisting the sameness or indifference of the transcendent privilege without abandoning its potentiality. In the case of Simone de Beauvoir, what Anderson says is that, like the sculpture of Eve, she is still partly captured within the vision of incapacity—which in traditional Christian theological terms is sinfulness—that prevents her having the confidence to claim herself as a philosopher in the way that she sees Sartre to be. And yet, at the same time, in her work she demonstrates precisely that capability—and this is also demonstrated in re-visiting the processes of translation (Latour, 1999) through which the material nature of embodied relations has arrived at the abstractions of gender hierarchies (Anderson, 2010, 177).

> Beauvoir's particular historical and social gender-type meant that she wanted a man who was intellectually superior to her in philosophy and this is what she got. But she also transformed for us the imagery of gender,

Thinking Otherwise—Gender in the Mix 87

including the myth of Eve as virgin or mother, which in Beauvoir's time and context, would have prevented her from recognising and challenging sexist oppression at all. So her philosophy gives to us new confidence for the lived body in the transformation of gender. In other words, she unwittingly helps us to recognise transcendence incarnate as the lived body's form of confidence and so as the possibility for new personal discoveries in relation to the lived through world.

It is still hard, in the 21st century, to discount the epistemic privilege afforded by the pervasive metaphors of gendered hierarchy discussed above, including that of transcendence over incarnation. Nevertheless, as Anderson—not forgetting Beauvoir and Gislebert—demonstrates, it is possible to challenge and perhaps even to begin to change this practice of privilege, starting by making the translations that have taken place to get to this abstraction more visible. Adopting transcendence incarnate as a form of *conceptual persona* for dissolving the dominant subject position in educational spaces can also be read as a line of flight (Deleuze and Guattari, 2003, 88) involving the deterritorialising of masculinist philosophical assumptions and the reterritorialising of curriculum spaces or epistemic cultures with new agenda that are as attuned to the potential of incarnation/embodiment and the capacity to be affected as they are to the power to transcend the limitations of embodied subjectivity.

Here, then, we have tried to shift the normative style of reasoning in line with a re-vised understanding of transcendence incarnate and the lived body, discussed here as a kind of *conceptual persona* or tool that can help us get started on growing a new framework of gender relations. Of course, this conflicts with current educational thinking at some points—this is one of the arguments of the chapter and the book. Even so, and even before beginning the work of trying to rekindle a conversation on these things between RE practitioners and researchers at different levels, potential partners in this dialogue are not at every point in disagreement. Arguably, transcendence incarnate as understood by Anderson has something in common with the widely stated aim of education to be about developing and supporting the confidence of students. The idea of cultivating 'confident individuals', for example, is one of the four purposes of education set out in the Scottish *Curriculum for Excellence* (2010), and it would surely be hard to find an educational document that did not aspire to a similar outcome. The argument of the chapter is that current thinking about educational policy (particularly the way in which RE is framed officially) has not yet been able to free itself from the overarching influence of metaphors that have distorted issues of gender within educational spaces and about which there continues to be an unnerving complacency at all levels. However, it could also be said that an understanding of confidence informed by Anderson's work on transcendence incarnate and the lived body otherwise maps rather well onto discussions of educational purposes outlined, for example, in the work of educational theorist Gert Biesta (2009). Looking at Anderson's paper from the perspective of Biesta's work on educational purposes, we see

88   *Thinking Otherwise—Resisting Indifference*

marked evidence of a parallel concern in both with critical and philosophical analysis—Beauvoir's or, by implication, Giselbert's analysis of gender binaries, for example—that addresses the purpose of equipping students with demonstrable critical skills. Just as significantly, Anderson's imaginative readings resonate strongly with what Biesta (2009, 40) calls the educational purpose of subjectification, something that he says

> . . . is precisely not about the insertion of 'newcomers' into existing orders, but about ways of being that hint at independence from such orders; ways of being in which the individual is not simply a 'specimen' of a more encompassing order.

In other words, subjectification in Biesta's terms is not about helping people to fit in or conform, however important it may be in some contexts, for communities and individuals to function according to certain norms. Subjectification as an educational purpose is about enabling people to be and act whether or not they are in alignment with the norms, something that has strong affinities with Julia Kristeva's understanding of female genius (Jasper, 2012), which is all about the capacity—specifically of women—to think, make relationships and bring new projects to birth in unpropitious circumstances marked by normative gender values. In this example, transcendence incarnate, as Anderson defines it, characterises departure from the dominant subject position of binary gendered hierarchy and accords with the work of building a woman or girl's confidence to say, 'I can'. For Anderson, this is what women and girls need: affirmation and approval in relation to their pre-reflective embodied capability unaffected by contingent and cultural disapprobation. Anderson's metaphor of transcendence incarnate as a way of understanding how we desire to be differently, shows us why, and one way how, we must dismantle the existing metaphorical framework of gendered binary distinction. Interestingly, as a comment to the side, it also suggests ways in which the legacy of Christianity's version of transcendence incarnate might also be read as a way to deconstruct the hierarchy with which it is normally/normatively associated.

(iii) Neighbourliness

It is hard to hold onto difference/s—we default to translations (into cognate terms) very quickly and have an instinct to '[cover] the other with clothes, images or speeches which render this other familiar to us' (Irigaray, 2004, 29). We are fearful of too much 'otherness' and wish to protect ourselves from the challenge it inevitably presents in class and lecture rooms, too. Of course, some of us are more adventurous or less risk averse than others; anthropologist and educator Helen Verran is actively interested in difference and in avoiding the lapse/collapse into sameness identified with translations. She proposes that differences should flourish alongside each other, a practice

Thinking Otherwise—Gender in the Mix 89

we identify here in terms of the *conceptual persona* of 'neighbourliness', hopefully capturing both experiences of differences and of simultaneity and the capacity to go along together without having to resolve everything in terms of hierarchies or exclusions, as has been the pattern in relation to styles of reasoning that are gender-inflected. Drawing on the work of John Law, Verran employs the term 'disconcertment' to get closer to the experience of difference before translations occur (Verran, 2001). In this way, she tries to identify feelings of confusion of 'delight and suspicion, failure and success' accompanied by 'a sort of visceral laughter . . . that grows from seeing a certainty disrupted to become a different sort of certainty: a certainty that sees itself' (Verran, 1999, 140). One of Verran's best-known illustrations of this experience is set in a classroom within which Nigerian (Yoruba) teachers and children are working on measurement. What sets things off is the realisation that in learning about how to measure height (in this class, 'length in our bodies' (1999, 137)), her student teacher, Mr Ojo, had presented the key concept of extension in a way that confounded the metaphorical structure of her own understanding of height, i.e., the perceived visual extension of a piece of string that represented the child. Instead of pieces of string laid out to be measured as a visual representation of the child and therefore of his or her height, the student teacher had focused the class's understanding of measurement on a notion of multiplicity: how many times could the string that measured the height be wound around a card of a standard size?

Verran renders the power relations in this situation carefully—she is anxious not to represent her feelings simply as a prompt to 'correct' the ways in which measurement is being understood in conformity with her own position of authority, and equally, she wants to avoid presenting this as the kind of clichéd story 'of powerful Yoruba resistance and Western impotence' (1999, 141). For Verran, what the experience draws attention to is a 'complex and subversive dance of mimesis and alterity in routines, generating new ways to go on, and re-generating old ways' so that they can go on together (142). In response to this experience of disconcertment, she examines the patterns of 'accommodation and resistance' that she detects in her own thoughts and behaviours (143). Attentiveness to these feelings of confusion or disempowerment—for example, recognising as part of this experience how messy and untidy the whole process of adding and calculating is (for example, using one's fingers differently, in English and Yoruba fashion (149)) in comparison with the ideal notion of quantifying—provided a way into understanding two similarly sophisticated routines and rituals. It alerted her to the possibility of using both. It showed her that whilst each way of doing/saying something provides us with a kind of certainty as a product of different sets of complex interconnected routines and rituals, it also makes us realise that certainty is, in the end, something of a 'hoax' (151). And in this sense, we see immediately how this might have relevance to ways of negotiating gender structures within educational spaces also dedicated, like RE, to negotiating other kinds of difference/s.

90 *Thinking Otherwise—Resisting Indifference*

These reflections inform a proposal to put 'the neighbour' or 'neighbour-liness' forward as another way of addressing in/difference, as a *conceptual persona* with potential to direct or focus our thinking beyond the dominant subject of male hegemony and exclusively Western styles of reasoning with their prioritisation of abstraction, distance and control. The idea is to combine Verran's way of understanding how new and old ways can go along together—acknowledging both the certainty and the hoax involved in their different positions—and the notions of proximity and relationship that are supported by the metaphor of the neighbour. A Verran-like reading of neighbourliness should then help to make it possible for, say, locational feminist and post-colonial insights to illuminate RE spaces more easily. Hopefully, it can be seen as a premise for moving forward in these areas critically, ethically and in a spirit of experimentation without necessarily having to abandon everything learned usefully from the past.

This reference to neighbourliness, like transcendence incarnate, invokes memories of a Christian biblical metaphor that is similarly invested with potential to represent critical, ethical and experimental approaches to difference or to undermine dominant frameworks or styles of reasoning and move in a more equal or inclusive direction. In the New Testament, the author of the Gospel of Luke places a story about neighbourliness (Luke 10:25–37) in the mouth of Jesus in answer to a lawyer who asks him how he can inherit eternal life. The story suggests that the neighbour with whom Jesus wants the lawyer to engage on familiar terms—helping, touching and expending money on him—is the Samaritan. For the lawyer, the Samaritan is a kind of familiar stranger or 'other' who lives close by but is separated by profound cultural differences (Whitworth, 2014). The biblical story does not describe the lawyer's response in terms of disconcertment, but it could be read as the shock of acknowledgement that neighbourliness, like measuring children's heights, can be done differently: it can be both a narrower responsibility to deal well with family and clan and, equally, a wider appeal to deal well with the dangerous and unlikeable stranger in front of you on the road making a similar request for help or just treatment. In this New Testament context, the two are juxtaposed; they go on together.

In UK contexts, educational spaces are now policed in terms of equality legislation that theoretically sustains and supports our difference/s insofar as they do not unduly restrict our neighbours' freedoms. But, as has been said already, it can be very hard to maintain even the awareness of difference/s let alone to resist slipping back into either rejection and exclusion or 'more of the same', for example, through slipshod translations or colonising behaviours that take over and eliminate unsettling or potentially stimulating differences. Becoming aware of different yet conterminous spaces, through the kinds of disconcertment to which Verran refers, reveals the dominant subject position (Braidotti, 2011, 12) and is a critical first step in the direction of undermining or dissolving this by becoming familiar with new ways of conceptualising a process of 'going-on together' on more equitable terms. Of course, this

Thinking Otherwise—Gender in the Mix 91

isn't necessarily guaranteed. Recently, an undergraduate student referenced her teaching practice in her dissertation and the shock—we could call this disconcertment—of recognising that 'popular boys' were wearing fake tan and drawing in their eyebrows. This was a kind of behaviour that she argued would have had serious social and perhaps even physical consequences in her own school days a few years earlier because of the implicit challenge to the rigid boundaries of male gender enforced in educational spaces. In Verran's terms, what would be important here is whether the laughter born of disconcertment at realising this different way of 'performing the male' in an educational space could be accepted as such, as a possibility of the widening acceptance of being male and female together in different ways that recognises the hoax, the game, the playfulness of being male as one of a number of practices of being male or female or transgender or gender queer going on together. In Verran's terms, the danger would be that this disconcertment might go no further, that these participants might simply be involved in changing the appearance of the still-dominant male subject position, rather than recognising their roles as 'participants who tell stories as part of [their] participation' (Verran,1999, 151) in a process of changes and transformations that produce a significant affect and begin to let the difference in.

Nevertheless, the idea of telling stories about the coterminous neighbourliness of different ways of doing a whole range of things is an attractive one. Neighbourliness is a metaphorical construction built on well-established patterns of human association that already has broader cultural currency and some proven potential to resist sameness and allow for creative exploration. It is attractive in its capacity to model ways in which differences can go along together, side by side, but still separately. Neighbours who live their lives closely together may not, in fact, always be 'there for one another'; they may turn out to be unsettling or even hostile strangers. However, the concept combines spatial proximity, and thus a necessary intimacy, with expectation of reciprocal responsibilities and obligations, including spaces for differences to flourish. The feminist philosopher Luce Irigaray draws attention to the spatial understanding of neighbour/neighbourliness as a context for a story of 'dwelling' together reflecting on the best way to live—go- along—together as lived and thus differently gendered bodies. Understanding the Other or the Otherness of gender in a positive sense, Irigaray believes different genders—she primarily references two, but her argument might be applied to more—do not speak, evaluate or react to situations in the same way. Her own fieldwork in the area of gendered discourse analysis (Irigaray, 2004, 35) convinces her that whatever the causes, differences exist and that therefore accommodating these differences remains important; that means providing some kind of dwelling place or space for these gender differences without reducing this to the sameness of, say, patriarchal segregation. In the past in the UK, boys and girls had different entrances into schools— still molded or etched into the walls of older school buildings—and patterns of perceived gender differences dictated the curriculum. These patterns

92 Thinking Otherwise—Resisting Indifference

have been adapted over the years in relation to the equality and diversity agenda—itself a conceptual metaphor that has shown some capacity to eliminate gendered privilege. And yet, there is still the danger of remaining content with equal access to values and practices that are themselves inherently gendered. In this context, Irigaray's work has something to offer as an alternative to differential patterns that simply serve to sustain certain kinds of gendered epistemological or pedagogical privilege; in other words, 'more of the same'. She emphasises the need for neighbourly (close, but not merged) spaces within the intimacy of male and female relationships: '[w]ithout a return into oneself, how still to approach the other?' (Irigaray, 2004, 29). In other words, Irigaray is also exploring Verran's question, 'How should we live?' (1999, 136), and the Gospel response to the lawyer whose question about the ultimate purpose and value of human life is redirected towards the business of getting on with the disconcerting stranger-neighbour (Luke 10:25). In her reflections on dwelling places, Irigaray notes that houses are generally built according to a view of mere subsistence, encompassing 'shelter, recuperation through eating and sleeping and provision of basic hygiene' (2004, 123). Her view is that, presently, these architectural spaces—and we might experiment with educational spaces here, too—do not 'respond to desires, which are supposed to define the human as such' (123). She suggests architects and designers should acknowledge other motivations, most particularly the necessity of having time and space in which to prepare for 'the moment for encounter' (29–30) with the Other of whatever gender. Whether we like the specific details of her designs, her reflections suggest that we have the capacity to colonise these spaces, imposing our own 'normative' framings on them or, alternatively, that the spaces will themselves colonise our lived experiences. However, these neighbourly spaces—modelling educational and RE spaces too—cannot be perceived as neutral. Her aim is thus not to create 'neutral' spaces but to arrange our dwellings in such a way as to allow for a continually creative, neighbourly encounter with the Other. In its combination of proximity, contiguity and separation from and/or desire for the Other, Irigaray's reflections (126) lend another layer of meaning to this proposal of neighbourliness as a metaphor for developing forms of thinking and going along together, new and old, that can be applied to educational spaces in ways that are critical, ethical and experimental.

> Instead of centering the house around a dining-room, a lounge, and a bedroom, which are mundane, functional and undifferentiated spaces that have often assimilated the family into a collective unity founded on a loss of individual identity, why not build the home on the basis of that which is particular to each one? Why not rebuild it starting with two small one-room apartments, which would replace the dining-room, lounge and shared bedroom? Would not this spatial topography be more suited for today's requirements? Would not this represent an economy of space that makes room for what is one's own and that which remains foreign to us, to one's own world and the closeness with the other, to

Thinking Otherwise—Gender in the Mix 93

an individual's singularity as well as to the foundation or re-foundation of a community: the community of a couple or a family, among others.

Although this might be thought to be remote from the classroom/seminar room context, the key point here is that Irigaray raises issues about the significance of design and architecture for gendered relationships. This form of neighbourliness, accommodating difference/s without relinquishing differentiation could, then, also apply to the living spaces of RE, where dominant models or ideologies can potentially also be shifted, knocked down and rebuilt both literally and metaphorically in order to make room/s that allow for difference/s and more going along together. These might be about changing locations and spaces—moving outdoors, for example—to accommodate or facilitate a different kind of encounter with the material world in the neighbourly and leafy spaces characteristic of 'outdoor learning' initiatives (Knight, 2013; Ogilvie, 2013). It could be about shifting the emphasis from formal assessment. Even existing/normative spaces, however, if they are framed differently, are opened to new accommodations and might allow different kinds of relationships to take place without risking the undifferentiated return to sameness. A classroom set up with desks and chairs for traditional teaching and note-taking practices that is redesigned through cooperative determination with all those involved, including children and young people, could become a work room, dedicated to different non-discursive practices, as a Glasgow RE classroom became for us—the authors—a space in which conversations about the practices and purposes of RE led to the eventual emergence of a project focused on fabricating objects and organising an event (I'Anson and Jasper, 2011).

Arguably, as we began in this section, there will still be a tendency to resolve difference/s and realign them with the normative in ways that are variously defined here as the lack of differentiation (Irigaray) or too much willingness to make *'foundationist'* interpretations (Verran); in other words, to default to more or less slipshod forms of translation into the familiar. Rather than struggle to accommodate the difference/s to which we are sometimes alerted by the visceral feelings of disconcertment that Verran illustrated in her work on Nigerian classrooms or the student experienced in her encounter with male cosmetics, it is much easier to return to the beaten track. Working with a group of very intelligent but also hard-headed young people in Glasgow on the project already referred to, we invited them to take off on a kind of 'walk in the park', deliberately without clear objectives or targets in mind, in order to discover something initially unknown. Unsurprisingly, this proved difficult and sometimes very uncomfortable; the questions 'What are we doing?' and 'Why are we doing it?' seem fair enough, after all. Although some of the research team quickly recognised the potential and freedom of this space in their weekly curriculum, the project moved uncertainly at times, and the pressures to resolve this uncertainty in conformity with various positions of authority (Verran, 1999, 141) were strong, emanating in particular from some of the young people themselves, unaccustomed or resistant to

94   Thinking Otherwise—Resisting Indifference

this lack of external direction and the responsibilities as well as the freedoms it afforded participants to encounter such unknown difference/s in a neighbourly way.

To conclude: the Bible presents a picture of neighbourliness through the parable of the Good Samaritan (Luke 10 29–37) that has been used here as a *conceptual persona* representing the work of relating to 'the Other', going beyond a conventional sense of familiarity, whether in terms of a theological, an ethical or an imaginative goal. And this critique of familiarity—or rather, of a tendency to sink all distinctions into the view from a dominant subject position—is presented in the parable, as well as by Irigaray and Verran, as a key obstacle to the task of living well in a neighbourly way as that *conceptual persona* or attempt to find adequate representation (Braidotti, 2011) has been mobilised here. Verran's (1999, 142) subversive dance of mimesis and alterity speaks to Irigaray's plea for separation in intimacy and the biblical challenge to discrimination. All three effectively challenge the dominant subject position, not by setting up another foundationist perspective, but through neighbourly cooperation and mutual respect of difference/s that demonstrate the ethical and creative possibilities of going on together. In Irigaray's words (2004, 133):

> Living an existence of one's own requires an awareness of one's own specific world, whose contents and limits must be recognised and affirmed. Only beyond these contents and limits can the other be encountered, desired and loved; provided that his or her own world is respected, and without infringing its frontiers.

(iv) Re-Vising Spirituality

Conceptual personae are attempts to find better or more appropriate representations that challenge indifference and, more specifically in this section of the book, try to dissolve the dominant male-normative subject characterised by detachment, abstraction and a lack of connection to people's lived experiences. The third of these thought experiments takes us into the territory described in terms of 'spirituality' or 'the spiritual'. Judging by the number of books, websites and publications, there has been a marked increase of interest in these concepts in recent years. However, Carrette and King (2005, 1) suggest that this is because

> . . . spirituality is taken to denote the positive aspects of the ancient religious traditions, unencumbered by the 'dead hand' of the Church, and something which provides a liberation and solace in an otherwise meaningless world.

In other words, the popularity of 'spirituality' is directly related to the ambiguities associated with the term 'religion'. Perhaps, in this sense, it could be seen as a way to revitalise interest and address some of the issues of the

Thinking Otherwise—Gender in the Mix 95

persistently male-normative context of the RE spaces that we diagnose and the crisis of plausibility (Berger, 1971) we have already identified in Chapter One. However, there are clearly some dangers in adopting spirituality as a style for thinking through difference. Carrette and King (2005, 5–6) point to the way in which spirituality, in the context of this new enthusiasm, has also been ruthlessly commodified and subjected to a powerful impetus towards sameness or indifference, precisely resisting the kind of change and transformation we have identified with the educational.

> What is being sold to us as radical, trendy and transformative spirituality in fact produces little in the way of a significant change in one's lifestyle or fundamental behaviour patterns (with the possible exception of motivating the individual to be more efficient and productive at work). By 'cornering the market' on spirituality, such trends actually limit the socially transformative dimensions of the religious perspectives that they draw upon by locating 'the spiritual' firmly within a privatised and conformist space.

Richard Roberts (2012, 9) makes a similar point about the forces of conformity and indifference in the context of contemporary management practices that appear to offer 'spiritually empowered human resources management'. Within an apparently benign frame of reference that claims to provide those who are managed with a sense of meaningful purpose (encouraging employees, for example, to identify with 'the brand' or to articulate purpose and values that transcend the individual as a member of the team), he argues that HR management, as a clearly identifiable form of the dominant subject, actually aims for 'a totalising form of social construction'. That is to say that it simply assumes the identity of interests between management and those who are managed, one that is fundamentally focused on corporate profit (10). In other words, the project of finding new styles of reasoning that avoid the tendency towards indifference will not be served if the conceptual framework we choose cannot be disentangled from male-normative subject positions such as the neoliberal or human resource management models of spirituality described above, both of which are clearly primed towards ever greater conformity with dominant subject positions.

Arguably, however, even if corporate neoliberalism is trying to exploit forms of non-Western wisdom (Carrette and King, 2005) for its own ends under this heading, these concerns do not have to be completely definitive for our purposes. There are, moreover, examples of work on spirituality that do not follow this pattern. For example, in his extensive and scholarly body of work on spirituality, Philip Sheldrake (2012; 2013; 2014) identifies and explores notions of spirituality that go well beyond the confines of the Christian Church whilst also providing critical reference to what he identifies as the spiritual dimensions of secular government policy, management and business practice. He draws, for example, on the non-Christian philosopher Pierre Hadot, approving the way in which Hadot (1995) expands the claims

96 *Thinking Otherwise—Resisting Indifference*

of philosophy from a strictly abstract intellectual exercise to a process of learning 'to be' (Sheldrake, 2012, 66) through attentiveness to a set of principled teachings that incorporate contemplative and ascetic practice as an aspect of communal and civic responsibility in a way that perhaps mirrors some of the conclusions about 'spirituality' addressed in Chapter Three in relation to Foucault and Spinoza under the sign of 'care of the self'.

Sheldrake's work is rooted in Christian thought and practice, even when this is not directly invoked. He acknowledges that the word 'spirituality' was first used within a Christian context (2012, 2). Derived from the biblical Greek, Latin and later vernacular translations, it indicated a contrast with 'fleshly', which meant worldly or contrary to God's spirit', and implied a distinction between 'two approaches to life' in which, a spiritual person (4)

> . . . was simply someone who sought to live under the influence of God whereas a 'fleshly' (or worldly) person was concerned primarily with personal satisfaction, comfort or success.

However, though this work acknowledges that the Christian Church's dominant position is challenged in the global context of the 21st century, it is less clear how it stands on the question of Christianity's gendered heritage. Forms of Christianity and powerful biblical narratives have routinely projected male shame and anxiety about embodiment and mortality onto women (Jantzen, 1998; Beattie, 2006; Clough, 2014). In tying the origins of the word 'spirituality' to a Christian distinction between flesh and spirit, Sheldrake (2012, 4) puts his finger on a key problem for feminist readers, who see in this gendered binary, the way in which male-dominated systems have sought to distance themselves from, and exert control over, both women and the material world, bringing to bear on the business of ascribing a privileged form of disembodied spirituality the whole weight of Christian divine endorsement (Isherwood and Stuart, 1998; Jasper, 1998). So it is at once clear that the term spirituality is not proof against normalising forces, whether these are aligned with the kind of gendered hierarchy of traditional forms of Western Christianity, post-Cartesian thought or with neoliberal exploitation.

It is also important to note at this point that the term 'spirituality' already has a place within the official settlement reached in relation to RE and that it continues to figure in policy documents at the school level as an educational good. At the same time, thinking on the subject does not appear to have developed very far since the 1944 Education Act in England and the 1945 Education Act in Scotland were published (National Archives, 1944; 1945). Here, it is stated that the education provided under its jurisdiction will address the child in terms of his or her spiritual, alongside moral, mental and physical, development (Erricker and Erricker, 2000, 36). Interestingly, the act also ruled out the identification of spiritual development with purely Christian formation, although it is not clear what alternative form it was supposed to take instead beyond a generalised notion of moral

Thinking Otherwise—Gender in the Mix 97

development. In the English context, there have been changes of nuance since 1944. Engagement with the idea of the child's spiritual development in the Education Reform Act in England (National Archives, 1988) focused on 'the importance of the development of the individual and the uniqueness of each individual's conception of spirituality' (Erricker and Erricker, 2000, 39), although this interpretation generated a critical response from some commentators who felt the emphasis was now too individualistic, failing to reference issues of wider human responsibility and justice (Thatcher, 1991) or making it more difficult for children to bring their contextualised experiences of spiritual nurture or direction from outside school into the classroom, thereby impoverishing any reference to the spirituality of students (Wright, 1997). By the 1990s, new regulatory bodies like Ofsted—heralding the beginnings of the now dominant focus on assessibility—were beginning to be set up. The critical issue at this point—given the limited nature of the available terms of reference—became the establishment of 'criteria and contexts in which [spiritual] development could be assessed' (Erricker and Erricker, 2000, 38).

Meanwhile, the idea that spirituality in these broader educational contexts continues to be widely viewed and used as a synonym for 'religion' is supported by the fact that references to spirituality are still generally located—perhaps isolated would be a better word—within RE. In the section of the Scottish *Curriculum for Excellence* setting out statutory requirements in relation to the provision of RE and Religious Observance (RO), in conjunction with the provision of RE (Education Scotland, 2011a, 2, *emphasis added*), there is reference to the value of increasing

> . . . children and young people's awareness of the *spiritual dimension* of human life through exploring the world's major religions and views, including those which are independent of religious belief, and considering the challenges posed by those beliefs and values.

The separate document referring to statutory provision of RO within the Scottish *Curriculum for Excellence* also refers (Education Scotland, 2011b, 1) to 'spiritual development' or 'needs' in the context of 'faith' perspectives. Some effort is made to indicate that this spirituality might also be derived from 'non faith' perspectives and that it is important to remain sensitive to this fact; yet what is significant is that discussion of this 'non faith' perspective is still being located in relation to RO. Similarly, even though Scottish Government Ministers have accepted the definition and aims of religious observance (Education Scotland, 2011b, 2, *emphasis added*) as being

> . . . community acts which aim to promote the *spiritual development* of all members of the school's community and express and celebrate the shared values of the school community,

98 *Thinking Otherwise—Resisting Indifference*

this still comes under the auspices of the Religious Observance Review Group. In their report (Scottish Government, 2004, 18), the discourse of spirituality is still lodged alongside religion—with a sideways glance at ethos.

> The review group acknowledged the need to balance the frequency of religious observance to be such as to impact on the spiritual develop-ment of the school community with providing a valuable and inclusive experience of religious observance.

The *Curriculum for Excellence* in Scotland does make some reference to 'spir-itual wellbeing' outside documents relating to RE, in the section relating to health and wellbeing (Education Scotland, 2011c). However, whilst in rela-tion to 'principles and practices' and to 'experiences and outcomes', health and wellbeing are clearly described, there is no corresponding explanation of spirituality. If the Scottish *Curriculum for Excellence* is at all typical, we can say then that spirituality will generally be located within contexts that range from areas of private 'self-orientation' (Sheldrake, 2012, 6), through the territory of religion viewed more or less suspiciously as institutional, to matters more to do with the importance of establishing an ethos of shared moral values (Besley, 2005).

So although spirituality appears to be embedded within this official account of RE, its present capacity—as some kind of *conceptual persona* to provide an alternative framework representing critical, ethical and experi-mental discussions that undermine or dissolve the indifferent and dominant subject—would seem to be somewhat doubtful as this point. However, the title of this section of the book makes reference to 're-vision', and this is to index a concept made familiar by Adrienne Rich (1971), concerned with a process of re-reading the texts and practices of the old patriarchal order from a new, critical direction. In this sense, there are very good reasons for making the effort to come at this somewhat ambivalent trope from a new critical direction, reclaiming it as a *conceptual persona* as that has been understood so far in this chapter as a space of experimentation and play, subverting the dominant subject. In the 1970s and 80s, a groundbreaking feminist reader in religion was published under the title *Womanspirit Rising* (Christ and Plaskow, 1979). In this and in many subsequent feminist publi-cations (Christ and Plaskow, 1979; 1989; Ruether, 1992; King,1993; 1994; Isherwood and Stuart, 1998; Isherwood, 2007), the adoption of a discourse of spirituality marks, as in the case of Anderson's transcendence incarnate, a refusal to subject feminine flesh to privileged disembodied and abstracted notions of masculine spirit sustained by Cartesian and Christian styles of reasoning. This was the pathway followed by theologian Carol Christ, who pointed out in her earliest work (Christ, 1979, 279–80) that these configu-rations of Christian spirituality had wide-ranging ramifications.

> Women were denigrated because they seemed more carnal, fleshy and earthy that the culture-creating males. The misogynist anti*body* tradition

Thinking Otherwise—Gender in the Mix 99

in western thought is symbolised in the myth of Eve who is traditionally viewed as a sexual temptress, the epitome of women's carnal nature. This tradition reaches its nadir in the *Malleus Maleficarum* (*The Hammer of Evil-Doing Women*), which states, 'All witchcraft stems from carnal lust, which in women is insatiable'.

In response, she and her co-authors employed spirituality in the nomadic sense of a theoretical, navigational tool (Braidotti, 2011, 12) precisely to deterritorialise the existing exclusively masculine and disembodied frame of reference and claim the word for a praxis that was more liberating and socially just. Spirituality, aligned to this liberatory intent, picks up on a different set of underlying material and embodied associations of spirit with life and breath within Christian and Hebrew contexts, amongst others. Luce Irigaray emphasises that the process of breathing—this cosmic characteristic—links women and the universe. They do not need to set themselves apart from it or quit their bodies and leave themselves to reach the divine, and listening to one's breathing is a form of communication with the soul of the world which prioritises not just words or even breath, but also touch as a fundamentally embodied experience (Irigaray, 2004, 167).

If Irigaray also associates breathing with an attentiveness that links or bridges the human and cosmic world, the liberatory intention of spirituality in this 'feminine economy' (2004, 166) could, in this way, be linked to the exhilaration of singing, another kind of breathing that animates, enlivens and creates. Another example that comes to mind as a way of illustrating the possibilities of this kind of nomadic spirituality focused on breath and breathing for challenging the dominant subject in educational spaces is the performances of Pussy Riot. Pussy Riot was a punk collective formed in Moscow in 2011. Their songs and music were vehement, outspoken protests against the administration of the Russian President, Vladimir Putin, and especially its oppressive attitudes towards women and the LGBT community. Through their music, they petitioned for liberation, solace and a meaningful response to their calls for justice and fairness. They came to prominence in 2012 when they challenged the collaboration between the Kremlin and the Orthodox Church against sexual non-conformity by performing their 'punk prayer' in Moscow's Christ the Saviour Cathedral. Their protest was certainly 'educational' in the sense understood in this book. They advocated a new and more ethical understanding of 'the good' that gave breathing space for those who were different and challenged the illusion of Russia as a safe and harmonious place for all its citizens, seeking instead to map out the untold story of oppression. As a result, three of the women were arrested and silenced; two of them being charged with hooliganism and, significantly, hatred against religion. A small collective of young women, the actual physical threat they posed was tiny in comparison to the threat that their animating breath represented, revealing, in the words of Carol Rumens's (2012) English translation, this 'holiness crap' that misidentified God and the Virgin as allies with tyrannical misogyny

100 *Thinking Otherwise—Resisting Indifference*

and homophobia in an age-old struggle against women and other sexual dissenters (Christ, 1979; Ussher, 2006).

Spirituality in this context, then, is revolutionary animation. For bell hooks, education as a whole can be seen in these revolutionary, transgressive terms (1994; 2003; 2010) so to speak, breathing new life into researchers, students and communities. Education is characterised as 'the practice of freedom', and the antithesis of the indifference our book attempts to define as a kind of resistance to being affected or changed. Conversely, nomadic spirituality in terms of 'patterns of becoming' and the development of what Braidotti (2002, 91) calls a 'rhizomic sensibility' in educational spaces inevitably resists 'more of the same'. Reflecting this insight, part of Clive and Jane Erricker's frustration with approaches to RE in schools at the end of the 20th century was precisely the implicit view of spirituality in school spaces as the context for inculcating a set of rigid values and principles that resisted change or held it at bay. For them, the idea of learning and education had less to do with rehearsing the authorised laws and customs, including patterns of gender sustained by the prevailing styles of reasoning and approved by policy makers or parents, and more to do with 'the child as a person' (2000, 87) and with their capacity to breathe and to animate or enliven others. (Nomadic) spirituality then stands opposed to sameness and indifference and, as a *conceptual persona*, is a tool for negotiating change and 'unjamming the machine' (Deleuze and Guattari, 1987) so that processes, people and other intersubjective multiplicities are not pointlessly dammed up.

(v) Becoming Undone

Judith Butler's (2004) understanding of 'undoing gender' provides a starting point or jumping-off ground for the final proposed metaphorical framework or *conceptual persona* (Braidotti, 2002, 12) evoked to 'mobilise creative possibilities in order to change the dominant subject position' and resist indifference in an ongoing search to find adequate representations for the people we—ourselves and our students—want to become. The target 'subject position' relates particularly in this chapter to the normative and gendered framework that still dominates educational spaces in the discourse of the official account or settlement that is RE in schools and universities. Sometimes, this discourse is simply elitist and Western-centred—referencing a particular kind of Western Protestant Christianity, for example—and often it is exclusive or dismissive of any difference/s, including, but not limited, of course, to gender difference/s. The creative possibilities indicated by the title of this section encompass the modality of becoming but also invoke Butler's idea of undoing as an active, if not risk-free process, of non-conformity to standard patterns of gender. This takes us into a more self-conscious discussion of genders and, in this chapter specifically, transgender. 'Trans' is used here to describe anyone who desires or seeks actively to embody their gender

Thinking Otherwise—Gender in the Mix 101

in non-conventional ways, including their forms of presentation, dress or by undergoing body-changing surgery for so-called gender reassignment. Trans people may be biologically male or female at birth or intersex (with biological characteristics of both biological sexes). They may be gay or lesbian or heterosexual or perhaps not regard themselves as any of these. They may simply want to change from one relatively conventional gendered position to another, or they may recognise their need or freedom to create or become something different from what has been embodied conventionally, so far. Equally, their relationships are likely to be as varied—or as narrow—as in the population as a whole (Monro, 2005).

Butler (2004, 1), of course, suggests that gender is always 'a kind of doing' or what she has called 'a practice of improvisation within a scene of constraint'. She has also developed an idea of performativity whereby gender is constituted by the repeated performance of certain stipulated gestures or actions that actively construct not simply the body as one gender or the other, but also the illusion of a particular, inner essence. According to Butler (1999, 172–3), this is

> . . . discursively maintained for the purposes of the regulation of sexuality within the obligatory frame of reproductive heterosexuality.

Performativity, as Butler understands it, describes the powerful impact of gender conditioning—or socialisation—upon subjectivity that is thus experienced as real and inescapable by many people and as very difficult to challenge for all. However, in what follows, we will adopt Butler's underlying position and not assume that gender is, in fact, something essential, necessary or unchanging. Arguably, instead, gender performativity should be understood as a matter of something that is ultimately unfinished. Butler implies that normative gender performativity cannot be warranted except *de facto* by the continual performances going on around us all the time, right from our earliest moments. 'Becoming undone', in gender terms, is thus not something that is to be achieved quickly or painlessly—or even—for many people, at all. Of course, at the same time, the rules of normative heteropatriarchy clearly do not suit everyone; there is also pain in conforming to the norm. But the consequences of flouting the rules and endeavouring to perform differently may be equally unconscionable. As Butler (2004, 2–3) says,

> If I desire in certain ways, will I be able to live? Will there be a place for my life, and will it be recognisable to the others upon whom I depend for social existence?

To resist playing the game or to refuse the gender role to which one has been assigned at birth is to bring down on oneself the still extraordinary weight of significance placed on this (comparatively minor) distinction between the biologically male and female. Moreover, in the words of one trans woman

102 *Thinking Otherwise—Resisting Indifference*

(Serano, 2007, 41), the trope of the performance of these roles—that is, as self-deception in contrast to a real essence—is often itself used in representations of trans women (those who are/were biologically male at birth but who identify with female gender) to shame them.

> In virtually all depictions of trans women . . . the underlying assumption is that the trans woman wants to achieve a stereotypically feminine appearance and gender role. The possibility that trans women are even capable of making a distinction between identifying as female and wanting to cultivate a hyperfeminine image is never raised. In fact . . . the media often dwells on the specifics of the feminisation process, showing trans women putting on their feminine exteriors. It's telling that TV, film, and news producers tend not to be satisfied with merely showing trans women wearing feminine clothes and makeup. Rather, it is their intent to capture trans women in the act of putting on lipstick, dresses, and high heels, thereby giving the audience the impression that the trans woman's femaleness is an artificial mask or costume.

At the same time, the inherited patriarchal framework of Western society continues to sustain the apotheosis of hypermasculinity, even without the symbolism of Christian theology to support it. The theological nature of this gender symbolism was first established by early second-wave feminist theologians like Mary Daly (1968; 1973) and Rosemary Radford Ruether (1983). Daly, for example, though she did not use the term hypermasculinity, nevertheless put her finger (Daly, 1973, 13) on these previously hidden structures: 'If God in "his" heaven is a father ruling "his" people, then it is in the "nature" of things and according to divine plan and the order of the universe that society be male-dominated'. What is more, the exaltation or privileging of masculinity is not just an historical memory. Although we have had access to types of feminist analysis for a century and more, reviewing this vast history of intellectual and active reflection on gender still does not, in general, form part of our basic educational curriculum. This is perhaps not so surprising when we consider the multi-billion-pound investment in a sense of patriarchal and masculinist entitlement represented, for example, by the digital pornography industry that still largely turns on the unexamined tastes of male consumers (Dines, 2011). There is still a great deal to play for in the exploitation of normative gender relations, and historically, educational spaces like schools and universities have been places where this socialisation along conventional gendered lines is powerfully enacted and performances are honed with little formal training being given in the analysis of this powerful determinant for future roles. Children and young people may encounter the idea in some educational spaces that diversity is a good thing and that men and women are equal, but without any tools for understanding the fabrications of conventional gender performances outside or across these formal spaces—for example, in the material circumstances of

Thinking Otherwise—Gender in the Mix 103

'growing up male'—it is unlikely that they will be able to understand this process or to come to acknowledge the possibility of difference/s or change. At the same time, as Serano (2007) and others attest, there are clearly elements of gender dysphoria within the population as a whole for whom a non-medicalised and non-pathologised study of RE dedicated to the exploration of difference/s could perhaps provide an element of reassurance and context.

Butler remains upbeat; she believes that undoing a normative conception of gender can lead to greater livability (2004, 1) for those who, for whatever reasons, find the existing constructions constricting. And of course, as Nelson Rodriguez notes, the queer theory with which Butler's more positive idea of 'undoing' can be associated has always been 'an anti-identitarian politics of difference' (2012, 272) that points to this potential for change. Drawing on Butler's work, Rodriguez points to a potential for difference that goes beyond normative binaries like male/female or gay and lesbian versus straight desire. Rodriguez's approach to queer in the 'women's and gender studies' classroom develops difference in terms of a particular kind of pedagogy; exposing students to the implicit generosity of trans people who tell their stories and whose struggles are not simply narratives of how someone travels from one gender to the other, but open up a range of possibilities for new becomings or forms of embodiment that readers/viewers, as well as writers or researchers, can draw on to flesh out Butler's notion of greater livability. In educational spaces, Rodriguez's pedagogy of generosity becomes the means of evoking a similar generosity in students who, through their own negotiation of gender in the light of what they come to recognise as its fluidity and instability, begin to create the conditions for future becomings for themselves—or, in Braidotti's terms, to evoke and mobilise creative possibilities. In other words, they are directed to reflect or focus not only on this queer embodiment, but also on its status as 'a language of possibility' (Rodriguez, 2012, 287). And arguably, in the RE classroom, in a similar way, a commitment to openness and generosity in acknowledging difference/s has the capacity to indicate different ways of achieving greater livability in answer to Butler's (2004, 2–3) questions: 'Will there be a place for my life, and will it be recognisable to the others upon whom I depend for social existence?'

Illustrating this practice of pedagogic generosity in more detail, Rodriguez focuses on two films he uses in educational spaces—specifically, his gender studies classroom. First *Ma Vie en Rose* (Berliner, 1997) tells the story of a seven-year-old transgendered child, Ludovic Fabre, whose biological sex is male but whose gender identity is, as he expresses it himself, 'boy/girl'. This child is 'being undone' not simply because a proclivity towards transgender confuses and distresses him/herself, but also because, as a result, it unsettles Ludovic's family, who have apparently no problems with conventional gender. The impact of Ludovic's gender dissonance is felt by the family, who are also ostracised by their community and, in response, take this out on

104 *Thinking Otherwise—Resisting Indifference*

Ludovic, as he tries to answer Butler's questions: can s/he find 'a place for his/her life'? Eventually, in this fictional setting, Ludovic's struggle brings about a change, creating 'the critical transformative conditions' for his/her family to come to a new, more generous understanding (Rodriguez, 2012, 267). In other words, this embodied struggle is itself the starting point for other positive forms of undoing. The kinds of patterns of social conformity and belonging within a family and a community that were undoing Ludovic in the sense of driving him to thoughts of suicide were also, in Rodriguez' view, limiting that community and family by fixing its understanding of the human in spite of the evidence that gender is subject to its historical context and has often been constructed through forms of extremely hostile, ethically problematic exclusions or 'othering' (Butler, 2004, 13). Thus undoing— initiated from both conscious and unconscious sites of resistance—is, for Rodriguez (2012, 268), ultimately a good way of doing gender for Ludovic.

By the film's end, one might say that Ludovic and his family have developed a critical consciousness—that is, an experientially informed and cultivated level of 'criticality'—in relation to gender and sexual norms that has enabled them, at least to a certain extent, to live 'queerly' alongside such norms. Here, then, queer forms of embodiment challenge or disrupt hegemonic forms of gender normativity that operate within families, themselves a product of social, gender normativity. Crucially, also in this 'pedagogic' context, this can be perceived as a process of creative development that extends from the film to the classroom or other educational spaces where it is encountered.

The second film to which Rodriguez refers is a documentary called *Gender Rebel* (Epstein, 2006). This documentary follows three biological females who identify as gender queer (Rodriguez, 2012, 276), that is to say, as gendered in an unconventionally male sense, and who are seeking to achieve a more conventionally masculine or a more idealised masculine-looking body. In the course of this journey or transition, one of the three, Jill, like Ludovic, manages to elicit from her family—or more exactly, her mother—alongside a profound sense of grieving and loss, a generous response, as she acknowledges the loss of her 'daughter' but tries to move towards a more accepting relationship with her 'child' (Rodriguez, 2012, 280). As the documentary indicates, there are many less hospitable responses to these potentially 'pedagogic' initiatives and many tears are shed.

Rodriguez's pedagogical practice, of course, is to introduce students to the stories and images of queer trans embodiments within his work as a lecturer in women and gender studies in a mode of generosity, in celebration of what he clearly regards in relation to gender and embodiment, as the positivity of difference. This is, in Deleuzian terms (Rodriguez, 2012, 285), furnishing students with a new vocabulary for 'becoming queer masculine body' as

> . . . one that challenges the arborescent logic of structuring biological sex, gender, and sexuality in a hierarchical system of truth and value,

Thinking Otherwise—Gender in the Mix 105

whereby biological sex is situated not only as static but also as connected to, and therefore, the root or base of the truth of gender and sexuality.

So, Jill binds her breasts to flatten them, whilst Kim, becoming Ryan, follows the more radical path of taking testosterone and undergoing surgery to remove them. Yet s/he doesn't see this as becoming conventionally male in all respects—or as hostile towards women and women's bodies—so much as becoming gender queer and having the body s/he wants and feels comfortable with. In Deleuzian terms, this behavior instigates 'lines of flight' that can deterritorialise gendered bodies by disturbing boundaries and demarcations (Rodriguez, 2012, 281). But of course, even the suggestion of hostility towards the female is a good illustration of what is at stake in these (pedagogical) practices (Rodriguez, 2012, 283).

> . . . it is precisely because the queer masculine embodiments of biological females, such as in Kim's case, run the risk of being positioned across any number of cultural and social locations as a threatening 'Other', especially in relation to delimited understandings of the category woman, that a pedagogy of trans generosity becomes a necessary critical intervention to challenge such a viewpoint.

This particular focus on becoming queer masculine body—in a pedagogic context—necessarily raises questions about the relative power or status of persons represented by themselves or others as masculine; what, if anything, does this kind of becoming or possibility have to do with the way in which men are viewed within male-normative societies as powerful, autonomous subjects in contrast to women, whose subjectivity is still often viewed as derivative and problematic? In seeking to be comfortable in their own skins, how much are transgender people—transitioners, or nomads, perhaps—influenced by the affordances of more mainstream gender? It also raises very serious questions about what underpins the assumption of a warranted authority on the basis of 'masculinity' when this is clearly something that can increasingly be taken on a voluntary basis and all the more so within a Western context within which the wealth and medical technology is readily available. And it certainly raises issues for those who—differently—view patterns of gender socialisation as, say, divinely or scientifically warranted.

Nevertheless, in terms of an ethical responsibility to difference/s, Rodriguez's pedagogics is acutely sensitive to the pain that is caused by limitation, closure and the rejection of difference/s without implying that this is simply about one interest group against another. What characterises his examples and the way in which he handles them in educational spaces is the way in which he draws attention to how trans people have to negotiate their relationships across communities of dissonance. In one way or another, they are constantly challenged to relate across difference/s, to find ways of loving and letting go. In other words, representations of 'otherness' are positioned

106   *Thinking Otherwise—Resisting Indifference*

in relation to generosity rather than hostility or threat, a generosity that goes both ways. The embodiment of 'becoming (queer) masculine body', for example, is itself a generous self-giving that elicits a corresponding generosity, as Kim's girlfriend Michelle—like Jill's mother—wrestles with Kim's desire for a new kind of embodiment that is at variance with her own identification and expectation as a lesbian woman. In this documentary, she still seeks to re-establish a relationship of love thrown out of that form of convention.

Pedagogically speaking, this practice demands more of those occupying educational spaces that could be said to be particularly suited to dealing with forms of difference such as RE, even as it is presently conceived and practised. As noted already, the dimension of *embodiment*, for example, goes against the grain of much standard educational practice that is still predominantly about abstract and discursive knowledge practices. And the kind of generosity Rodriguez has in mind is not so much related to examinable knowledge as to bringing about a form of empathy or changing sensibility that may be tested to some extent in the classroom but crucially impacts outside of it in the wider world. The pedagogics of *generosity*, then, involves all participants making the effort to move towards the expression of difference/s and a willingness not to cut off that movement in the interests of safety or sameness, but to aim towards mobilising creativity and challenging the dominant subject nor simply for the sake of it, but in the effort to achieve some kind of greater livability. As Serano points out (2007, 86), from the perspective of trans people, choosing to transition away from conventional gender is an attempt to escape considerable internal pain. In her words:

> . . . the hardest part about being trans has not been the discrimination or ridicule that I have faced for defying societal gender norms, but rather the internal pain I experienced when my subconscious and conscious sexes were at odds with one another . . . Sometimes people discount the fact that trans people feel any actual pain related to their gender. Of course, it is easy for them to dismiss gender dissonance: It's invisible and (perhaps more relevantly) they themselves are unable to relate to it. These same people, however, do understand that being stuck in a bad relation or in an unfulfilling job can make a person miserable and lead to a depression so intense that it spills over into all other areas of that person's life. These types of pain can be tolerated temporarily, but in the long run, if things do not change, that stress and sadness can ruin a person . . . by the time I made the decision to transition, my gender dissonance had gotten so bad that it completely consumed me; it hurt more than any pain, physical or emotional, that I had ever experienced.

And in this sense, of course, a pedagogics of generosity in RE certainly resonates with Education Scotland's (n.d., 19)—no doubt typical aspiration within policy contexts—to 'embrace and celebrate . . . difference'.

Thinking Otherwise—Gender in the Mix   107

In sum, this approach presents a creative challenge to a dominant—heterosexual—subject position by developing—as Rodriguez frames his pedagogy—through the interventions of a marginalised/different sector of the community some understanding of what new spaces of greater livability might be opened up and look like. A key feature here is the sense in which this intervention effectively derives from the different/minority position itself, that, through laying itself open in and with filmmakers, allows narratives of transition to be used to grow or develop greater empathy and flexibility and make it more possible to accommodate and be accommodated to difference/s. The level of challenge will appear very high in some relatively closed or exclusive contexts. As the work of Serano and others indicates, hostility is not an uncommon response to trans people generally. It is interesting, then, that Rodriguez references college or university-level classes in gender studies rather than other educational spaces, such as in schools. Having said this, if it is important to address forms of gender difference/s in educational spaces, then some provision of gender or feminist analysis would seem to be essential as part of a core curriculum for the 21st century at all levels. This is particularly true for RE if it is going to be understood as a space for developing hospitality to difference/s as a process requiring care, attention, engagement and willingness to risk getting lost in order the better to understand that loss of certainty and vulnerability that comes with a desirable transformation in terms, for example, of subjectification (Biesta, 2009).

A second illustration of the kind of pedagogics Rodriguez talks about—that it, so to say, refers to something that presents a challenge to limited and limiting dominant subject positions—is taken from one of six film shorts (*Examined Life*, 2010) that document the thoughts of a number of philosophers. In this example, asking what a body can do, Judith Butler, playing the role of privileged subject and educator, takes a walk on two feet. Her conversation partner is artist and animal rights campaigner Sunaura Taylor who—in the spirit of Rodriguez's pedagogics of generosity—offers herself as a kind of enacted challenge to—or undoing of—Butler's privileged form of embodiment from her wheelchair. The film begins with a collage of people moving on foot, on bicycles, in cars, pushing pushchairs with a stick, before focusing in on the two women 'taking a walk' together, wheelchair user and non-wheelchair user, talking about what a body can do differently. Applying Rodriguez's analysis of her actions in terms of pedagogic generosity, Sunaura allows herself, her actions and her reflections to address that question, so that in the first instance, we are made to understand Sunaura's 'undoing' through the contrast with others who are conventionally able-bodied in a world designed largely in accordance with these conventions. At the same time, the 'walk' itself incorporates examples of, or reflections on, what Sunaura—and thus what 'the body'—does differently. Thus, Sunaura herself moves along pavements and into shops in her wheelchair. Sometimes she has to ask for help. Once, she acknowledges that her city has been built by those who try hard to accommodate the differently abled. She refers, for example, to sometimes using her

108 *Thinking Otherwise—Resisting Indifference*

mouth rather than her hands to carry a cup in order to avoid a crippling social isolation that would ensue if her movements had to be limited to a certain kind of acceptable and conventional 'able-bodied' doing. And at the same time as these things are being recorded, and whilst the conversation starts with the theme of 'what a body can do', the viewer is made powerfully aware, not so much of any specific answer to the question in discursive terms, as of the way in which the women relate to each other. Sunaura and Judith do not simply illustrate what a body can do by entering a shop and buying a cardigan, but, through the empathetic nature of their relationship with each other, the viewer becomes aware of how normative, conventional assumptions about what the body can do, drawing on notions of individual autonomous action, are set aside in what they are able to achieve together. Sunaura needs help putting on the cardigan, and her generosity in allowing Judith Butler to help her through a tenderly, bodily action enables the viewer to come to an unexpected, different and far more interesting answer to the original question.

And so the conceptual persona of becoming undone with its resonances of terror and disintegration, as well as of flight, change and transformation, represents the last of this quarternity, indicating some of the risks and opportunities of proposing alternative metaphorical frameworks or styles of reasoning that allow us—if we are cautious and careful (Latour, 2004, 246)—to begin to see things differently, lessening our preoccupation with neutrality and processes of distancing based on the normative masculine Western perspectives in order to bring the complex relational and contextual factors of gender into play so that we can begin to unpick or dissolve the dominant subject position.

(vi) Conclusion

In this chapter, we have looked at how an orientation that engages both critically and ethically with imagining and re-imagining—sense-making expressed through different conceptual personae and styles of reasoning—can move towards new representations through pedagogies and forms of experimentation that unsettle or rearrange the framings and metaphorical patternings of the past in search of something more adequate for becoming subjects in our unstable worlds. In the terms of Thrift (2004) and Rodriguez (2012), this chapter has been about developing resources for a 'politics of imaginative generosity' within educational sites where different cultures connect— particularly as demarcated and identified through the mobilisation of gender. In this sense, then, we lay claim to being educational insofar as this 'leads out' from what is known already and seeks not to re-inscribe existing assumptions but, in Stengers' (1997) terms, to bring about new 'mapping[s] into knowledge'. This is something that we will return to in further detail in Chapter Six.

Note

1. Some parts of this chapter rework two previously published articles (Jasper, 2015a; 2015b).

Bibliography

Althaus-Reid, M., 2000. *Indecent theology: Theological Perversions in Sex, Gender and Politics*. London and New York: Routledge.

Althaus-Reid, M., 2004. *From Feminist theology to Indecent theology*. London: SCM Press.

Anderson, E., 2013. *H. D. and Modernist Religious Imagination: Mysticism and Imagination*. London: Bloomsbury.

Anderson, P.S., 2010. 'The lived body, gender and confidence'. In: P.S. Anderson ed., *New Topics in Feminist Philosophy of Religion: Contestations and Transcendence Incarnate*. Dordrecht, Heidelberg, London and New York: Springer, pp. 163–180.

Anderson, P.S., 2012. *Re-visioning Gender in Philosophy of Religion: Reason, Love and Epistemic Locatedness*. Farnham, Surrey and Burlington, VT: Ashgate.

Barad, K., 2007. *Meeting the Universe Halfway: Quantum Physics and the Entanglement of Matter and Meaning*. Durham, NC and London: Duke University Press.

Battersby, C., 1989. *Gender and Genius: Towards a Feminist Aesthetics*. London: The Women's Press.

Beattie, T., 2006. *New Catholic Feminism: theology and Theory*. London and New York: Routledge.

Beauvoir, S. de, 1949. Paris: Editions Gallimard. *The Second Sex (Le deuxieme sexe)*. C. Borde and S. Malovany-Chevallier eds., 2011 ed. London: Vintage.

Beauvoir, S. de, 1958. Paris: Librairie Gallimard. *Memoirs of a Dutiful Daughter Mémoires d'une jeune fille rangée*. 1963 ed. Harmondsworth and Middlesex, UK: Penguin Books.

Berger, P.L., 1971. *A Rumour of Angels: Modern Society and the Rediscovery of the Supernatural*. Harmondsworth: Penguin.

Berliner, A., 1997. *Ma Vie en Rose*.

Besley, T., 2005. 'Foucault, truth telling and technologies of the self in schools'. *Journal of Educational Enquiry*, vol. 6, no. 1, pp. 76–89.

Biesta, G., 2 December 2009. 'Good education in an age of measurement: On the need to reconnect with the question of purpose in education'. *Educational Assessment, Evaluation and Accountability*, vol. 21, pp. 33–46.

Braidotti, R., 2002. *Metamorphoses: Towards a Materialist Theory of Becoming*. Cambridge and Malden, MA: Polity Press.

Braidotti, R., 2011. *Nomadic Subjects: Embodiment and Sexual Difference in Contemporary Feminist Theory 2. Embodiment and Difference*. New York: Columbia University Press.

Brown, W., 2005. *Edgework: Critical Essays on Knowledge and Politics*. Princeton and Oxford: Princeton University Press.

Butler, J., 20 March 1999. 'A "bad writer" bites back'. New York: The New York Times. Available from https://pantherfile.uwm.edu/wash/www/butler.htm.

Butler, J., 2004. *Undoing Gender*. New York and London: Routledge.

Carrette, J. and King, R., 2005. *Selling Spirituality: The Silent Takeover of Religion*. London and New York: Routledge.

Chanter, T., 2006. *Gender: Key Concepts in Philosophy*. London and New York: Continuum.

Christ, C., 1979. 'Why women need the goddess: Phenomenological, psychological, and political reflections'. In: *Womanspirit Rising: A Feminist Reader in Religion*. J. Plaskow ed., 1992 ed. New York: HarperCollins, pp. 273–287.

Christ, C. and Plaskow, J., 1979. New York: HarperCollins. *Womanspirit Rising: A Feminist Reader in Religion*. 1992 ed. New York: HarperSanFrancisco.

110 Thinking Otherwise—Resisting Indifference

Clough, M., 2014. *Shame: The Church and Female Sexuality*. PhD Thesis. University of Bristol.

Crenshaw, K., 1991. 'Mapping the margins: Intersectionality, identity politics and violence agains women of color'. *Stanford Law Review*, vol. 43, pp. 1241–1279.

Daly, M., 1968. *The Church and the Second Sex*. 1985 ed. Boston, MA: Beacon Press.

Daly, M., 1973. *Beyond God the Father*. Boston, MA: Beacon Press.

Daly Goggin, M. and Fowkes Tobin, B., 2009a. *Material Women, 1750–1950*. Farmington, Surrey and Burlington, VT: Ashgate.

Daly Goggin, M. and Fowkes Tobin, B., 2009b. *Women and the Material Culture of Needlework and Textiles, 1750–1950*. Farmington, Surrey and Burlington, VT: Ashgate.

Daly Goggin, M. and Fowkes Tobin, B., 2009c. *Women and Things, 1750–1950*. Farmington, Surrey and Burlington, VT: Ashgate.

Davies, B., 2014. *Listening to Children: Being and Becoming*. London and New York: Routledge.

Deleuze, G. and Guattari, F., 1987. Paris: Les Éditions de Minuit. *A Thousand Plateaus: Capitalism and Schizophrenia*. 2003 ed. London and New York: Continuum.

Dines, G., 2011. *Pornland: How Porn Has Hijacked Our Sexuality*. Boston, MA: Beacon Press.

Eddo-Lodge, R. 2014. 'Calling the Williams sisters 'scary' isn't just sexist, it's racist too'. *The Daily Telegraph* 20th October 2014.

Education Scotland, February 2011a. 'Curriculum for Excellence: Religious and moral education and religious education in non-denominational schools and religious education in roman catholic schools'. Available from www.educationscotland.gov. uk/resources/c/genericresource_tcm4650441.asp.

Education Scotland, February 2011b. 'Curriculum for Excellence: Provision of religious observance in schools'. Available from www.educationscotland.gov.uk/resources/c/genericresource_tcm4650441.asp.

Education Scotland, 2011c. 'Curriculum for Excellence: Health and well-being'. Available from www.educationscotland.gov.uk/learningandteaching/curriculumareas/healthandwellbeing/eandos/index.asp.

Education Scotland, n.d. 'Promoting diversity and equality: Developing responsible citizens for 21st century Scotland: A report to support schools and centres in promoting diversity and equality through all aspects of planned learning'. Available from www.educationscotland.gov.uk/Images/Promoting_DE080313_tcm4-747988.pdf.

Epstein, E., 2006. *Gender Rebel*.

Erricker, C. and Erricker, J., 2000. *Reconstructing Religious, Spiritual and Moral Education*. London and New York: RoutledgeFalmer.

Examined Life—Judith Butler and Sunaura Taylor 720p.avi , 6 October 2010. Available from www.youtube.com/watch?v=k0HZaPkF6qE.

Fitzgerald, T., 2007. 'Encompassing religion, privatized religions and the invention of modern politics'. In: T. Fitzgerald ed., *Religion and the Secular: Historical and Colonial Formations*. 2007 ed. London and Oakville, CT: Equinox, pp. 211–240.

Fricker, M., 2003. 'Life-story in Simone de Beauvoir'. In: C. Card ed., *The Cambridge Companion to Simone de Beauvoir*. Cambridge: Cambridge University Press, pp. 208–227.

Friedman, S.S., 2001. 'Locational feminism: Gender, cultural geographies and geopolitical literacy'. In: M. Dekoven ed., *Feminist Locations: Global and Local, Theory*

Thinking Otherwise—Gender in the Mix 111

and Practice. New Brunswick, New Jersey and London: Rutgers University Press, pp. 13–36.

Hadot, P., 1995. *Philosophy as a Way of Life: Spiritual Exercises From Socrates to Foucault*. Malden, MA, Oxford, Melbourne and Berlin: Blackwell Publishing Ltd.

Hersch, J. 1985. 'Eve ou la Naissance éternelle du Temps'. *Textes*. Fribourg: le Feu de Nuict.

Hill Collins, P. and Bilge, S., 2016. *Intersectionality*. Cambridge and Malden, MA: Polity Press.

hooks, b., 1994. *Teaching to Transgress: Education as the Practice of Freedom*. New York and London: Routledge.

hooks, b., 2003. *Teaching Community: A Pedagogy of Hope*. London and New York: Routledge.

hooks, b., 2010. *Teaching Critical Thinking: Practical Wisdom*. London: Routledge.

Hultman, K. and Taguchi, H.L., 2010. 'Challenging anthropocentric analysis of visual data: A relational materialist methodological approach to educational research'. *Qualitative Studies in Education*, vol. 23, no. 5, pp. 525–542.

I'Anson, J. and Jasper, A., 2011. '"Religion" in educational spaces: Knowing, knowing well, and knowing differently'. *Arts and Humanities in Higher Education*, vol. 10, no. 3, pp. 295–314.

Irigaray, L., 2004. *Key Writings*. London and New York: Continuum.

Isherwood, L., 2007. *The Fat Jesus: Feminist Explorations in Boundaries and Transgressions*. London: Darton, Longman and Todd.

Isherwood, L. and Stuart, E., 1998. *Introducing Body theology*. Sheffield: Sheffield Academic Press.

Jantzen, G.M., 1998. *Becoming Divine: Towards a Feminist Philosophy of Religion*. Manchester: Manchester University Press.

Jasper, A., 1998. *The Shining Garment of the Text: Gendered Readings in John's Gospel*. Sheffield: Sheffield Academic Press.

Jasper, A., 2007. 'Body and word'. In: A. Hass, D. Jasper and E. Jay eds., *The Oxford Handbook of English Literature and theology*. 2007 ed. Oxford: Oxford University Press, pp. 776–792.

Jasper, A., 2012. *Because of Beauvoir: Christianity and the Cultivation of Female Genius*. Waco, TX: Baylor University Press.

Jasper, A., 2015a. 'Womanspirit still rising? Some feminist reflections on "Religious Education" in the UK'. *Feminist theology*, vol. 23, no. 3, pp. 240–253.

Jasper, A., 2015b. '"RE/RME/TRS is a girl's subject": Talking about gender and the discourse of "religion" in UK educational spaces'. *Feminist theology*, vol. 24, no. 1, pp. 69–78.

Johnson, M.P., 2008. *A Typology of Domestic Violence: Intimate Terrorism, Violent Resistance, and Situational Couple Violence*. Boston, MA: Northeastern University Press.

Keller, C., 2003. *Face of the Deep: A theology of Becoming*. London and New York: Routledge.

Kelly, L. and Radford, J., December 1990. '"Nothing really happened." The invalidation of women's experiences of sexual violence'. *Critical Social Policy*, vol. 10, no. 30, pp. 39–53.

King, U., 1993. *Women and Spirituality: Voices of Protest and Promise*. London: Palgrave Macmillan.

112 *Thinking Otherwise—Resisting Indifference*

King, U., 1994. *Feminist theology From the Third World: A Reader*. London: SPCK.

Knight, S., 2013. *Forest School and Oudoor Learning in the Early Years*. London, California, New Delhi and Singapore: Sage.

Kristeva, J., 1980. *Powers of Horror: An Essay on Abjection*. 1982 ed. New York: Columbia University Press.

Kristeva, J., 1999. Fayard. Hannah Arendt. In: *Female Genius: Life, Madness, Words— Hannah Arendt, Melanie Klein, Colette*. New York: Columbia University Press.

Kristeva, J., 2002. Fayard. *Colette*. In: *Female Genius: Life, Madness, Words—Hannah Arendt, Melanie Klein, Colette*. New York: Columbia University Press.

Kristeva, J., 2012. *The Severed Head: Capital Visions*. New York and Chichester West Sussex: Columbia University Press.

Latour, B., 1999. *Pandora's Hope: An Essay on the Reality of Science Studies*. Cambridge, MA: Harvard University Press.

Latour, B., Winter 2004. 'Why has critique run out of steam? From matters of fact to matters of concern'. *Critical Inquiry*, vol. 30, no. 2, pp. 225–248.

Law, J. and Lin, W., 2010. 'Cultivating disconcertment'. *The Sociological Review*, vol. 58, no. S2, pp. 135–153.

Law, J. and Mol, A.-M., 2002. *Complexities: Social Studies of Knowledge Practices*. Durham, NC: Duke University Press.

Le Dœuff, M., 1980, Éditions Payot. *The Philosophical Imaginary, L'Imaginaire Philosophique*. 1989 ed. London and Stanford, CA: Athlone Press and Stanford University Press.

Le Dœuff, M., 1998. Paris: Aubier. *The Sex of Knowing Le Sexe du savoir*. 2003 ed. London and New York: Routledge.

Lippy, C.H., 2009. 'Miles to go: Promise keepers in historical and cultural context'. In: B. Krondorfer ed., *Men and Masculinities in Christianity and Judaism: A Critical Reader*. London: SCM Press, pp. 319–332.

Lloyd, G., 1984. *The Man of Reason: 'Male' and 'Female' in Western Philosophy*. Minneapolis, University of Minnesota Press: Methuen.

McFague, S., 1987. *Models of God: theology for an Ecological, Nuclear Age*. Minneapolis, MN: Fortress Press.

Mohanty, C.T., 1991. *Third World Women and the Politics of Feminism*. Bloomington: Indiana University Press.

Mohanty, C.T., 2003. *Feminism Without Borders: Decolonizing Theory, Practicing Solidarity*. Durham, NC: Duke University Press.

Monro, S., 2005. *Gender Politics: Citizenship, Activism and Sexual Diversity*. London and Ann Arbor, MI: Pluto Press.

Morten, N., 1986. *Journey Is Home*. Boston: Beacon Press.

National Archives, 1944. *Education Act, 1944*. Available from www.legislation.gov. uk/ukpga/Geo6/7-8/31/enacted.

National Archives, 1945. *Education (Scotland) Act, 1945*. Available from www. legislation.gov.uk/ukpga/Geo6/8-9/37/contents.

National Archives, 1988. *Education Reform Act, 1988*. Available from www. legislation.gov.uk/ukpga/1988/40/contents.

National Archives, 2010. *Equality Act 2010* [viewed 7 November 2016]. Available from www.legislation.gov.uk/ukpga/2010/15/contents.

Newman, E. 2015. 'No room for body image criticism in Serena Williams' Grand Slam chase'. *Sports Illustrated*, 14th July 2015.

Ogilvie, K.C., 2013. *Roots and Wings: A History of Outdoor Education and Outdoor Learning in the UK*. Lyme Regis, Dorset: Russell House Publishing.

Plaskow, J. and Christ, C.P., 1989. *Weaving the Visions: New Patterns in Feminist Spirituality*. New York: Harper Collins Publishers.

Rich, A., 1971. 'When we dead awaken: Writing as re-vision'. In: B.C. Gelpi and A. Gelpi eds., *Adrienne Rich's Poetry and Prose*. 1993 ed. New York: W. W. Norton, pp. 166–177.

Roberts, R.H., 2012. 'Contemplation and the "Performative Absolute": Submission and identity in managerial modernity'. *Journal of Management, Spirituality and Religion*, vol. 9, no. 1, pp. 9–29.

Rodriguez, N., 2012. 'Queer imaginative bodies and the politics and pedagogy of trans generosity: The case of Gender Rebel'. In: J. Landreau and N. Rodriguez eds., *Queer Masculinity: A Critical Reader in Education*. Dordrect, Heidelberg, London and New York: Springr, pp. 267–288.

Ruether, R. Radford, 1983. *Sexism and Godtalk*. Boston, MA: Beacon Press.

Ruether, R. Radford, 1992. *Gaia and God: An Ecofeminist theology of Earth Healing*. 1993 ed. London: SCM Press.

Rumens, C., Monday 20 August 2012. 'Pussy Riot's Punk Prayer is pure protest poetry'. The Guardian. Available from www.theguardian.com/books/2012/aug/20/pussy-riot-punk-prayer-lyrics.

Scottish Government, 2004. *The Report of the Religious Observance Review Group*. Edinburgh: Scottish Executive. Available from www.gov.scot/Publications/2004/05/19351/37062.

Serano, J., 2007. *Whipping Girl: A Transsexual Woman on Sexism and the Scapegoating of Femininity*. Berkeley, CA: Seal Press.

Sheldrake, P., 2012. *Spirituality: A Very Short Introduction*. Oxford: Oxford University Press.

Sheldrake, P., 2013. *Spirituality: A Brief History*. Malden, MA, Oxford and Chichester: John Wiley and Sons Ltd.

Sheldrake, P., 2014. *Spirituality: A Guide for the Perplexed*. London: Bloomsbury.

Spice, R.C., August 2016. *Strong Is the New Slim: A Study of the Body and Gender Amongst Female Free Weights Users*. MPhil Thesis, University of Stirling. Faculty of Health and Sports Science.

Spivak, G.C., 1984. 'Can the subaltern speak?' In: L. Chrisman and P. Williams eds., *Colonial Discourse and Post-Colonial Theory: A Reader*. New York: Columbia University Press, pp. 66–111.

Stengers, I., 1997. *Power and Invention: Situating Science*. Minneapolis, MN: University of Minnesota Press.

Thatcher, A., 1991. 'A critique of inwardness in religious education'. *British Journal of Religious Studies*, vol. 14, no. 1, pp. 22–27.

Thatcher Ulrich, L. and Carter, S.A., 2015. *Tangible Things: Making History Through Objects*. Oxford: Oxford University Press.

Thompson, L., 1999. *The Wandering Womb: A Cultural History of Outrageous Beliefs About Women*. Amherst, New York: Prometheus Books.

Thrift, N., 2004. 'Summoning life'. In: P. Cloke, P. Crang and M. Goodwin eds., *Envisioning Human Geographies*. London: Arnold, pp. 81–103.

Trible, P., 1984. *Texts of Terror: Literary-Feminist Readings of Biblical Narratives*. Minneapolis, MN: Fortress Press.

114 Thinking Otherwise—Resisting Indifference

Ussher, J.M., 2006. *Managing the Monstrous Feminine: Regulating the Reproductive Body*. London and New York: Routledge.

Verran, H., 1999. 'Staying true to the laugher in Nigerian classroom'. In: John Law and John Hassard eds., *Actor Network Theory and After*. Oxford, UK: Blackwell Publishing, pp. 136–155.

Verran, H., 2001. *Science and an African Logic*. Chicago: Chicago University Press.

Whitworth, P., 2014. *Gospel for the Outsider: The Gospel in Luke and Acts*. Durham: Sacristy Press.

Wright, A., 1997. 'Embodied spirituality: The place of culture in contemporary educational discourse on spirituality'. *International Journal of Children's Spirituality*, vol. 1, no. 2, pp. 8–20.

Young, I.M., 2005. *On Female Body Experience: 'Throwing Like a Girl' and Other Essays (Studies in Feminist Philosophy)*. Oxford: Oxford University Press.

5 Thinking Otherwise—The Anthropology of Islam

(i) Introduction

The focus of Chapter Five, as the third chapter in Part Two that explores a variety of different styles of reasoning and practice, is the anthropology of Islam. In recent years, misgivings have been expressed in regard to the representation of Islam, especially as regards Western media portrayals and the aim of articulating approaches that move beyond negative framings and associations that are both contentious and severely limiting. Although such an intent is positive, some of these proposals re-inscribe a 'world-view' and 'world-religions' approach to the study of Islam, which is also problematic, if for different reasons. Not the least concern is that 'world- religions' approaches tend to go hand in hand with the kinds of epistemic frameworks and translations that were a focus of critique in Part One. In working beyond approaches that inscribe generalised narratives that abstract from the particularities of day-to-day negotiations, this chapter articulates a different approach to the study of Islam, drawing upon recent work associated with an anthropology of Islam. This, we contend, enables a concern with a broader range of factors, including indigenous concepts, imaginative concerns and embodied commitments.

An anthropology of Islam draws upon the notion of a 'discursive tradition of inquiry' in relation to 'Islam' as a matter of concern. The notion of a discursive tradition, it will be argued, can acknowledge difference, which a 'world religions' approach tends to erase. A case in point is the significance of dream states, which modernist approaches tend to excise, since these do not translate easily into Western preoccupations and categories.

Secondly, exploration of a given discursive tradition provides concepts from within the tradition itself that may be helpful for practices of sense-making in relation to that tradition. Here, we draw upon al-Ghazālī's concept of *dihlīz* that moves beyond the imposition of a subject–object binary in the encounter with difference. Such a concept calls into question some of the assumptions that inform Western approaches to the subject as autonomous.

Thirdly, we then consider the case of 'possessed states', which raise a series of critical issues in regard to understanding, surfacing a series of ontological fault lines that call into question settled assumptions about where a

116   *Thinking Otherwise—Resisting Indifference*

subject begins and ends. The issues raised by this are not 'merely academic', but touch down in practical situations where different ontologies collide. A case in point is how to make sense of *jinn*, where traditional Islamic understandings and Western psychiatric discourses draw upon widely differing ontologies and remedies. These different ontologies and remedies variously collide, intersect and diffract in Western health centres, where these issues are of urgent concern and consequence.

Such an inquiry will, in turn, contribute to a critical reconsideration of the concepts, such as the imagination, which the other chapters in Part Two take up and within whose terms considerable work of cultural translation takes place.

(ii) Points of Departure

In a chapter that begins with a consideration of uprisings in the Middle East since 2011, Bush (2015) draws attention to the presence of poetry on various placards that were part of these demonstrations. The presence of poetry within the context of a protest or revolutionary movement is immediately disconcerting to Western sensibilities: at the very least, there would appear to be a category error here, where incompatible practices are uncomfortably conjoined. And yet, the surprise that attends such an undoing of expectation and of familiar ordering is a recurrent experience in the encounter with Islam, as will be seen in what follows. Put another way, the issues of framing and translation that were discussed in Part One are likely to become especially salient as far as the study of 'Islam' is concerned. And if, as Anjum (2007, 656) has observed, the would-be student of Islam strives to make sense in ways that are *not* essentialist 'and insensitive to the change, negotiation, development, and diversity that characterises lived Islam', they are immediately confronted with a series of dilemmas. Not the least of these dilemmas is a question as to *what the study of Islam might consist in* if essentialised approaches (such as 'the 5 pillars of Islam') are left behind. But a second issue lies with the conditions of communicability at all, for in describing a particular practice or meaning, it becomes wrested from a living and contingent history. This in some ways parallels the difference between a static drawing of a chaffinch in a nature guide, as compared with the complex patterns and interactions that become visible when one attends to a chaffinch visiting a bird table.

Then there are key issues here as to how Islam, as a matter of concern, might be characterised. If the focus of orientalists tended to be texts, usually produced at some distance in the past, anthropologists, in response to this, tended to focus upon Islam as being constituted through a range of distinctive social practices (Gilsenan, 1982). For some influential writers, such as Geertz (1968) and Gellner (1981), Islam thereby became a blueprint for social order.[1] However, such a focus upon diverse traditions and situations

Thinking Otherwise—The Anthropology of Islam 117

immediately raises the issue of 'multiple Islams': given the astonishing variety of different forms of expression, is there *a minimal commonality* that is necessary to affirm in order for a particular articulation to be regarded as 'Islam'? In other words, this is to raise a series of complex questions *apropos* the limits of heterogeneity, how these are decided—and by who. When facing these questions, it is easy to see how and why current 'world-religions' approaches have taken the form that they have—since the appeal to abstract beliefs and particular practices, such as pilgrimage, as being in some sense definitive, settles some of the more intractable issues of definition. Through such means, a form of complexity reduction is practised where such dilemmas fall into the background (Osberg and Biesta, 2010).

For el-Zein (1977), the object of analysis is the experience of particular expressions of Islam as lived. With such a focus, it is easy to see how the study of Islam becomes formidably difficult, especially once its diversity is acknowledged. Indeed, it is perhaps not surprising that the conclusion that el-Zein reaches is that such study is not in fact possible. Quite apart from its practical execution, there are also difficulties with the limits imposed through a focus upon experience alone. One such limitation is that philosophical and theological issues that are raised become effectively 'black boxed' and, in becoming hidden from view, are no longer of live concern to the would-be student of Islam within these terms.

The approach taken by Asad (1986) marks something of a departure from these previous analyses insofar as he is concerned with how 'Islam' as a category might be theoretically conceptualised and the implications of this as a matter of concern for the practice of anthropology (1993). Asad identifies a number of problems with previous framings, whether these are the limitations associated with reducing Islam to the study of texts (the tendency in play with the Orientalist position) or the reductionism inherent in equating Islam with a particular social structure (such as the approaches found in Gelner and Geertz). In response to this, Asad (1986) charts a new way forward, and this includes a critical reading of Western translations of Islam through (an unproblematised) mobilisation of Western concepts. If, as we have seen, 'poetry' cannot be easily disassociated from 'politics' in the case of Islam, neither can Western categories—such as 'religion'—be appropriately taken up in efforts to make sense of Islam.

This critical reading is informed by wide reading that includes Asad's (1986) engagement with the writings of Alasdair MacIntyre. In particular, Asad finds MacIntyre's (1984) concept of a discursive tradition helpful to his project in re-thinking approaches to the study of Islam. In this connection, MacIntyre (1984, 222) characterises a discursive tradition as consisting of

> . . . an historically extended, socially embodied argument extended through time, and an argument precisely in part about the goods which constitute that tradition . . .

118 *Thinking Otherwise—Resisting Indifference*

In terms of Asad's deployment of this concept in relation to Islam, according Moumtaz (2015, 128), this consists in 'texts, discourses, and authorised speakers and practitioners'. Within these terms, the unification that is distinctive to Islam is to be found in its extended dialogue—through time—with the *Qu'ran* and *Hadith* as founding texts. Whilst there are clearly other texts that are also drawn upon in this ongoing dialogue, the *Qu'ran* and *Hadith* have a foundational authority that is non-negotiable (Asad, 1986). The discursive tradition includes the varieties of ways in which practitioners engage with the resourcefulness of the tradition to forge meaningful connections with their own conditions and circumstances.

There are a number of distinct advantages to Asad's drawing on the concept of tradition as an interpretative tool in the study of Islam. First of all, it brings together a focus upon texts and practices; with the concept of a discursive tradition, these are intrinsically interlinked rather than being artificially prised apart, as was the case in many orientalist and previous anthropological approaches that we discussed above. Secondly, with such a framing, official texts inform, authorise and partially constitute practices that are oriented towards particular goods. In other words, texts and practice are in a dialectical relationship to one another, and to separate these for purposes of analysis is to severely limit the kinds of insight possible. A third consequence of such a re-framing is that this re-works the concept of tradition in ways that can acknowledge that tradition is not necessarily anti-rational and a-critical. This was an assumption of many Enlightenment thinkers, who dismissed tradition as the antithesis of rational inquiry, and, as MacIntyre (1988, 7) points out, sometimes they were right in this claim. However, this obscures a more important point, that traditions can—and frequently do—mobilise standards of rational justification that are socially embodied in 'argument[s] extended through time' (12). Consequently,

> . . . standards of rational justification themselves emerge from and are part of a history in which they are vindicated by the way in which they transcend the limitations of and provide remedies for the defects of their predecessors within the history of that same tradition.
>
> (MacIntyre, 1988, 7)

The ways in which a particular conception of rationality is understood therefore have a broader history, and as such, this needs to be set within a broader narrative. Thus, according to MacIntyre (1988, 8), '[t]o justify is to narrate how the argument has gone so far'.

Fourthly, approaching Islam as a discursive tradition also broadens the scope of analysis, bringing within its purview the imaginative, affective and dispositional work involved in its ongoing production. Another consequence of Asad's focus upon tradition is that this puts centre stage issues of power and authority—especially as regards different conceptions of what is authentic Islam and how in different times and contexts this has been determined.[2]

Thinking Otherwise—The Anthropology of Islam 119

(iii) Islam as a Tradition

(a) Al-Ghazālī

Instead of ordering inquiry through concepts that derive from outside a tradition of inquiry, therefore, approaching Islam as a discursive tradition of inquiry encourages the would-be student to draw upon resources from within the tradition in question, so as to provide conceptual and methodological resources for approaching its study. Here, we provide a brief illustration of the concept of discursive tradition in relation to Islam so as to illustrate some of its affordances and difficulties, before examining how the concept of discursive tradition might be applied in more empirical directions, in terms of an anthropology of Islam, along the lines suggested by Asad.

One example of deploying the concept of a discursive tradition in relation to Islam would be to engage the writings of al-Ghazālī, (1058–1111 CE), who is of an equivalent stature to Aquinas in Christianity or Maimonides within Judaism (Bowker, 1978, 194). Although al-Ghazālī is regarded by many as both 'an enigmatic and agonistic figure' (Moosa, 2005, 35), there are, nevertheless, powerful reasons for engaging his thinking, especially in relation to encounters with heterogeneous knowledge traditions. Al-Ghazālī was brought up in a highly complex cultural situation where, by the 11th century, Islam extended from Spain to Afghanistan, and so embraced considerable diversity (Thomas, 2015). Although initially more or less unified, the Islamic area had split into a series of semi-autonomous regions. This fragmentation was mirrored at an intellectual level where, broadly speaking, there were three rival traditions of inquiry into the nature of the world and how the action of God was to be understood in relation to this. Each of these traditions of inquiry led in very different directions, with the philosophers, Mu'tazila's, drawing upon ibn Sīnā (better know in the West as Avicenna), maintaining that reason was the ultimate arbiter, the mystics promoting instead practices that led to a direct personal experience, and then there were the conservatives, who argued for a literalistic interpretation of the *Qu'ran* (and who looked back to the 9th century scholar Aḥmad ibn Ḥanbal).

Within this complex situation, al-Ghazālī was exercised especially by questions concerning the kinds of knowledge and subjectivity that were appropriate to his time (Moosa, 2005, 39). This led to his extended engagement with and reinterpretation of the Islamic tradition in ways that included taking up metaphorical tropes. According to Moosa (2005, 217),

> This tension between the literal and the figurative, the corporeal and the allegorical, creates a semantic space that offers wide latitude for interpretive maneuver, ambiguity, and productive imagination.

An example of such a concept that mediates between the literal and the figurative, and between a binary conception of subject and object, is al-Ghazālī's

120 *Thinking Otherwise—Resisting Indifference*

concept of *dihlīz*—as an interspace or 'inbetween-ness' (Moosa, 2005, 57). *Dihlīz* is a Persian word that translates as 'that space between the door and the house'; in Moosa's (2005, 48) words:

> [*Dihlīz*] is the critical intermediate space between outside and inside, between exoteric (*ẓāhir*) and eso-teric (bāṭin). And it is also the space that one has to traverse in order to enter or exit, which is the real function of a threshold area.

Consequently, viewed as a spatial metaphor, *dihlīz* signifies a plurality of meanings and, taken up within the context of al-Ghazālī's writings, the *dihlīz* becomes the basis for a 'new locus of epistemic and political enunciation' that troubles and undoes totalitarian modes of being and thought (Moosa, 2005, 49). Such a style of reasoning is manifestly non-totalitarian since it problematises the boundaries that inform clear-cut styles of reasoning: it is both inside and outside, depending upon one's location. As such, *dihlīz* departs quite radically from post-Enlightenment ecologies of thinking, which Crang and Thrift (2000, 8), for example, have characterised as implying a much more definite and bounded sense of self: 'a self defined through disciplining boundaries, and a process of mastery and control'.

Consequently, mobilising the trope of *dihlīz* affords al-Ghazālī[3] the possibility of 'a new locus of epistemic and political enunciation' (Moosa, 2005, 49). This enables the would-be student to see how al-Ghazālī drew upon this notion as a creative response to some of the tensions of his time—but also, more generally, how the concept of a discursive tradition sets the ongoing development of a line of argument through time. And then, in entertaining a different conceptual figure, there is the further possibility of seeing whether such a concept might contribute to other debates, such as the tension described in Chapter Two above, between proximate and distant subject positions in relation to RE, for example.[4]

(b) Do Dreams Matter?

Asad's approach to Islam as a discursive tradition has shifted in focus since this was first elaborated in his 1986 essay. As Moumtaz (2015) observes, whereas the focus of inquiry was initially upon debate within a discursive tradition, the focus in Asad's more recent works has shifted to embodiment (Asad and Scott, 2006). This, in turn, has enabled productive contributions to more recent work on sensibility, affect and, in particular, work on ethical self-formation that has followed from Foucault's last phase of work (see Chapter Three). This includes Mittermaier's (2011) anthropological fieldwork in Cairo on the productive role of the imagination and in particular on the significance of dreams in 'undreamy times'. The issue of dreams is important—both as a thematic and as a particular matter of concern. This

Thinking Otherwise—The Anthropology of Islam   121

is because the topic of dreams tends to be overlooked in Western accounts, since such phenomena are viewed as ambivalent. And secondly, given their exclusion from consideration, the potential work that dreams do within a tradition where they *are* taken seriously is likely to be missed.

Within the Islamic tradition, dreams, amongst other things, introduce an 'Elsewhere' (*al-ghayb*) within peoples' lives that is quite other than a reduction to (mere) fantasy. To this extent, dream visions 'carry ethical and political weight because they draw attention to the very conditions of inter-relatedness, the in-between, and alterity' (Mittermaier, 2011, 237). Dreams are understood to function as a kind of prophetic enactment of the future, insofar as prophetic action is intended to be anticipatory: the prophet enacts in the present what will in future come to pass.[5] Within contemporary expressions of Islam, dreams were taken seriously by many involved in the so-called 'Arab Spring' across the Middle East in 2011, where in Egypt, after 18 days of protest, the regime of Mubarak was brought down. Mittermaier (2015, 107) remarks on the irruption of dream talk at this time, with dreams referencing 'a future-orientedness; the reach for something not yet fully graspable; a space of shared, collective hopes'. Nevertheless, the understanding of dreams and miracles also requires engagement with textual traditions, whether theological or popular, that continue to inform and shape their interpretation, even if they exceed these terms, too (Mittermaier, 2015, 113). This acknowledges Asad's point, above, that it is important that an arbitrary divide is not created between text on the one hand, and other foci, such as sociality and experience on the other, since in practice, the two mutually inform sense-making practices. Consequently, dreams 'are deeply social and are always narrated and interpreted' (Mittermaier, 2015, 119).

(c) Different Types of Dreams

Dreams as a focus of concern also potentially challenge and complicate the would-be student's theoretical and analytical horizons of possibility insofar as the implications of taking dreams more seriously raises difficult questions regarding the ontological status of the imagination that move beyond the assumption of autonomous individualism. Such engagement might also call into question the ways in which the West draws a dichotomy between waking and dream-life, and, as Mittermaier (2011, 239) observes, this might in turn interrupt a number of taken-for-granted co-ordinates.

> A widened vision, one attuned to (in)visible realities, might then also invite us to reconsider our broader epistemological, political, and anthropological outlooks.

Whilst within the West, dreams are usually regarded as located within the individual, the Islamic tradition entertains the notion 'that certain dreams *come*

122   *Thinking Otherwise—Resisting Indifference*

to the dreamer as opposed to being *produced by* her or him' (Mittermaier, 2012, 248). In broad terms, therefore, dreams can be seen as falling into three distinct categories:

(*i*) *hadīth nafsī*—originating within the dreamer's own self
(*ii*) *hulm*—inspired by jinn or evil spirits (often nightmares)
(*iii*) ru'yā—divinely—inspired dream—vision or night vision that gives pro-
       phetic insight.

(Mittermaier, 2012, 249)

Such a categorisation radically departs from Western assumptions regarding the significance of dream states insofar as this assumes the possibility of the subject being acted upon. Such understandings of being acted upon (*passionnes*) have tended to fall into abeyance within contemporary Western self-understandings, given the focus upon an autonomous individualism in which the self being in control is valorised (Heelas and Lock, 1981). Furthermore, insofar as '[t]he subject is subjected to what it is not and does not control', to use Winquist's (1998, 232) words, these factors are typically located *within* the subject, rather than exercising agency from without. Dreams problematise the assumption of a unified subject and, moreover, serve as a reminder that—notwithstanding commitments to autonomous agency—humans are always embedded in an extended web of relations. This, in turn, has potentially significant consequences for an ethics of passion and an ethics of relationality (Mittermaier, 2012).

These considerations gesture towards a different framing of subjectivity in which humans are potentially spoken-through rather than speaking (Keller, 2002). To this extent, the trope of 'possession' articulates a key fault line, since the English word 'possession' holds together two distinct meanings: on the one hand, something that is owned or controlled by a subject, and on the other, the overcoming of that subjectivity by a supernatural will, spirit or entity (Johnson and Keller, 2006). Clearly, the two renderings of possession are not the same, but according to Johnson and Keller (2006, 112, 113), their juxtaposition can be a useful hermeneutic device for opening up new perspectives, beyond the 'so-called self-possessed or autonomous agent around which western models of jurisprudence, medicine and property have largely evolved' (Johnson and Keller, 2006, 116). Moreover, the notion of possession also calls into question a number of other binary constructions, such as that between spirit and matter, the animate and inanimate, as people can become 'possessed by' material realities as well as, for example, supernatural entities.

The issue of location with respect to dream states also raises a number of issues in regard to their ontology. For in the traditional typology noted above, only the first type of dream is traceable to factors within the individual; the second and third types draw upon an ontology that accords reality to external

Thinking Otherwise—The Anthropology of Islam 123

realities that are characterised as jinn and as God, respectively. It is to a consideration of the first of these putative realities, jinn, that we now turn.

(d) Are Jinn Actants?

Whilst discussion concerning the ontological status of jinn might at first appear appear to be somewhat remote from an educational concern with lived experience, there are actual situations in professional practice where the framing of such issues—and decisions that are taken in response to these—have both a practical and urgent impact. A case in point is with regard to different explanatory models of illness and, more specifically, the early detection and management of psychosis. In this connection, McCabe and Priebe (2004) found that in the UK, 'Black patients' (comprising Bangladeshis, African-Caribbeans and West Africans) were more likely to attribute their symptoms to supernatural causes, whereas 'White' patients tended to assume a biological aetiology. More recently, Singh *et al.* (2015), in their Birmingham-based study, found that Asian patients were significantly more likely to attribute the cause of their illness to supernatural activity as compared with either 'Black' or 'White' patients, who tended to make no attribution for symptoms. Furthermore, in terms of their treatment pathways, both 'Black and Asian' patients reported a significantly higher proportion of faith-based encounters as compared with 'White' patients (Singh *et al.*, 2015, 6).

Whilst there have been calls designed to elicit a person's own explanatory models of illness (such as Kleinman, 1988), clinicians have tended to privilege their own biomedical orientations that exclude other framings (Bhui and Bhugra, 2002). This has tended to be the case despite evidence from empirical research that suggests that patients are generally more satisfied in situations where the psychiatrist shares how they understand the patient's distress and course of treatment (Callan and Littlewood, 1998; Bhui and Bhugra, 2002, 6). In contrast to many traditional healing approaches that encourage dialogue and collaboration, Western biomedicine has tended to go hand in hand with an esoteric conception of knowledge that is held by the professional. Here, the tasks of diagnosis and treatment tend to foreclose the possibility of a broader engagement with indigenous understandings and their associated healing pathways (Patel, 1995).

And yet, as Latour (2003, 235) has observed, writing in a different context,

> . . . actors still insist they are made to do things by those real entities 'outside' of them! Ordinary persons don't want them to be just an object of belief and so those entities have to come from the outside after all.

Faced with such claims, which exceed a Western practitioner's ontological repertoire, a typical response is, as Latour (2003, 234) puts it, to 'bracket their existence out, and locate them firmly in the believer's mind. We would literally

124 *Thinking Otherwise—Resisting Indifference*

have to *invent a believer*'. And, by so doing, the respondent's account would be translated into another ontological plane, such as the biomedical account described above, in order that some remedy might be found. The alternative way forward would appear inconceivable for many. In Latour's (2003, 235) words:

> Why not say that in religion what counts are the beings that make people act, just as every believer has always insisted? That would be more empirical, perhaps more scientific, more respectful, and much more economical than the invention of two impossible non-existing sites: one where the mind of the believer and the social reality are hidden behind illusions propped up by even more illusions.

This is in some respects to anticipate Latour's own (2004) critique of critique, which points to the limitations of adversarial positioning where one side simply projects onto another a set of assumptions. There is, in consequence, no meeting point between the two positions as both are firmly entrenched in their views, and, moreover, no possibility of moving beyond this point of departure (see below, Chapter Six, for a discussion of this). Happily, in respect of spirit possession, there has been movement beyond such a stalemate. Thus, for example, Johnson and Keller (2006, 116) have noted 'a new respect for possession traditions among western-trained mental health professionals'. They continue:

> spirit possession is no longer dismissed as archaic fancy, but rather analysed as an idiom with which one can develop effective treatment for people whose community understands psychic health to be related to the needs and actions of a supernatural force that is using human illness to communicate with its human community.

So in what ways might this 'new respect' be played out in practice? One response is for practitioners to begin by finding out about the particular indigenous systems of healing and their associated rationales and justifications that a particular person identifies with. The aim of this is to gain a perspective as to how that person construes events and happenings before attempts are made to find a suitable treatment. With such an approach, however, it would still appear that medical explanations still claim the upper hand, with a tendency to translate a patient's own account into specific biomedical diagnostic categories and related care pathways (Bhui and Bhugra, 2002).

In practice, however, the situation is made more complex in view of the fact that patients may *themselves* draw upon multiple framings rather than attribute their distress to a single cause, and these attributions may, in turn, be quite fluid. Thus, for example, McCabe and Priebe (2004, 29) noted that this may be especially relevant in relation to people of different ethnic

Thinking Otherwise—The Anthropology of Islam   125

origins 'who will vary in degree of acculturation and so may draw on multiple social and linguistic resources in narratives about illness'. According to Singh *et al.* (2015, 7),

> . . . Black and Asian patients are likely to use both faith-based and mental health services concurrently. This underscores the importance of increasing collaboration between EIS [Early Intervention Services] and faith-based organisations to ensure the delivery of holistic, person-centred care.[6]

And so, in a number of situations, traditional accounts may be drawn upon alongside medical framings, the latter being only one of several different ontologies in play. Given this complexity, Singh *et al.* (2015) researched ways in which pathways to care differed according to ethnicity—with particular reference to situations where multiple cultures intersect, such as in Birmingham, UK. Patients within the Islamic tradition may attribute their symptoms to jinn and seek remedy through religious means. However, this is not necessarily the case: they may choose not do so, and/or patients may seek remedy through medical pathways, too.

(iv) Case Study: Jinn and Multiple Ontologies

Some of these issues were surfaced in a recent episode in the BBC (2015) Radio 4 'One to One' series, which included an interview conducted by Selina Scott, which focused on the work of Yasim Ishaq, who is a teacher in Rotheram. She also works as a counsellor with Muslims possessed by jinn. Within the Islamic tradition, the word jinn literally means 'something hidden', and this refers to ghost—like entities that are believed to have been created before the advent of people and most of which live without impacting upon human affairs.[7] However, there are malevolent jinn that do possess people, and Ishaq's role is to work with these people to alleviate their suffering and trauma. From the outset of the interview it is clear that Ishaq believes jinn exist—and she justifies this claim since they are specifically mentioned in the *Qur'an* where it is said that jinn are created from smokeless fire. One of the tests for jinn possession is their action when the *Qur'an* is recited; there will be no discernible effect if the cause of the malady is not jinn related, but there will be sometimes dramatic and violent consequences if a jinn is present. However, one of the critical issues in practice is whether a person is actually suffering from the action of these entities or from some other factor, such as mental health issues. Consequently, Ishaq always advises people to undergo treatment from the health service at the same time as they seek a remedy through traditional treatments, even though in practice, most people she sees do not, in fact, take this advice. As Ishaq put this, 'It isn't about one or the other. I believe in complementary therapies'. And as if to underline this, Ishaq's concluding remark in the interview focused upon the

126   *Thinking Otherwise—Resisting Indifference*

effects of jinn possession: no one could doubt their existence if they had seen these effects in practice.

> There needs to be more awareness around: what is correct and authentic from the *Qur'an* and that which is completely, you know, made up . . . But as for belief in the jinn, I absolutely believe in jinn: I've seen far too many strange things and unexplainable things to dismiss them and say well, no, it doesn't exist or there aren't any things . . .
>
> (BBC, Radio 4, 2015)

Once again, there is a clear connection between the authority of a holy text, the *Qu'ran*, and efforts to make sense in practice. In this case, the choice of ontology is not determined *a priori*, but through an ongoing experimental engagement in which decisions are taken in the light of new evidence that becomes available. This would appear to have links with the kind of open-ended approach taken by al-Ghazālī through the concept of *dihlīz*. According to Moosa (2005, 153), al-Ghazālī lived in a 'mental *dihlīz* when it came to philosophy and theology', and this can account for at least some of the apparent contradictions to be found in al-Ghazālī's works. As we have seen, the cultural situation at his time was highly complex, and so he was 'forced to negotiate multiple antithetical positions'. According to Moosa (2005, 140), this led to a certain undecidability to be found in his writings, both on account of his refusal to take a totalitarian line and his openness to the possibility of reconstruction.

   This capacity to hold multiple ontologies in creative tension, without thereby dismissing alternative accounts, has been a focus of work undertaken by Helen Verran (2005; 2007), which she conceives as a practice of 'doing ontics'. This is to recognise how practices are enmeshed in producing particular accounts of the real, whilst also opening up new possibilities once a given ontological performance is recognised as only one of a range of alternatives. Thus, the Yolngu of north-east Arnhem, in Australia, provide an example of what this might mean in relation to land management practices (Verran, 2005; 2007). Here, Yolngu knowledge traditions acknowledge different ways of 'doing place' according to the situation in hand. When it comes to firing a particular territory, Aboriginal clan members collectively perform places in ways that parallel the kinds of pragmatic ordering that would be instantly recognised by a Western ranger, with carefully cordoned areas to keep the fire under control. However, this is not the only way of doing place: an account can also be given in terms of 'the dreamtime' (*Wangarr*) in which these activities are related to stories of ancestors. This way of doing place is one in which specific activities are never closed but always open to an imaginary that is, at all times, present and ongoing. Yolngu, according to this account, 'do ontics' in ways that are not restricted to a single account of the real; they acknowledge that place can be constituted differently according to different

Thinking Otherwise—The Anthropology of Islam 127

requirements. The choice of ontology is situation dependent: it is not a case of necessarily deciding definitively between one ontology and another.

There would appear to be parallels between this capacity to entertain multiple ontologies and approaches to difference that are valorised by al-Ghazālī through his concept of *dihlīz* and the open approach taken by Yashim Ishaq in relation to the different ontologies that might be drawn upon in relation to possession by jinn. In 'doing ontics', the translation of one ontology into the terms of another is suspended; the different practices and gatherings are not reducible to one another—it is a question, as suggested already, of 'going along together' (see also Chapter Four above). Of course, this is to go against the grain of many habitual assumptions that inform the modern project, especially as regards the project of a unified and singular outlook.

It is here too, that Latour's (2013) project of modes of existence, which we encountered initially in Chapter Two, above, is especially valuable, since this recognises that each distinct 'mode of existence' has its own felicity conditions that cannot be translated into the terms of another's. Thus 'law', as a mode of existence (Latour, 2013, 358–9, emphasis in original text)

> ... has its own force [. . .] its own mode of veridiction, certainly different from that of Science, but universally acknowledged as capable of distinguishing truth from falsity *in its own way*.

Due legal process is what is aimed for within law, and it would be mistaken to assume that law was primarily concerned with the kinds of accurate representational thinking that informs the felicity conditions required for science, which has its own distinctive forms of veridiction. Acknowledging these distinct modes—in the case of possession, as discussed here—those of 'religion' and 'science'—leads to a broader imaginative compass, in which different practices and gatherings issue in different *diffractive* potentialities that can be explored.

(v) The Work of Imagining

These studies have far-reaching implications not only for how a particular tradition of enquiry is engaged, but also in terms of their unsettling a series of assumptions that inform modernity. According to Lambek (2010, 725),

> The questions raised by spirit possession cast a reflection on the Western discourse of mind, challenging cherished assumptions concerning the unity of consciousness, the duality of mind/body, and the rational basis of ethical judgment.

In this connection, the understanding of the imagination is also crucial and will be consequential as regards the kinds of sense that become possible.

128 *Thinking Otherwise—Resisting Indifference*

As Mittermaier (2015, 109) observes, the imagination, according to the O.E.D., is

> [the human] power or capacity to form internal images or ideas of objects and situations not actually present to the senses [. . .] often with the implication that [these very ideas and images do] not correspond to the reality of things.

Such ambivalence is reflected in everyday situations when it is remarked that 'you only imagined that', or, 'it was only a dream', with the implication that imaginative productions are of lesser import than other tokens and cannot be relied upon. Furthermore, imaginative productions are viewed as necessarily located within an individual psyche and may well be considered the outcome of repressed feelings and reactions etc. The idea that the imagination may be open to, and traversed by, a broader relationality and, moreover, be a scene for insight into future action and happenings is largely missing from the Western account. Consequently, inquiry into Islam is unlikely to foreground—let alone consider—dreams and waking visions, nor the ontological claims with which these are imbricated.

However, there remains the (*edu-cational*) possibility of re-configuring understandings towards a more open understanding of imaginative possibility. Within this, entertaining dreams and 'doing ontics' in relation to possession may offer new spaces for 'meaning-making, negotiation, and (re)-imagining' (Mittermaier, 2015, 116). Becoming attentive to a different tradition, on this reading, involves a questioning of the limits and translations that are mobilised in its interpretation *and* an openness towards its 'articulatory potential' (Boddy 1989, 141, in Mittermaier 2015, 117). And it is in this sense that engaging Islam, as a matter of concern, can become a 'space of surprise' (Rothenberg, 2004) that leads out in new critical, experimental and ethical pathways.

Notes

1. See Asad (1993) for detailed critiques.
2. Although a detailed consideration lies outwith the focus of this chapter, it is worth noticing that there have been critiques of this focus upon Islam as a tradition, insofar as this can lead to an exaggerated sense of coherence, both as regards practitioners and the tradition itself, as compared with the contingent challenges and interruptions that might be foregrounded (Schielke, 2010). However, as Moumtaz (2015, 140) has observed, *the aspiration for coherence* within a context is itself noteworthy and does not necessarily undermine the potential productiveness in mobilising 'tradition' as a mode of inquiry.
3. It might be noted that al-Ghazālī's concept of *dihlīz* has some parallels with Winnicott's (1971) conception of transitional space—the space of play that initially emerges in relation to an infant's negotiation between what is and is not 'me'. Transitional objects (such as a piece of cloth or a teddy bear) help the child accomplish the work involved in moving from primary identification with the mother

Thinking Otherwise—The Anthropology of Islam 129

to the creative use of objects in relation to which the self is-and-is-not identified. According to Winnicott, the successful establishment of the capacity for engagement with such transitional phenomena provides the basis for successful cultural pursuits in adult life. What is also noteworthy in Winnicott's approach is that the transitional space is located *within* the psyche, whereas for al-Ghazālī, the equivalent concept of *dihlīz* is located in social space. As such, *dihlīz* provides a framing that works beyond some of difficulties associated with an 'inner-outer' divide, which haunts forms of Cartesianism. In relation to Islam in particular, *dihlīz* might enable a broader understanding of relationality, given the significance of dreams and being acted upon by external agencies (Mittermaier, 2011; 2012; 2015).

4. The concept of *dihlīz* has been taken up by Sabry (2011, 6) to explore the threshold position of Arab-American women. '. . . the Arab-American diasporic experience is a *dihlizian* space where various material, political, social and economic conditions are negotiated opening up the Arab-American diasporic experience to a multitude of possible positionalities'.

5. An illustration from within the New Testament of a prophetic action would be *Acts* 21:10–12, where Agabus tied his own hands and feet with Paul's belt as a forewarning of the latter's future arrest and imprisonment.

6. McCabe and Priebe (2004, 26) categorised these causal attributions into four categories: 'biological (physical illness/substance misuse); social (interpersonal problems/stress/negative childhood events/personality); supernatural (supernatural); and non-specific (do not know/mental illness/other)'.

7. Traditionally, according to the *Qur'an* and the *Sayings of the Prophet*, jinn exist alongside the world of humans, but the two worlds are separated by a veil (*hijāb*, Qur'an 41:5); see Suhr (2015) for background, including reference to studies on the interaction of *jinn* and humans.

Bibliography

Anjum, O., 2007. 'Islam as a discursive tradition: Talal Asad and his interlocutors'. *Comparative Studies of South Asia, Africa and the Middle East*, vol. 27, no. 3.

Asad, T., 1986. *The Idea of an Anthropology of Islam Occasional Paper Series.* Washington, DC: Center for Contemporary Arab Studies, Georgetown University.

Asad, T., 1993. *Genealogies of Religion: Discipline and Reasons of Power in Christianity and Islam.* Baltimore, MD: Johns Hopkins University Press.

Asad, T. and Scott, D., 2006. 'The trouble of thinking: An interview with Talal Asad'. In: D. Scott and C. Hirschkind eds., *Powers of the Secular Modern: Talal Asad and His Interlocutors.* Stanford, CA: Stanford University Press, pp. 243–303.

BBC Radio 4, 2015. 'Selina Scott talks to Yasim Ishaq'. BBC Radio 4 'One to One' series, (Broadcast 14/7/15). Available from www.bbc.co.uk/programmes/b061qsdf/.

Bhui, K. and Bhugra, D., 2002. 'Explanatory models for mental distress: Implications for clinical practice and research'. *The British Journal of Psychiatry*, vol. 181, no. 1, 6–7.

Boddy, J., 1989. *Wombs and Alien Spirits: Women, Men and the Zar Cult in Northern Sudan.* Madison: University of Wisconsin Press.

Bowker, J.W., 1978. *The Religious Imagination and the Sense of God.* Oxford: Clarendon Press.

Bush, J.A. 'The Politics of Poetry'. In: In: *A Companion to the Anthropology of the Middle East.* Hoboken, NJ: John Wiley & Sons, pp. 188–204.

Callan, A. and Littlewood, R., 1998. 'Patient satisfaction: Ethnic origin or explanatory model?'. *International Journal of Social Psychiatry*, vol. 44, pp. 1–11.

130 Thinking Otherwise—Resisting Indifference

Crang, M. and Thrift, N., eds., 2000. *Thinking Space: Critical Geographies*. London and New York: Routledge.

El-Zein, A.H., 1977. 'Beyond ideology and theology: The search for the anthropology of Islam'. *Annual Review of Anthropology*, vol. 6, pp. 227–254.

Geertz, C., 1968. *Islam Observed: Religious Development in Morocco and Indonesia*. New Haven: Yale University Press.

Gellner, E., 1981. *Muslin Society*. Cambridge and New York: Cambridge University Press.

Gilsenan, M. 1982. *Recognizing Islam* London: Croom Helm.

Heelas, P. and Lock, A., 1981. *Indigenous Psychologies*. London: Academic Press.

Johnson, P.C. and Keller, M., 2006. 'The work of possession(s)'. *Culture and Religion*, vol. 7, no. 2, pp. 111–122.

Keller, M., 2002. *The Hammer and the Flute: Women, Power, and Spirit Possession*. Baltimore and London: Johns Hopkins University Press.

Kleinman, A., 1988. *Rethinking Psychiatry: From Cultural Category to Personal Experience*. New York: Free Press.

Lambek, M., 2010. 'How to make up one's mind: Reason, passion, and ethics in spirit possession'. *University of Toronto Quarterly*, vol. 79, no. 2, pp. 720–741.

Latour, B., 2003. *Reassembling the Social: An Introduction to Actor-Network-Theory*. Oxford and New York: Oxford University Press.

Latour, B., Winter 2004. 'Why has critique run out of steam? From matters of fact to matters of concern'. *Critical Inquiry*, vol. 30, no. 2, pp. 225–248.

Latour, B., 2013. *An Inquiry Into Modes of Existence: An Anthropology of the Modern*. Cambridge, MA: Harvard University Press.

McCabe, R. and Priebe, S., 2004. 'Explanatory models of illness in schizophrenia: Comparison of four ethnic groups'. *British Journal of Psychiatry*, vol. 185, no. 1, pp. 25–30.

MacIntyre, A., 1984. *After Virtue: A Study in Moral Theory*. Notre Dame: University of Notre Dame Press.

MacIntyre, A., 1988. *Whose Justice? Which Rationality?* London: Duckworth.

Mittermaier, A., 2011. *Dreams That Matter: Egyptian Landscapes of the Imagination*. Berkeley: University of California Press.

Mittermaier, A., 2012. 'Dreams from elsewhere: Muslim subjectivities beyond the trope of self-cultivation'. *Journal of the Royal Anthropological Institute (N.S.)*, vol. 18, pp. 247–265.

Mittermaier, A., 2015. 'Dreams and the Miraculous'. In: *A Companion to the Anthropology of the Middle East*. S. Altorki ed., Hoboken, NJ: John Wiley & Sons, pp. 107–124.

Moosa, E., 2005. *Ghazālī and the Poetics of Imagination*. Chapel Hill and London: University of North Carolina Press.

Moumtaz, N., 2015. 'Refiguring Islam'. In: S. Altorki ed., *A Companion to the Anthropology of the Middle East*. Hoboken, NJ: John Wiley & Sons, pp. 125–150.

Osberg, D. and Biesta, G., 2010. *Complexity Theory and the Politics of Education*. Rotterdam: Sense.

Patel, V., 1995. 'Explanatory models of mental illness in sub-Saharan Africa'. *Social Science Medicine*, vol. 40, pp. 1291–1298.

Rothenberg, C., 2004. *Spirits of Palestine: Palestinian Village Women and Stories of the Jinn*. Lanham, MD: Lexington.

Sabry, S.S., 2011. *Arab-American Women's Writing and Performance: Orientalism, Race and the Idea of the Arabian Nights*. London and New York: I.B. Tauris.

Schielke, S., 2010. *Second Thoughts About the Anthropology of Islam, or How to Make Sense of Grand Schemes in Everyday Life*. Berlin: Zentrum Moderner Orient Working Papers.

Singh, S.P., Brown, L., Winsper, C., Gajwani, R., Islam, Z., Jasani, R., Parsons, H., Rabbie-Khan, F. and Birchwood, M., 2015. 'Ethnicity and pathways to care during first episode psychosis: The role of cultural illness attributions'. *BMC Psychiatry*, vol. 15, no. 1, p. 287.

Suhr, C., 2015. 'The failed image and the possessed: Examples of invisibility in visual anthropology and Islam'. *Journal of the Royal Anthropological Institute*, vol. 21, no. S1, pp. 96–112.

Thomas, D., 2015. 'Al-Ghazali and the Progress of Islamic Thought'. In: E.E. Lemcio ed., *A Man of Many Parts: Essays in Honor of John Bowker on the Occasion of His Eightieth Birthday*. Eugene, OR: Pickwick, pp. 181–195.

Verran, H., 2005. 'Knowledge traditions of aboriginal Australians: Questions and answers arising in a databasing project'. Available from www.cdu.edu.au/centres/ik/pdf/knowledgeanddatabasing.pdf.

Verran, H., 2007. 'Software for educating aboriginal children about place'. In: D.W. Kritt and L.T. Winegar eds., *Education and Technology: Critical Perspectives and Possible Futures*. Lanham, MD: Lexington Books, pp. 101–124.

Winnicott, D., 1971. *Playing and Reality*. London: Tavistock.

Winquist, C.E., 1998. 'Person'. In: M.C. Taylor ed., *Critical Terms for Religious Studies*. Chicago and London: University of Chicago Press, pp. 225–238.

Part 3

Remediation—Beyond Indifference?

Introduction to Part Three

On the basis of our historical and spatial analysis of the present difficulties besetting RE in Part One, together with our exploration of alternative trajectories in Part Two, Part Three is concerned with looking at new gatherings of ideas, people and relationships that might constitute a new arrangement for RE and with outlining ways in which innovative pathways might be realised through further dialogue between multiple stakeholders.

More specifically, we identify a key difficulty facing RE at the present time as being the failure to initiate an ongoing tradition of inquiry in the field, which has led to a settlement that has privileged a particular and fixed account that is no longer fit for purpose. So what we offer/attempt here is to choreograph a new way forward on the basis of an approach that is simultaneously, experimental—in its openness to the new, critical—in its preparedness to interrogate the dominant subject, and ethical—in its hospitality to, and negotiations with, difference. On this basis, we hope this could inaugurate new practices that are educational—in the broadest sense—and that move decisively beyond an indifference that has tended to characterise a gathering that has been settled for too long. In a sense, we are trying to take advantage of the present situation—where there is an openness to entertaining styles of reasoning that move beyond a modernity that never was—and which, we feel, is auspicious for this kind of theoretical exploration. In moving beyond indifference, therefore, these approaches afford new opportunities for transformation and change, such as, for example, the implications for students to become ethnographers in ways that enrich their readings of present-and-future contexts or imagined communities.

In Chapter Six we outline a new heuristic that identifies some of the key elements that might inform an ongoing tradition of inquiry and especially between the academy and the world of early years, primary and secondary schools. In moving towards a materially grounded stance, our approach is potentially also more inclusive given its relational and material orientations. Rather than emphasising the abstract and detached, it is our hope to engender forms of thinking and practice that remain in touch with these

134 Remediation—Beyond Indifference?

orientations. Finally, in Chapter Seven, we attempt to draw the key threads of this project together, in the hope that this might, in turn, encourage other researchers, practitioners and policy makers to take up the questions and have courage to take forward new ecologies of practice that are both forward looking and interdisciplinary in intent.

6 Remediation—Imagining Otherwise

(i) Introduction

Current knowledge practices in RE are nested in a conception of education that has severe limitations. In this chapter, we explore new ways in which students might be equipped to 'read' their cultural situations and explore different understandings of 'the good' that are culturally available.

Our analysis of the effects of neutrality as a governing trope in Part One argued that this is premised upon an assumption that knowledge can be decontextualised: under the sign of neutrality, the knower is positioned as detached from matters of concern, and this orientates thinking towards disembodied statements. Such an approach ultimately presents the illusion of a mastery of knowledge, where a successful educational outcome is a knower secure in their cognitive grasp of key beliefs and concepts that are taken as being constitutive of the 'religion' being studied (Strhan, 2010). In other words, such an approach installs a positivistic approach to knowledge that is concerned primarily with correct statements rather than with, for example, grappling with some of the difficulties that ensue in empirical situations where people's understandings and actions are not as transparent as at first thought and where different theoretical framings and assemblages will afford different kinds of focus and insight (Crang, 2000; 2003). In light of both the ethical and educational difficulties that such a style of reasoning presents, it is desirable to think and imagine in ways that are open to greater complexity and that can in turn acknowledge the limitations, as well as the advantages, of a particular approach to sense-making.

In re-thinking knowledge practices that might become constitutive of a distinctively educational approach to RE, we argue for the need to move away from a trope of neutrality to a more relationally complex approach, such as is foregrounded through the trope of diffraction discussed above (Chapters Three and Four). According to Barad (2007, 30), diffraction is concerned with 'how different differences get made, what gets excluded, and how these exclusions matter'. With such a relational account, the student is located in the midst of complex relational practices and assemblages that need to be acknowledged. We argue that instead of the dominance of

136   *Remediation—Beyond Indifference?*

writing practices that are oriented towards examinations, a greater variety of practices such as those developed within anthropology might better equip young people for more complex readings of diverse cultural imaginaries and horizons. Under the trope of neutrality, the default approach is to bracket one's own particular commitments in order to attend, in an open way, to the beliefs and practices of others. In practice, this has led to students' own cultural commitments falling into the background, without these becoming a focus for inquiry and analysis. An illustration of the consequences of this failure to address issues of cultural specificity and positionality can be found in the field of children's rights education, where it has been acknowledged that assumptions that inform Western (majority) childhoods have been taken as constitutive of childhood *as such*, rather than acknowledging this as both highly contingent and culturally specific (Valentin and Meinert, 2009; Tisdall and Punch, 2012). In this case, the absence of critical reflexivity leads both to the imposition of specific goods associated with Western childhood onto (minority) others, as well as a refusal to acknowledge other cultural constructions of childhood that may, for example, privilege relational responsibility through caring for others over other values, such as the promotion of individual autonomy (I'Anson, 2016).

A considered response to the diagnosis offered in Part One will necessarily have multiple implications that are at once epistemological, ontological and ethical in scope. In terms of practices, a key question is that of identifying ways in which students might begin to articulate their own positionality and imbrication within a distinct relational field. This has a number of implications: on the one hand, this acknowledges that the classroom space is literally a 'face-to-face' (Edgoose, 2001): it is a plurality in its own terms. Rather than privileging orientations to a knowledge that are always primarily oriented 'out there' (Law, 2011), away from the specificities and differences that are in play, we propose that the classroom space is instead recognised as a context for significant engagement with and debate concerning difference. The dynamics of people present in interaction therefore become constitutive of the possibility of insight and change, rather than simply remaining in the background and out of sight. On the other hand, this plurality is not restricted simply to a person-to-person dialogue and encounter. In light of new theoretical developments, it is also necessary to amplify the many non-human elements that are gathered together in the making of insight and events of understanding (e.g., Fenwick and Edwards, 2010; Fenwick *et al.*, 2011; Sørensen, 2011).

(ii) Mapping into Knowledge: From Epistemology to Ontology

In this section, we trace how theoretical developments within the academy move beyond a limited concern with epistemic questions. These new framings, we argue, underscore the significance of both ontological and ethical

Remediation—Imagining Otherwise 137

considerations. To raise these questions is to engage with some of the complexities associated with the knowledge production process conceived as a 'working together' rather than the exercise of an isolated and disembodied knower. It is a move beyond seeing knowledge production staged simply in terms of representation (where it is assumed that what matters is the 'fit' between language on the one hand and the world on the other), to one that can acknowledge the many different relations, translations and materialities that are gathered together in a given educational site. As such, the scene of education is acknowledged as being more complicated that at first thought, and this demands new tools with which to think such embodiment and new practices of sense-making, too. In this connection, as previously noted, Stengers (1997) has described this process of making sense as a 'mapping into knowledge'; this is a useful expression insofar as this foregrounds the many translations and mediations that are necessarily involved in the making of any kind of sense. Taking account of 'mapping into knowledge' has far-reaching implications for the kinds of educational practices that are taken to be central in relation to RE, not least because this entails moving beyond naïve assumptions as to how language connects with the world.

One way of drawing out some of the implications of 'mapping into knowledge' is through drawing a contrast between current practice in RE and changes that this new orientation entails. The approach to knowledge that we saw informing current assumptions about knowledge in examinations (Chapter Two) is primarily concerned with representation, with how language connects with reality (Thrift, 2008). This is a legacy of the Enlightenment, which translates into education being conceived as primarily an epistemological enterprise (Biesta, 2006). However, if the various entanglements that together comprise the educational scene are foregrounded, it is no longer possible to regard the subject as simply set over against the material, which it has to describe. This is because all kinds of material artefacts—from pencils, computer algorithms and desks to the idiosyncrasies of a building's architecture—are materially implicated in *any* act of knowing and have material consequences (Sørensen, 2011): in short, the particular gathering of people, concepts and things that together comprise such a heterogeneous assemblage make a difference (Law, 2008).

Rather than deciding in advance what is to count (and thereby downplaying the influence of material entities), a socio-material approach aims to be more open and inclusive with regard to the multiple assemblages in the midst of which we find ourselves. And this involves critically examining the practices and concepts that are deployed in routine acts of sense-making and acknowledging their effects. Thus, for example, the concept of 'belief' orientates analysis towards an abstract plane that tends to be forgetful of material entities and the detailed practices that are implicated (Chapter Two). If the distance between the subject and the world presupposed in conventional accounts (such as the current settlement in RE) can no longer be sustained, it becomes necessary to interrupt the conventional 'word-world' settlement

138 *Remediation—Beyond Indifference?*

(the ways in which words are assumed to refer to reality) and to re-figure the ways in which language is believed to connect with reality as such. This raises questions as to how reality is 'mapped into' knowledge and the kinds of practices that become appropriate once the subject's implication within complex socio-material assemblages is recognised.

For once the educational subject is conceived as entangled within complex gatherings that materially affect that very process, the task of making sense is, to borrow a phrase from Todd May (2005, 20), more a question of 'palpating' the real than of exercising cognitive mastery over it: as when a doctor carefully examines a patient's wound through a variety of tactile moves that enables him/her to sense what is at issue. If the educational project conceived as the exercise of achieving mastery through creating distance, mediated via language, is no longer plausible, then it becomes necessary to articulate another grammar. Hence, for example, the *conceptual personae* that are a focus in Chapter Four are not a means to acquire comprehension of reality through mastery, but might be regarded as a way of engaging with difference through palpating reality in this broader sense.

So, to begin *in medias res*, in the middle of things and practices, is, by contrast, to begin with the complexity of relations and then to begin describing the processes through which these become mapped into knowledge.[1] This changes the key question from 'what can I know about x'—which is a primarily an epistemological issue—to a more ontologically focused question: 'how, and in what ways, does the world make itself known?' (Whatmore, 2003). The upshot of this is that in place of seeing education as limited to epistemological questions, acknowledging these broader relational assemblages supplements an epistemological focus through raising questions that are at once ontological and ethical in scope (Chapter Three). Although it is tempting to regard such a theoretical and methodological re-orientation as of recent provenance—especially associated with the work of socio-material theorists, some of whose work informs this study—the genealogy of the key ideas informing these approaches is complex and actually pre-dates the current settlement in RE by some years. In this connection, it is noteworthy that there are a number of points at which the process of 'mapping into knowledge' takes up William James's (2003 [1912]) project concerning the significance of relational understandings, and a brief excursus into this will assist in drawing out some important implications for re-imagining RE.

(iii) William James's Relational Universe: Towards a Radical Empiricism

The significance of James's writings for current theorising has been remarked upon by Latour (2011; 2013a) in relation to empirical philosophy and by Carrette (2013) in relation to 'religion'. Latour credits James's philosophy as marking a philosophical breakthrough in his proposal for a radical empiricism in which *what is given in experience* becomes of central concern. In

James's analysis, it is precisely *relations* that are given in experience, and this provides a valuable point of departure for approaches that are attuned to events, such as 'assemblage theory' and 'mapping into knowledge', that are oriented to the empirical. An exploration of prepositions—words that concern the quality and kind of relations that particular entities have with one another—is an especially valuable way of paying attention to what is given (Latour, 2013a; see in particular, James, 1996 [1909]; James, 2003 [1912]). James (2003, 50) describes prepositions in the following terms

> Prepositions, copulas, and conjunctions, 'is', 'isn't', 'then', 'before', 'in', 'on', 'beside', 'between', 'next', 'like', 'unlike', 'as', 'but', flower out of the stream of pure experience, the stream of concretes or the sensational stream, as naturally as nouns and adjectives do, and they melt into it again as fluidly when we apply them to a new portion of the stream.

The significance of attending to the kinds of relations and their qualities that are given in experience is described by Latour (2013a, 57) as follows:

> . . . each of these prepositions plays a decisive role in the understanding of what is to follow, by offering the type of relation needed to grasp the experience of the world in question.[2]

In relation to cultural and religious difference, a prepositional approach informs Latour's (2013b) own project to identify distinct and incommensurable modes of existence, and 'religion' is identified as a distinct mode; Latour's (2013b) *Rejoicing: Or the Torments of Religious Speech* is an extended exploration of the relational and prepositional implications from an 'insider's standpoint.[3] In the same vein, Strhan (2012) has pointed to advantages of mobilising a prepositional approach in relation to the understanding of 'secularism', the study of which has gained considerable ground in recent years. With regard to RE, an analysis concerning what is given in experience in practice takes a different pathway from phenomenological bracketing. The latter, as translated into educational practice within current approaches has, as we have seen, tended to excise from analysis individual experience itself. So James's radical empiricism provides a theoretical orientation that has affinities with Smart's (1969) valorisation of experience, but through attending to relations as they are given in experience, opens up an enhanced empirical approach, which we will later take up in relation to ethnographic practice.

The significance of James's relational approach as regards the understanding of 'religion', which has tended to be obscured through a critical focus on other aspects of James's corpus of writings, is the target of Carrette's (2013) study. Aside from tracing some of the theoretical sources of James's approach, Carrette's (2013, 191) work is especially valuable in drawing out the ethical implications of such a relational understanding.

140 *Remediation—Beyond Indifference?*

Our capacity to relate differently depends on our ability to bring the periphery to the centre in reading (con)texts and create new forms of relation. James returns thought and practice to the ethics of our relations and the ethics of our noticing.

Taking such a relational approach therefore brings with it an ethical attentiveness: the ethical consequences of taking a particular approach to mapping into knowledge are foregrounded over a (putative) neutrality in regard to knowledge production.

(iv) Some Ontological Implications of James's Radical Empiricism

A critical analysis of the kinds of relations in play within experience can help to surface a number of assumptions that are so basic that they remain unseen until they are attended to. And such assumptions can have far-reaching consequences for how sense is made, for what is valued and discounted and for how a different cultural ordering and categorisation is viewed. When we experience the red glow of a sunset, we may well regard this as beautiful; however, if we have been schooled within a modern, Western context, we are likely to concede that this is simply our own 'subjective' impression and that what we're *really* experiencing is a particular configuration of radiation, molecules and electrons. What is presumed in this habitual ordering is that a fundamental distinction can be drawn between 'nature' and 'culture'—between, that is, primary qualities and secondary qualities. Only primary qualities are properly basic; it is the *mind* (culture) that *brings to experience* the particular kinds of relations that lead to the red sunset being regarded as aesthetically beautiful. With such a reading, in other words, only the radiation and electrons are real; these are the primary qualities, and the secondary qualities are relegated to lesser account. This is an illustration that Whitehead (1920) himself gave as an example of what he termed the *bi-furcation of knowledge*.

This bi-furcation of knowledge, wrought through a division of experience in which only certain relations are regarded as primary, is associated with a long line of thinkers extending from Galileo and Locke to the present (Stengers, 2014) and, as an approach to empiricism, is deeply inscribed within a post-Enlightenment imaginaries. According to Whitehead (1920), it was William James (1996 [1909]) who was the first to move beyond these terms through his radical empiricism, according to which *everything* is experienced. In Whitehead's (1920, 29 and see Stengers's (2014, 33) commentary) words,

. . . everything perceived is in nature. We may not pick up and choose. For us the red glow of the sunset should be as much part of nature as are the molecules and electric waves by which men of science would explain the phenomenon.

Remediation—Imagining Otherwise 141

Rather than simply assuming, *a priori*, that what is experienced can be divided into primary and secondary qualities, Whitehead draws the conclusion that the different qualities are *given in* experience and cannot without further ado be simply set aside. Whitehead's analysis, via James's radical empiricism, overcomes powerfully ingrained assumptions that construct a particular account of 'nature' as basic and primary with culture as so many *perspectives* upon that fundamental reality. This way of dividing up experience has haunted Western thinking, and surfacing this assumption potentially allows for the entertaining and recognition of different gatherings and orderings and their affordances. One of the implications of moving beyond the bi-furcation of knowledge is the possibility of a re-enchantment with materiality and vibrant matter (Bennett, 2010; Braidotti, 2013). Such a re-orientation potentially moves beyond metaphors of inert matter and provides resources with which to respond to Jantzen's (2004) critique of Western philosophical approaches being pre-occupied with violence and death (Chapter Three, above). Another implication is that thinking and discussion about ecological concerns, especially in the aftermath of the *anthropocene*—which marks the era in which human activity has had a significant impact upon global ecology—has to be reframed. This is because talk of 'nature' (as distinct from 'culture') within these terms actually re-inscribes the bi-furcation of reality, which might be seen as a fundamental part of the ecological problem itself (Latour, 2014).

There are parallels between the radical empiricism of James and forms of experimental phenomenology, such as the practices informing Ihde's (1986) account. Both approaches, for example, involve a rigorous interrogation of the relations given in experience with the possibility of interrupting ingrained assumptions ('sedimentation' in Ihde's terms) on the basis of new insight that is the outcome of a radical attention to experience. However, insofar as bracketing does not problematise an existing ordering of relations, these will simply remain in play. In terms of our discussion here, the ontological implications of the bi-furcation of knowledge point to the inadequacy of limited forms of bracketing—such as those that inform current practice in RE (see above, Chapter Two). The intention to simply bracket our initial judgments is clearly insufficient—when the very starting point from which we make sense at all is structured by an *already assumed* bi-furcation of knowledge. In other words, the (epistemological) practice of bracketing takes place within a framing that has already been resolved in a particular (ontological) way; unless critique extends beyond epistemological practice to consider the kinds of ontology that are being performed, questionable assumptions—that have far-reaching implications—will not even be noticed.

(v) Towards an Ontology of the Virtual

If there are far-reaching ontological issues rising from the practice of a radical empiricism for RE, the same might be said with regard to unearthing assumptions about material assemblages with which it is implicated and

142 *Remediation—Beyond Indifference?*

how potentiality is conceived in the light of this. In Chapter Three we saw that Spinoza observed that we never know in advance what a particular entity is capable of, and this insight has implications for the kind of ontology that is assumed and the ensuing orientation to practice in RE. In other words, acknowledging the wider socio-material relations broadens the potentiality for a new inventiveness beyond previously determined forms of measurability.

The implications of this have been extended further with assemblage theory—since one never knows in advance what particular entities *in relation to each other* are capable of. As Strathern (2014, 4) summarises this: 'relations open up the capacities of properties in unexpected ways and capacities come into existence through new relations'. This is to gesture to a different ontology from that which usually informs educational perspectives, where possibility is usually conceived as *already* determined.[4]

However, as Deleuze (1988, 98, italics in original) has observed, such a framing privileges an actual that, in being already determined, is, in fact, only one possible outcome out of a whole set of virtual potentialities.

> [W]e give ourselves a real that is ready-made, preformed, pre-existent to itself, and that will pass into existence according to an order of successive limitations. Everything is already *completely given*.

The process of evolution, when approached through some such actual ontology, is regarded as consisting in the unfolding of what is already given, where nothing new enters the scene, such as when an acorn is perceived to contain within it all that will become the oak tree in future.

Strathern's (2014) insight moves beyond such a restriction in noticing that a gathering of relations can release consequences that have not been, and could not in principle be, pre-determined in advance of an event. In Deleuze's (1988) terms, this is to acknowledge an ontology of the virtual: that is, the field of potentialities that *may* become actual at a given point in time but may not in fact be actually realised. An ontology of the virtual is the set of potentialities that inheres in a given relational ordering—and its distinction from that which is contingently played out—the actual—is a significant implication of moving away from the 'word-world settlement' into 'mapping into knowledge' approaches. An ontology of the virtual, in being open to the emergence of the new and unforeseen, gestures, therefore, towards a new ecology of practice that does not foreclose what may happen in advance. As such, this ontology sits uneasily with a 'word-world settlement' approach, which presumes a stable world continuing along predictable lines, on the basis of what is known already. A virtual ontology has much clearer affinities with 'mapping into knowledge', since this is attuned to standpoint and the precariousness of translations that are made. Choreograph an RE or classroom assemblage differently, and very different potentialities will emerge.

Remediation—Imagining Otherwise 143

In the following section, we take up the insights from this discussion in framing a heuristic that might inform both ways in which a dialogue between higher education and schools might be instituted and ways of re-thinking practices within RE in the light of this.

(vi) Towards a Heuristic for Re-Connecting Higher Education and Schools

Such an acknowledgement makes it all the more important to consider carefully the reasons how and why we 'cut' relational networks for specific purposes or whether the ways these have been determined in the past are still desirable. As we have previously observed, the relations between higher education and school-based contexts in regard to theorising RE have tended to be one way, with higher education initially providing a framing that successfully addressed the issues faced by the subject in the early 1970s. Since that time, as has already been noted, there has been surprisingly little ongoing exchange between the two sectors, and there have been calls for new dialogue in light of far-reaching change within the academy (I'Anson, 2004; Baumfield, 2014). A consequence of this has been that higher education has moved in new theoretical directions, whereas the basic grammar of the approach to RE in schools and colleges has remained largely unchanged (Cush and Robinson, 2014). Whilst there have been developments in this interregnum as regards pedagogy, including the development of more student-centred approaches, active learning etc., the subject has remained knowledge-focused; such developments as there have been as regards insight and practice have not extended to include a critical reading of the very framings and assumptions that inform the construction of the subject (see above, Part One).

In the diagnosis performed in Part One, we argued that one of the problems with the current settlement is that it was, if anything, *too successful* in addressing a series of critical issues at the time of its construction (Chapter One). The approach to knowledge production that was its outcome fitted seamlessly with the qualifications economy as described in Part One, which is likely to discourage thinking in other terms (Conroy *et al.*, 2013). This, coupled with a failure to institutionalise ongoing relations between schools and the academy, has left a gathering of concepts, tropes and practices that are no longer fit for purpose, in light of critiques within the academy, a changed cultural situation and new policy imperatives. Current knowledge practices are focused more on the risks associated with a largely uncritical approach to 'religion' than with developing an educational rationale for the subject. In the light of this, an urgent question concerns ways in which thinking and practice in schools might re-connect both with educational questions and with the academy, such that a two-way dialogue becomes possible, and theoretical and methodological developments within higher education might enable fresh thinking about the project of RE. Simultaneously, specific problematics, issues and practices developed within schools might in

144   *Remediation—Beyond Indifference?*

turn inform ongoing critical inquiry and pedagogy within higher education contexts (Cush and Robinson, 2014). This might include, for example, identifying ways in which an awareness of students' development needs (Cush and Robinson, 2014) inform curriculum design and interactions, in terms, for example, of taking up 'scaffolding' interactional approaches (Bruner, 1978) in the light of constructivist educational theory (e.g., Vygotsky, 1978 [1933]), or identifying the particular sequencing of concepts in ways that enable the student to recognise the actual translations involved.

In the following section, we develop a heuristic designed to facilitate such a dialogue between higher education and schools in regard to RE. This will also provide a framing for re-imagining practices in RE that moves beyond the current state of affairs that, we have argued, has produced indifference.

(vii) Three Elements of RE: Towards a Heuristic

The notion of heuristic derives from the ancient Greek *heuretikos* and is concerned with articulating some of the most important considerations involved in processes of discovery. Here, our specific purpose is to try and articulate key elements that might inform such discovery *vis-à-vis* knowledge exchange between higher education and schools in relation to RE. In identifying our proposed heuristic in terms of 'Three Elements of RE',[5] we are not suggesting that these provide an exhaustive mapping of the field or, indeed, that these eclipse other ways of going on. We put these forward as a contribution to remediation: drawing out key elements that inform both our diagnosis and imagining otherwise, that in turn might promote ongoing dialogue and exchange between higher education and school contexts. Each element is, after a brief introduction, set out successively; however, in practice, we envisage each of the three elements being mutually constitutive and mutually interdependent.

Our discussion above concerning the wider implications of attending to 'mapping into knowledge' moves beyond accepting a series of unproblematised assumptions about knowledge. We have, more generally, explored some of the implications of acknowledging embodied and relational dimensions that often become invisible once a settled understanding has been achieved. As such, a critical line has been taken as regards surfacing the many different practices, entities and assumptions involved in the production of knowledge. This *critical element* is, we contend, a key element in developing a heuristic, and in the following we explore some of the theoretical background that informs this. In taking the line that knowledge is never simply given but is the outcome of a complex assemblage that comprises relations between entities and practices, there is necessarily an *experimental element* in play. We argue that this openness to exploration is inherently educational and is linked to an educational ontology that is open to the incoming of the new. From what has been written already, it is clear that the account offered is one that is

Remediation—Imagining Otherwise   145

relational through and through: to this extent, an *ethical element* is of fundamental importance in thinking through the implications of educational practice, especially with regard to the knowledge/ontic practices involved in RE.

As noted at the outset of this section, in practice these three elements are dynamic, mutually constitutive and inter-determined, and their separation into distinct critical, experimental and ethical dimensions is simply to enable their initial outline. Thus, for example, if we take the process of 'mapping into knowledge' described above, it becomes immediately apparent that the practices involved cut across all three elements. Insofar as its point of departure moves beyond a passive reception of knowledge that has already been achieved, there is a critical element necessarily involved in the deconstructive moment in eschewing a naïve reception for one that critically inquires into how a given position has been fabricated. There is an experimental element involved in thinking through how such an investigation might be carried out, which may involve some kind of empirical inquiry in the field and analysis of findings in light of this. Inquiry, therefore, aims to be open-ended, rather than simply tracing framings that have been determined in advance, although it is recognised that a given ordering will always exceed our cognitive grasp. And finally, at each stage of this exercise in becoming aware of how knowledge is produced, there is a collaborative process that involves the 'working together' of people and of entities that is ethical through and through.

Having initially outlined the three elements of RE, the critical, experimental and ethical, we will now say a little more about each of these constitutive elements, linking these to issues that we have addressed in our diagnosis. Relevant theory, together with specific considerations arising from the effort to imagine and practice otherwise, will also be addressed.

(a) The Critical Element

We have earlier (Chapter Two) drawn parallels between root meanings of education as leading out and the discourse of religion as entailing multiple re-readings. This implies that an important element of any enterprise that concerns education is being critical of horizons that restrict or limit possibilities of insight, comparison and considered practice, including, in this book, the use of the term 'religion' itself. Accordingly, the critical element involves commitment to a critical reflexivity *apropos* the various concepts, tropes and practices that are engaged in the making of particular kinds of sense. This also involves a preparedness to interrupt familiar ways of going on and to become aware of the limits of particular framings and approaches. Of course, the critical element, although initially challenging the adequacy of a given standpoint or framing, may itself be part of a broader process of diagnosis and remediation (such as that outlined by Rabinow and Bennett, 2007) that in turn leads to new imaginative construction and horizons of possibility.

146   *Remediation—Beyond Indifference?*

The critical element is necessarily linked with some particular account of what it means to be critical. One of the advantages of MacIntyre's (1985; 1988) work on traditions of inquiry is that this situates practices of argument and critique within traditions of inquiry that are extended through time. This affords the identification of the specificities of language, time and culture in relation to continuing work that has a narrative structure. As we have seen above, such an approach has been of value in approaching Islamic and gendered traditions of thinking (Chapters Four and Five) and is of value, too, in identifying university traditions of argumentation through time. It is therefore desirable to identify the particular tradition(s) of critique that are being appealed to.

Within Western university contexts, present-day understandings of critique derive from what is, broadly speaking, characterised as the Enlightenment, with Kant's writings, especially *The Critique of Pure Reason* (1965, [1781]) and *The Critique of Judgment* (1987, [1790]) usually being taken as key points of reference. However, it is in his essay 'An Answer to the Question: What is Enlightenment?' that Kant (2009 [1784]) distils what he regards as some of the main contours informing what it is to be critical, even though parts of this text are somewhat opaque. It was in this work, according to Foucault (1988), that Kant articulated two critical traditions that have continued to divide philosophy to this day. On the one hand, analytic philosophy responds to the question as to the conditions necessary for the possibility of attaining true knowledge. On the other, however, a different kind of question is posed; this instead asks the questions: 'what is our actuality? and 'what is the present field of possible experiences?' This is to address the sorts of concern that might be characterised as an ontology of ourselves, the present and our actuality. Foucault (1988, 154–5) then interrogates what practices of critique within such an ontology might consist of.

> [C]ritique is not a matter of saying that things are not right as they are. It is a matter of pointing out on what kinds of assumptions, what kinds of familiar, unchallenged, unconsidered modes of thought the practices that we accept rest . . . Criticism is a matter of flushing out that thought and trying to change it: to show that things are not as self-evident as one believed, to see that what is accepted as self-evident will no longer be accepted as such. Practicing criticism is a matter of making facile gestures difficult.

An illustration of such a practice of critique can be seen in regard to the limitations of the 'word-world settlement' as discussed above. In this connection, it will be recalled, we pointed to the limited ways in which language within the discourse of 'religion' is understood within naïve word-world settlement approaches, which can lead to misunderstanding, implausibility and indifference. Catherine Keller (2008, 3) points, for example, to the 'dispiriting polarization' that settles for antagonism between religious absolutism and

Remediation—Imagining Otherwise 147

secular relativism. Another case in point is a medieval monastic account, *Life of St Benedict of Nursia*, by Gregory the Great, believed to have been written around 594 CE, that describes an intense, and on the face of it, entirely implausible encounter between a monk and a dragon. As Ingold (2013) observes, present-day readers are likely to dismiss such accounts as mythological and hence incredulous. However, this is only because of the dominance of word-world settlement assumptions that inform this particular reading and the (negative) judgment that rises as a consequence. But once the terms of the word-world settlement itself are problematised, it then becomes possible to engage seriously with such accounts in ways that can acknowledge other than purely representational relations between word and world, that afford a much greater plasticity with regard to interpretation. Thus, Ingold, for example, offers an existential interpretation of the story, where, drawing upon a number of contextual details in the account, he suggests that what was at stake here was a fundamental crisis, which brethren at the time would have instantly recognised. Hence, in Ingold's words (2013, 736–7),

> The dragon was not the objective cause of fear; it was the shape of fear itself . . . in medieval ontology, the dragon existed as fear exists, not as an exterior threat but as an affliction instilled at the core of the sufferer's very being. As such, it was as real as his facial expression and the urgency in his voice. But unlike the latter, it could neither be seen nor heard save by the one who was himself afeared.

A critical re-reading of the reader's pre-existent horizon of understanding opens the text to encounters, and the possibility of new insight, beyond indifference. Moving beyond a limited word-world framing then affords openness to different ways of sense-making, acknowledging that in Homer, for example, powerful forces such as love (Aphrodite) and war (Ares) are described as external entities (Heelas and Lock, 1981).

However, whilst such a summary might initially appear to chime well with the practice of critique as mobilised within the academy at the present time, there have been some misgivings expressed as regards how such critique is exercised in practice. Latour (2004), for example, has pointed to the tendency for practices of critique to identify putative weaknesses in competing points of view, without that same level of critical insight being displayed with regard to interrogating the theory being defended. This leads to a situation where the practice of critique can render the point of view being proposed becoming invulnerable to change, whilst failing to give sufficient account to the affordances of different positions for different questions and purposes.

With this reading, critique is potentially valuable but is not inherently good, pursued as an end in itself. To this extent, the practice of critique also entails being cognisant of the limits of critique *per se* and the dangers associated with its mobilisation in practice. One might even say that the practice of critique always requires that it be mobilised in conjunction with both the

148 *Remediation—Beyond Indifference?*

experimental and ethical elements, since these might question some of the projections and limitations that might otherwise go unnoticed. In recognising some of the dangers associated with an agonistic account of critique, Wendy Brown (2005) has proposed a more eirenic metaphor of counterpoint as a means of acknowledging the affordances of different theories for different purposes. According to Brown (2005, 74), counterpoint

> . . . complicates a single or dominant theme through the addition of contrasting themes or forces. At once open-ended and tactical, counterpoint emanates from and promotes an anti hegemonic sensibility and requires a modest and carefully styled embrace of multiplicity in which contrasting elements, featured simultaneously, do not simply war, harmonize, blend, or compete but rather bring out complexity that cannot emerge through a monolithic or single melody.

In taking up the limitations associated with the practice of critique, it is noteworthy that an awareness of limitations of a particular experiment is an important element in scientific practice, which is included in a critical commentary on the procedures untaken. In Knorr Cetina's (2007, 366) work on scientific practice, she draws parallels between scientists' work with partial objects that are not clearly defined, and traditional forms of apophatic speech within theology, such as the *via negativa*.

> Negative knowledge is not non-knowledge, but knowledge of the limits of knowing that is gained from the disturbances, errors and uncertainties of research. In Christian theology, there was once an approach called the 'apophatic', which prescribed studying God in terms of what He was not rather than what He was, since no positive assertions could be made about His essence. High energy physics experiments show similar preferences.

The significance of apophatic approaches has become a focus in a number of disciplinary areas (Caputo, 1997; Franke, 2014; Henderson, 2014; Keller, 2015; Scrima, 2016 [1952]). Acknowledging limitations might then be conceived as part of enlarged repertoire of practices in RE that comes from a more reflexive approach that is promoted through engaging with various socio-material gatherings. A more considered practice would then be sensitive to the difference that different framings bring and proffer reasons for mobilising one such approach over another.

Socio-material approaches have further extended the kinds of questions that the critical element might encompass in acknowledging the wider, non-human elements and the roles that these play in all kinds of gatherings. In particular, the significant work of mediation and translation that is involved in the makings of sense in diverse fields of practice has become a focus of critical attention in recent years and in this chapter this has been

Remediation—Imagining Otherwise 149

taken up once again, with regard to Stengers' (1997) concept of 'mapping into knowledge'.

Such a conception of critique brings in its trail a series of questions that are attentive to the specificity of location and the ways in which this might be acknowledged in accounts that are constructed. Whilst acknowledging the complexity of embeddedness within heterogeneous assemblages, it is also necessary to be attentive to the kinds of *complexity reductions* that are in play (I'Anson, 2010b; Osberg and Biesta, 2010). Complexity reduction was a feature that Latour noticed in his account of the various translations that are effected in the making of knowledge, discussed in Chapter Two. As we have seen above, in our analysis of the current settled framing with regard to RE, such forms of complexity reduction are not infrequently hidden from view and have far-reaching effects *apropos* the kinds of sense that are made and the consequences of these for practice. Whilst some forms of complexity reduction are necessarily in play—especially in educational contexts—a justification for a particular form of reduction and an exploration of its effects is desirable.

(b) The Experimental Element

The experimental element is a key constituent of an ontology that rejects the assumption that education is primarily concerned with the already known. If, following Spinoza, we do not know in advance of what a particular being is capable, a key purpose of education becomes the fashioning of events and encounters that lead students out from their point of departure through open engagement and exploration.

In this connection, it is interesting to note that Bergson (1998 [1907]) characterised two movements in which this can take place. The first is through 'descent', which is the unfolding of a pre-determined rationale to which some kind of alignment is sought. This characterises educational practice where a field has been mapped in a particular way and the role of educators is to induct new students into established pathways and findings. This was seen to be a dominant educational assumption informing examinations (Chapter Two), but the assumption of a pre-existing mapping also informs theoretical approaches, such as Land *et al.*'s (2008) threshold concepts, where the precise learning of specific concepts, practices and their ordering, can, at least in principle, be outlined in advance. The extent to which such an orientation can be considered properly 'educational' is a question that has been taken up by a number of theorists (e.g., Biesta, 2006), as we have seen.

The other orientation Bergson characterises as 'ascent', which is the working out of new and emergent possibilities that are present within a particular relational context. As such, the direction of travel is unfathomable and undetermined, open as it is to the emergence of the new and unforeseen. Bergson's (1998 [1907]) style of reasoning, following upon that of Spinoza, was taken up by Deleuze and Guattari (1987) in their understanding of 'line of flight'

150   Remediation—Beyond Indifference?

and Braidotti's (2002, 27) notion of space of experimentation; this has become influential within recent educational theorising, such as thinking through the creative possibilities of early years education (Davies, 2014). It is important to note, however, that the two orientations, towards descent and ascent, are not to be viewed as necessarily mutually exclusive possibilities or, indeed, as respectively 'good' and 'bad'. This is because, as Davies (2014) observes, a particular trajectory that might otherwise be characterised as 'descent' can, in certain circumstances, be 'undone' or interrupted and thus become the occasion for new and previously unimagined possibilities. On the other hand, although there is a temptation to valorise ascent, or 'lines of flight', in Deleuze's terms, as promoting joy, they can also, as Deleuze and Guattari (1987, 205) remind us, be challenging, even tragic in their effects. Any particular line of flight therefore needs to be critically and ethically assessed.

Such considerations might suggest that a particular kind of experimental ethos is characteristic of a distinctively educational approach, especially insofar as this opens up questions regarding ways in which students might live and imagine the present otherwise. Again, following Spinoza, if we do not know in advance what a particular assemblage of people, technologies, concepts and practices is capable of, then an inquiring approach that is open to the incoming of the new is desirable, and this is also taken up in a range of more recent feminist approaches from Irigaray (2004) and Jantzen (1998) to Catherine Keller (2003), marking the difficult pathway from previous imaginations and forms of cultural practice clearly identified with Western male-normative approaches. Educational strategies that promote individual and collaborative forms of enquiry, together with a sensitivity to different audiences and the warrants required for justification, are some key features of an inquiring, experimental approach.

One way of marking the shift in both thinking and practice involved in the move to a more experimental approach is to focus upon the metaphors that are mobilised in making sense. Thus, Sfard (1998) has distinguished two metaphors that characterise approaches to education: that of acquisition, which is characterised as a process of knowledge appropriation by individual students, and participation, which involves social interaction and distributed cognition. The acquisition metaphor is especially associated with disciplinary learning and is characteristic of situations where a distinct field is mapped and the order in which concepts are to be acquired by an individual inquirer is set out. According to Paavola and Hakkarainen (2005, 538), with the participatory metaphor,

> [h]uman activity is indexically bound to its social and material environment. Knowledge does not exist either in a world of its own or in individual minds, but is an aspect of participation in cultural practices.

This approach, like that of learning as acquisition, can be conservative insofar as existing, already known cultural practice is foregrounded rather than

Remediation—Imagining Otherwise 151

being concerned with creative change to such practice and the construction of new artefacts or objects of knowledge. A move beyond this can be seen in Paavola and Hakkarainen's (2005) proposal for a third metaphor—that of knowledge creation—to supplement the earlier metaphors described by Sfard. Knowledge creation is where students collaborate to develop shared objects and artifacts (Paavola and Hakkarainen, 2005, 539). We will explore possible implications of mobilising such an approach below.

(c) The Ethical Element

Education is a fundamentally relational activity, and as such, an ethical element will be in play especially if, as Lambek (2015, 228) has put this, the ethical consists in an imminent, 'ongoing orientation, enactment, and evaluation of human activity and character as constituted in and through . . . the articulation of performance and practice'. The ethical element becomes all the more complex and interesting once it is accepted that the many 'different acts, criteria, and accounts' are distinct and cannot be collapsed into a single plane of sense-making (Lambek, 2015, 228). The acknowledgement of ethical difference, in other words, requires an approach that is able to register such difference whilst giving insight into the work of ethical composure that is necessary to realise a particular vision of the good.

One account of the constitution of the ethical domain is that provided by Foucault (2005) in his later writings, which we encountered in Chapter Three in connection with the discussion of some of the implications of Spinoza's philosophy. Foucault's account has a number of advantages; it is, as Faubion (2011, 4) observes, remarkable for its analytical and methodological parsimony in identifying four parameters of ethical subject formation. These are

(i) 'ethical substance', which refers to the focus of ethical work, be this the soul, carnal pleasures etc., that requires some kind of fashioning so as to produce the desired subject;

(ii) 'mode of subjectivation', which is the manner in which a given subject engages with the criteria so as to live up to or to become aligned with the particular qualities that characterise the desired state;

(iii) '*askêsis*' refers to the work that the subject has to undertake in order to become the desired subject (this derives from the Greek for training or exercise);

(iv) '*telos*' is the end or hope towards which the subject aims.

A further advantage of Foucault's approach is that it does not begin with some kind of normative approach as to what counts as ethics, but is instead concerned with mapping the contours of particular articulations as to what the ethical might be within specific cultural contexts and horizons. With this approach to ethics there is, therefore, a strong empirical dimension, insofar

152 *Remediation—Beyond Indifference?*

as there is an interest in the various assemblages of people, artefacts, texts and practices that together help choreograph a particular vision of ethical formation. Consequently, Foucault's four-fold axes of subjectification can be used to analyse diverse ethical practices, whether in relation to religious millenarianism or the *askêsis* associated with Portuguese elites (Faubion, 2011). Insofar as *askêsis* is primarily an exercise, it can be a means through which the subject becomes aware of her relationship to herself, a means through which she can transform this, as well as functioning as 'a diagnosis and a poetics of the present' (McGushin, 2007, 282). In other words, the axes of ethical formation afford an open-ended inquiry into the specific values and practices that are valorised in a particular culture and can inform an analysis as to how these ideals are worked out through socio-material practices.

However, the ethical element also comprises analysis of collective forms of ethics that move beyond individual practices of self-formation, important though these are. This is to raise, as Faubion (2011, 8) has put it, 'the question of the ethical—ontologically and epistemologically—to the level of the collective from the level of the individual'. Study of the ethical element is therefore multifaceted and includes both a focus upon actual practice and analysis of the particular virtues and ethical theories that inform the 'good' that is desired. Such an ethical framing can provide insight into a wide variety of ethical practices and theories; one such illustration is the study of the early rabbinic self-formation practices and ethical theory in relation to the *Mishnah*, a rabbinic legal text, as 'an intriguing site for the examination of practices of self-formation' (Balberg, 2014, 11). And thus,

> [t]he mishnaic discourse of purity and impurity constructs and develops certain ideas about the self and certain techniques of the self. These ideas and techniques pertain to the ways in which one govern's one's body, one's possessions [. . .] and one's behaviour, as well as to the ways in which one conducts oneself *vis-à-vis* the law and its rabbinic self-proclaimed representatives.
>
> (Balberg, 2014, 12)

So how might the three elements of the critical, experimental and ethical enable re-thinking educational practices within the context of RE that, in our view, should foreground relationality and awareness of the implications of socio-material gatherings?

(viii) The Three Elements in Practice

In the following section, we outline some ways forward that engage practices in RE after neutrality that in various ways acknowledge relationality in a broad sense as comprising the multiple assemblages of which we are a part and the ethical complexities that are a consequence of that. We also take on board 'mapping into knowledge' (Stengers, 1997) and the outcome of being attentive to ways in which we construct knowledge. In taking up the heuristic developed in Part Three, we address the three elements through students 'becoming ethnographer', a focus on interdisciplinarity, socio-materiality and, through the making of artefacts in aesthetic education, where these are found to impose their presence through acting back upon students. The illustrations presented here are simply that: we envisage that a more detailed programme would be the outcome of an ongoing practice of dialogue between practitioners from both higher education and school sectors.

In place of approaches that presume a detached knower and that take a capacity to re-iterate an abstract language as constitutive of successful learning, our analysis points in the direction of new practices that take seriously students' implication in complex cultural and relational practices that they might 'read' and engage in new ways. For this to be possible, a key aspect will be exercises that are empirically oriented and that issue in new capacities to 'read' and 'map into knowledge' within the diverse spaces, events and practices that students encounter in everyday life. In regard to school contexts, this is to take up a key insight from the New sociology of Childhood (James and Prout, 1997; James *et al.*, 1998) regarding the desirability of a critical focus on children and young people's *present* experience rather than this being deferred to a future 'adult' focus as primary. To this one might add that there also needs to be educational opportunities to *re-imagine present and future states*, together with giving an account that serves both as justification and as analysis of the steps that might be taken to implement these. This was a key point raised by David Harvey (2006, 88) in his Amnesty Lecture at Oxford, 'The Right to the City', given back in 2003, when he observed that:

> The right to change the city is not an abstract right, but a right that inheres in daily practices, whether we are conscious of that right or not. [. . .] How can I hope for an alternative possible urban world, even imagine its contours, its conundrums, and its charms, when I am so deeply immersed in the experience of what already exists?

To create moments 'in which our imaginations can wander and wonder about alternative possible urban worlds' (Harvey, 2006, 88) and to engage seriously with these kinds of questions is to fundamentally change the 'grammar' of RE as it is currently practised. This involves a re-imaging of the subject's educational potential and responsibility to children and young people as well as to the different cultures with which it engages.

However, there are also opportunities for a retrospective analysis that examines how particular events have in part formed present judgments and outlooks in regard to a particular issue or tradition. For example, within a higher education setting, Jasper (see I'Anson and Jasper, 2011) has re-designed an Introduction to Christianity module so that instead of beginning with an historical

154   *Remediation—Beyond Indifference?*

or doctrinal mapping, the point of departure is students' own encounters with Christianity through rites of passage, church attendance and so forth, so that diverse initial points of departure can be acknowledged and their impacts inform the future direction of travel. In the same institution, Stewart (2016) has introduced a module in material religion that addresses our relationship with the material dimension of our environment in terms, for example, of Foucault's 'care for the self' (1986; 2005), alerting students to the significance and transformative effects of engaging with the material world themselves and also in helping them to acknowledge this process in others.[6]

(ix) Re-Thinking Educational Practice Beyond Indifference: Towards Empirical Practice

If the project of mastery via a detached and disembodied standpoint is no longer plausible, new educational practices in which students' empirical exploration of their environment become conceivable. In this connection, it is noteworthy that Foucault regarded his own standpoint as primarily that of a 'reader' (Certeau, 1986); this gestures, as already noted above in Chapter One, towards a richer understanding of literacy than is currently practised that may involve a multi-modal reading of practices and texts (e.g., Jewitt and Kress, 2003).

The Warwick project, especially associated with the work of Jackson (1997; 2004; 2008), has done much to further empirically informed accounts being available within the classroom. Likewise, European explorations of contextual approaches have offered multiple justifications for practices that are sensitive to particularities (Skeie *et al.*, 2013). Such an ethnographic focus within RE, although welcome, has tended to focus on either the production, by adults, of ethnographical accounts of religious practice or the use of ethnographic methodologies to inform practitioner research in relation to different cultures and educational practice. This has not, to date, focused upon young people themselves 'becoming ethnographer' and engaging in practices of observing, listening and recording, followed by analysis. Without this further move to implicate students in this work of production—of mapping into knowledge—there is a danger that for all the sophistication of the ethnographic materials designed for use in the classroom, these are simply resolved back into the familiar subject positions and categories that we have critiqued above.

The ethnographic approach that we advocate here builds upon this rich stream of existing work and extends this to include children and young peoples' own ethnographic knowledge practices as having a constitutive role in sense-making within RE. Such an empirical orientation can draw upon the extensive material within anthropology that has been made accessible through recent work of the Royal Anthropological Institute (n.d.).

The experimental element comes to the fore within the context of interdisciplinary working, especially where this involves the creation of a new

Remediation—Imagining Otherwise 155

assemblage that does not quite fit what has gone before. For as Barry *et al.* (2008, 21) observe:

> . . . ideas of interdisciplinarity and transdisciplinarity imply a variety of boundary transgressions, in which the disciplinary rules, trainings and subjectivities given by existing knowledge corpuses are put aside or superseded.

Thus, the introduction of digital cameras as a tool for exploring relations can quite radically change relations within a particular gathering and lead to new educational diffractions beyond those anticipated (Sørensen, 2011). The use of cameras can also be used in practices such as photo-elicitation, originally developed as a tool to redress some of the power imbalances in ethnographic encounters. Here, students take images of significant concerns in relation to the issue at hand, and the ensuing dialogue, which is led by them, can also lead in unexpected directions (Mannion and I'Anson, 2004). However, approaches and insights from other areas, such as aesthetic education, can also provide resources for practising differently, especially as regards the creation of an aesthetic 'object' as a tool for inquiry, which then 'acts back' upon participants in unexpected ways, re-figuring relationships differently and potentially leading to new insight.

In terms of a radical attending to experience and a critical exploration of the relations that are given, there have been a number of new initiatives, especially in connection with the philosophy of education. Jan Masschelein (2010), for example, asks students to follow a particular line drawn upon a map and then report back what was seen, encountered and discovered through such wandering. On critically engaging with the accounts that they have constructed, students become aware of the extent to which they have brought particular assumptions to a situation that they have recounted and particular things that they have missed as compared with a fellow student's account. Such walking practices have been used to explore familiar themes such as 'home' (Myers and Harris, 2004), as well as ways of negotiating unfamiliar terrain (Vansieleghem, 2011).

Ethnographic practices such as interviewing afford significant opportunities for ethical engagement, and it is noteworthy that Bourdieu (1999, 614) has suggested that the practice of attending to another in an interview

> . . . can be considered as a sort of spiritual exercise that, through forgetfulness of self, aims at a true conversion of the way we look at other people in the ordinary circumstances of life.

Be that as it may, material from such encounters can be analysed using a variety of different approaches that foreground the kinds of relations that are present (prepositions), the different value positions that respondents desire and the means that are deployed to realise these in practice (the anthropology

156   Remediation—Beyond Indifference?

of the good). In other words, such a re-orientation towards the empirical and the material offers multiple opportunities for mobilising the three elements of RE in practice, wherein open-ended, experimental, critical and ethical elements are mutually in play.

In each of these different situations, new diffractions of educational possibility became actualised as part of an experimental exploration of the relations that are given in experience. Such an orientation does, however, lead to new pedagogical challenges for the practitioner, both as regards the design of educational context, where traditional behaviourist-informed approaches to lesson planning are unlikely to be of much use (Allwright, 2003), and as regards some of the affective challenges of living with the uncertainties that attend such experimentation (I'Anson, 2010a; I'Anson and Jasper, 2011).

Within the compass of the ethical element are specific topics that connect with students' own awareness and engagement in cultural practices. One such topic is that of the ethics of cultural appropriation, which cuts across many taken-for-granted assumptions about the availability and appropriation of diverse cultural artefacts (Young and Brunk, 2012). Such topics are likely to be of interest to students insofar as these connect with—and cut across—a number of cultural practices with which they themselves are imbricated. This might also include a critical investigation of the connections between capitalism and 'selling spirituality' (Carrette and King, 2005), together with ongoing critiques of the ethics and subject-forming practices associated with late capitalism (Goodchild, 2002; 2007). Moreover, the focus upon distinct understandings of the 'good' (as *telos*) and the diverse ways in which such imaginaries are realised in practice are also likely to be of interest in identifying—and critiquing—the presumption of Western ideals and framings.

Such connection with students' own practice is also a feature of pedagogical practice that takes 'mapping into knowledge' seriously, insofar as students themselves are encouraged to 'read' the diverse cultural settings they move within and encounter. It can be seen that the working out of the implications of such an educational approach takes up all three elements insofar as this involves a critical analysis, identification of key values and assumptions and an experimental/empirical orientation insofar as this involves a reading of current practice—for example, of consumers in a local shopping centre or participants in online communities or interactions.

The three elements taken together might therefore provide a point of departure for re-engaging conversations between higher education and school contexts in relation to future thinking and practice in RE. Beyond its value as a heuristic to encourage such dialogue, the three elements can also inform a re-imagining of practices within RE, especially in thinking through the implications of moving beyond approaches that are premised up the trope of neutrality.

Notes

1. As Stengers (2005) observes, for Deleuze the focus upon *le milieu* in French has a double sense: both that of beginning 'in the middle' but also in relation to the context within which such practice takes place.

2. This was also the approach taken by Souriau (2015) in his philosophy, which Latour (2011) has sought to make available to a broader audience, and many of whose distinct themes inform Latour's (2013a) project.
3. Latour (2010) has traced the roots of his approach in relation to the discourse of religion and has drawn out some of the implications for thinking about the relation of 'science' to 'religion' (Latour, 2008).
4. DeLanda (2006, 10) explores some of the broader implications of this way of thinking. As he has put this, '. . . there is no way to tell in advance in what way a given entity may affect or be affected by innumerable other entities . . .'
5. The 'three elements' is a framing that initially derives from Friedrich von Hügel's (1923) *magnum opus, The Mystical Element of Religion.* Whilst von Hügel's insights regarding the interconnected and mutually determining relational structure of the elements has been taken up, in most other respects, the understanding of the elements as advanced here is very different, focused, for example, upon RE as a practice, and drawing upon a very different theoretical repertoire that includes Foucault, Deleuze and Latour, amongst others.
6. In practice, there are competing institutional logics that severely compromise approaches that aim to be open-ended and recursive (see I'Anson and Jasper, 2011).

Bibliography

Allwright, D., 2003. 'Exploratory practice: Rethinking practitioner research in language teaching'. *Language Teaching Research*, vol. 7, no. 2, pp. 113–141.

Balberg, M., 2014. *Purity, Body, and Self in Early Rabbinic Literature.* Berkeley, Los Angeles and London: University of California Press.

Barad, K., 2007. *Meeting the Universe Halfway: Quantum Physics and the Entanglement of Matter and Meaning.* Durham, NC and London: Duke University Press.

Barry, A., Born, G. and Weszkalnys, G., 2008. 'Logics of interdisciplinarity'. *Economy and Society*, vol. 37, no. 1, pp. 20–49.

Baumfield, V.M., 2014. 'To teach is to learn'. *British Journal of Religious Education*, vol. 36, no. 1, pp. 1–3.

Bennett, J., 2010. *Vibrant Matter: A Political Ecology of Things.* Durham, NC: Duke University Press.

Bergson, H.L., 1998 [1907]. *Creative Evolution.* Mineola, NY: Dover Publications.

Biesta, J.J., 2006. *Beyond Learning: Democratic Education for a Human Future.* Boulder and London: Paradigm.

Bourdieu, P., 1999. *The Weight of the World: Social Suffering in Contemporary Society.* Cambridge: Polity Press.

Braidotti, R., 2002. *Metamorphoses: Towards a Materialist Theory of Becoming.* Cambridge and Malden, MA: Polity Press.

Braidotti, R., 2013. 'Posthuman humanities'. *European Educational Research Journal*, vol. 12, no. 1, pp. 1–19.

Brown, W., 2005. *Edgework: Critical Essays on Knowledge and Politics.* Princeton and Oxford: Princeton University Press.

Bruner, J., 1978. 'The role of dialogue in language acquisition'. In: A. Sinclair, R. Jarvella and W.J.M. Levelt eds., *The Child's Conception of Language.* New York: Springer-Verlag, pp. 241–256.

Caputo, J.D., 1997. *The Prayers and Tears of Jacques Derrida: Religion Without Religion.* Bloomington and Indianapolis: Indiana University Press.

Carrette, J., 2013. *William James's Hidden Religious Imagination: A Universe of Relations.* London and New York: Routledge.

158   Remediation—Beyond Indifference?

Carrette, J. and King, R., 2005. *Selling Spirituality: The Silent Takeover of Religion*. London and New York: Routledge.

Certeau, M.d., 1986. *Heterologies: Discourse on the Other*. Minneapolis: University of Minnesota Press.

Conroy, J.C., Lundie, D., Davis, R.A., Baumfield, V., Barnes, L.P., Gallagher, T., Lowden, K., Bourque, N. and Wenell, K., 2013. *Does RE Work? A Multi-dimensional Investigation*. London: Bloomsbury.

Crang, M., 2000. 'Relics, places and unwritten geographies in the work of Michel de Certeau (1925–86)'. In: M. Crang and N. Thrift eds., *Thinking Space*. London and New York: Routledge, pp. 136–153.

Crang, M., 2003. 'Qualitative methods: Touchy, feely, look-see?'. *Progress in Human Geography*, vol. 27, no. 4, pp. 494–504.

Cush, D. and Robinson, C., 2014. 'Developments in religious studies: Towards a dialogue with religious education'. *British Journal of Religious Education*, Vol. 36, no. 1, pp. 4–17.

Davies, B., 2014. *Listening to Children: Being and Becoming*. London and New York: Routledge.

Delanda, M., 2006. *A New Philosophy of Society: Assemblage Theory and Social Complexity*. London and New York: Continuum.

Deleuze, G., 1988. *Bergsonism*. Trans. H. Tomlinson and B. Habberjam. New York: Zone Books.

Deleuze, G. and Guattari, F., 1987. *A Thousand Plateaus: Capitalism and Schizophrenia*. Minneapolis: University of Minnesota Press.

Edgoose, J., 2001. 'Just decide! Derrida and the ethical aporias of education'. In: G.J.J. Biesta and D. Egéa-Kuehne eds., *Derrida and Education*. Abingdon and New York: Routledge, pp. 119–133.

Faubion, J.D., 2011. *An Anthropology of Ethics*. Cambridge and New York: Cambridge University Press.

Fenwick, T. and Edwards, R., 2010. *Actor-Network Theory and Education*. Abingdon and New York: Routledge.

Fenwick, T., Edwards, R. and Sawchuk, P., 2011. *Emerging Approaches to Educational Research: Tracing the Sociomaterial*. London and New York: Routledge.

Foucault, M., 1986. *The Care of the Self: The History of Sexuality 3*. New York: Pantheon Books.

Foucault, M., 1988. 'Practicing criticism'. In: L.D. Kritzman ed., *Politics, Philosophy, Culture: Interviews and Other Writings 1977–1984*. Trans. A. Sheridan and others. New York and London: Routledge, pp. 154–155.

Foucault, M., 2005. *The Hermeneutics of the Subject: Lectures at the College de France 1981–1982*. F. Gros ed. New York: Palgrave Macmillan.

Franke, W., 2014. *A Philosophy of the Unsayable*. Notre Dame, IN: University of Notre Dame Press.

Goodchild, P., 2002. *Capitalism and Religion: The Price of Piety*. London and New York: SCM.

Goodchild, P., 2007. *The Theology of Money*. London: SCM.

Harvey, D., 2006. 'The right to the city'. In: R. Scholar ed., *Divided Cities*. Oxford and New York: Oxford University Press, pp. 83–103.

Heelas, P. and Lock, A., 1981. *Indigenous Psychologies*. London: Academic Press.

Henderson, D. 2014. *Apophatic Elements in the Theory and Practice of Psychoanalysis: Pseudo-Dionysius and C.G. Jung*. London and New York: Routledge.

Hügel, F. von, 1923. *The Mystical Element of Religion as Studied in Saint Catherine of Genoa and Her Friends*, 2 vols. 2nd ed. London: J.M. Dent and Sons/James Clarke and Co.

I'Anson, J., 2004. 'Mapping the subject: Student teachers, location and the understanding of religion'. *British Journal of Religious Studies*, vol. 26, no. 1, pp. 41–56.

I'Anson, J., 2010a. 'After a rhetorics of neutrality: Complexity reduction and cultural difference'. In: G. Biesta and D. Osberg eds., *Complexity Theory and the Politics of Education*. Rotterdam: Sense, pp. 126–138.

I'Anson, J., 2010b. 'Pedagogy: After neutrality?'. *British Journal of Religious Studies*, vol. 32, no. 2, pp. 105–118.

I'Anson, J., 2011. 'Childhood, complexity orientation and children's rights: Enlarging the space of the possible?'. *Education Inquiry*, vol. 2, no. 3, pp. 373–384.

I'Anson, J., 2016. 'UNCRC at 25: A critical assessment of achievements and trajectories with reference to educational research'. In: J. Gillett-Swan and V. Coppock eds., *Children's Rights, Educational Research and the UNCRC Past, Present and Future*. Oxford: Symposium, pp. 17–37.

I'Anson, J. and Jasper, A., 2011. '"Religion" in educational spaces: Knowing, knowing well, and knowing differently'. *Arts and Humanities in Higher Education*, vol. 10, no. 3, pp. 295–314.

Ihde, D., 1986. *Experimental Phenomenology: An Introduction*. Albany: SUNY Press.

Ingold, T., 2013. 'Dreaming of Dragons: On the imagination of real life'. *Journal of the Royal Anthropological Institute*, vol. 19, no. 4, pp. 734–752.

Irigaray, L., 2004. *Key Writings*. London and New York: Continuum.

Jackson, R., 1997. *Religious Education: An Interpretive Approach*. London: Hodder Education.

Jackson, R., 2004. *Rethinking Religious Education and Plurality: Issues in Diversity and Pedagogy*. London: RoutledgeFalmer.

Jackson, R., 2008. 'Contextual religious education and the interpretive approach'. *British Journal of Religious Education*, vol. 30, no.1, pp. 13–24.

James, A., Jenks, C. and Prout, A., 1998. *Theorising Childhood*. Cambridge: Polity Press.

James, A. and Prout, A., 1997. *Constructing and Reconstructing Childhood: Contemporary Issues in the Sociological Study of Childhood*. London and New York: Routledge.

James, W., 1996 [1909]. *A Pluralistic Universe*. Lincoln: University of Nebraska Press.

James, W., 2003 [1912]. *Essays in Radical Empiricism*. Mineola, NY: Dover Publications.

Jantzen, G.M., 1998. *Becoming Divine: Towards a Feminist Philosophy of Religion*. Manchester: Manchester University Press.

Jantzen, G.M., 2004. *Foundations of Violence: Death and the Displacement of Beauty*, vol. 1. London and New York: Routledge.

Jewitt, C. and Kress, G., eds., 2003. *Multimodal Literacy*. New York: Peter Lang.

Kant, I., 1965 [1781]. *The Critique of Pure Reason*. New York: St. Martin's Press.

Kant, I., 1987 [1790]. *The Critique of Judgment*. Indianapolis: Hackett Publishing.

Kant, I., 2009 [1784]. *An Answer to the Question: What Is Enlightenment?* Harmondsworth: Penguin.

Keller, C., 2003. *Face of the Deep: A theology of Becoming*. London and New York: Routledge.

Keller, C., 2008. *On the Mystery: Discerning Divinity in Process*. Minneapolis, MI: Fortress Press.

160 *Remediation—Beyond Indifference?*

Keller, C., 2015. *Cloud of the Impossible: Negative theology and Planetary Entanglement.* New York: Columbia University Press.

Knorr Cetina, K., 2007. 'Culture in global knowledge societies: Knowledge cultures and epistemic cultures'. *Interdisciplinary Science Reviews*, vol. 32, no. 4, pp. 361–375.

Lambek, M., 2015. 'The hermeneutics of ethical encounters: Between traditions and practice'. *HAU: Journal of Ethnographic Theory*, vol. 5, no. 2, pp. 227–250.

Land, R., Meyer, J. and Smith, J., eds., 2008. *Threshold Concepts Within the Disciplines.* Rotterdam: Sense Publishers.

Latour, B., Winter, 2004. 'Why has crititique run out of steam? From matters of fact to matters of concern'. *Critical Inquiry*, vol. 30, no. 2, pp. 225–248.

Latour, B., 2008. 'What is the style of matters of concern?'. Spinoza Lectures at the University of Amsterdam, 2005. Amsterdam: Van Gorcum. Available from www.bruno-latour.fr/sites/default/files/97-SPINOZA-GB.pdf.

Latour, B., 2010. 'Coming out as a philosopher'. *Social Studies of Science*, vol. 40, no. 4, pp. 599–608.

Latour, B., 2011. 'Reflections on Etienne Souriau's *Les différents modes d'existence*'. In: G. Harman, L. Bryant, and N. Srnicek eds., *The Speculative Turn: Continental Materialism and Realism.* Melbourne: Re.press, pp. 304–333.

Latour, B., 2013a. *An Inquiry Into Modes of Existence: An Anthropology of the Moderns.* Cambridge, MA: Harvard University Press.

Latour, B., 2013b. *Rejoicing Or the Torments of Religious Speech.* Cambridge and Malden, MA: Polity.

Latour, B., December 2014. 'Anthropology at the time of the anthropocene—A personal view of what is to be studied'. Distinguished Lecture, American Association of Anthropologists. Washington. Available from www.bruno-latour.fr/sites/default/files/139-AAA-Washington.pdf.

Law, J., 2008. 'Actor-network theory and material semiotics'. In: Bryan S. Turner ed., *The New Blackwell Companion to Social Theory.* Oxford: Blackwell, pp. 141–158.

Law, J., 2011. 'What's wrong with a one-world world?'. Paper presented to the Center for the Humanities, Wesleyan University, Middletown, Connecticut on 19th September, 2011. Available from www.heterogeneities.net/publications/Law2011 WhatsWrongWithAOneWorldWorld.pdf.

MacIntyre, A., 1985. *After Virtue: A Study in Moral Theory.* London: Duckworth.

MacIntyre, A., 1988. *Whose Justice? Which Rationality?* London: Duckworth.

Mannion, G. and I'Anson, J., 2004. 'Beyond the disneyesque: Children's participation, spatiality and adult-child relations'. *Childhood*, vol. 11, no. 3, pp. 303–318.

Masschelein, J. 2010. 'The idea of critical e-ducational research: e-ducating the gaze and inviting to go walking'. In: I. Gurzeev (Ed.). *The possibility/impossibility of a new critical language in education.* Rotterdam: Sense, pp. 275–291.

May, T., 2005. *Gilles Deleuze: An Introduction.* Cambridge: Cambridge University Press.

McGushin, E.F., 2007. *Foucault's Askêsis: An Introduction to the Philosophical Life.* Evanston, IL: Northwestern University Press.

Myers, M. and Harris, D., 2004. 'Way from home'. *On the Page*, vol. 9, no. 2, pp. 90–92.

Osberg, D. and Biesta, G., 2010. *Complexity Theory and the Politics of Education.* Rotterdam: Sense.

Paavola, S. and Hakkarainen, K., 2005. 'The knowledge creation metaphor—An emergent epistemological approach to learning'. *Science and Education*, vol. 14, no. 6, pp. 535–557.

Rabinow, P. and Bennett, G., 2007. 'The work of equipment: 3 Modes'. *Anthropology of the Contemporary Research Collaboratory (ARC) Working Paper*, No. 10, University of Berkeley. Available from http://anthropos-lab.net/wp/publications/2007/08/workingpaperno10.pdf.

Royal Anthropological Institute, n.d. 'Discover anthropology—Teaching resources'. Available from www.discoveranthropology.org.uk/for-teachers/teaching-resources.html.

Scrima, A., 2016 [1952]. *Apophatic Anthropology*. Piscataway, N.J.: Gorgias Press.

Sfard, A., 1998. 'On two metaphors for learning and the dangers of choosing just one'. *Educational Researcher*, vol. 27, no. 2, pp. 4–13.

Skeie, G., Everington, J., Avest, I. and Miedema, S., 2013. *Exploring Context in Religious Education Research: Empirical, Methodological and Theoretical Perspectives*. Berlin: Waxmann.

Smart, N., 1969. New York: Charles Scribner's Sons. *The Religious Experience of Mankind*. 1971 ed. Glasgow: Fontana.

Sørensen, E., 2011. *The Materiality of Learning: Technology and Knowledge in Educational Practice*. Cambridge: Cambridge University Press.

Souriau, E., 2015. *The Different Modes of Existence*. Trans. E. Beranek and T. Howles. Minneapolis, MN: Univocal Publishing, Minnesota University Press.

Stengers, I., 1997. *Power and Invention: Situating Science*. Minneapolis, MN: University of Minnesota Press.

Stengers, I., 2005. 'Introductory notes on an ecology of practices'. *Cultural Studies Review*, vol. 11, no. 1, pp. 183–196.

Stengers, I., 2014. *Thinking With Whitehead: A Free and Wild Creation of Concepts*. Cambridge, MA and London: Harvard University Press.

Stewart, F., 2016. 'Blurring the educational lines? Material religion in the undergraduate classroom'. *Lines in Sand: Borders, Conflicts and Transitions*. Conference of the International Society for Religion, Literature and Culture. Paper given on 9th September 2016, University of Glasgow.

Strathern, M., 2014. 'Reading relations backwards'. *Journal of the Royal Anthropological Institute*, vol. 20, no. 1, pp. 3–19.

Strhan, A., 2010. 'A RE otherwise? An examination and proposed interruption of current British practice'. *Journal of Philosophy of Education*, vol. 44, no. 1, pp. 23–44.

Strhan, A., 2012. 'Latour, prepositions and the instauration of secularism'. *Political theology*, vol. 13, no. 2, pp. 200–216.

Thrift, N., 2008. *Non-Representational Theory: Space, Politics, Affect*. London and New York: Routledge.

Tisdall, E.K.M. and Punch, S., 2012. 'Not so "new"? Looking critically at childhood studies'. *Children's Geographies*, vol. 10, no. 3, pp. 249–264.

Valentin, K. and Meinert, L., 2009. 'The adult North and the young South: Reflections on the civilizing mission of children's rights'. *Anthropology Today*, vol. 25, no. 3, pp. 23–28.

Vansieleghem, N., 2011. 'Philosophy with children as an exercise in *Parrhesia*: An account of a philosophical experiment with children in Cambodia'. *Journal of Philosophy of Education*, vol. 45, no. 2, pp. 321–337.

162 Remediation—Beyond Indifference?

Vygotsky, L., 1978 [1933]. *Mind in Society: The Development of Higher Psychological Processes*. M. Cole, V. John-Steiner, S. Scribner and E. Souberman eds. Cambridge, MA: Harvard University Press.

Whatmore, S., 2003. 'Generating materials'. In: M. Pryke, G. Rose and S. Whatmore eds., *Using Social Theory: Thinking Through Research*. London: Sage, pp. 89–104.

Whitehead, A.N., 1920. *The Concept of Nature*. Cambridge: Cambridge University Press.

Young, J.O. and Brunk, C.G., 2012. *The Ethics of Cultural Appropriation*. Oxford: Wiley-Blackwell.

7 Teasing Out the Cross-Cutting Themes

This study has aimed to take a critical and fresh look at the area of RE across university, school and college sectors and at the prevailing state of play in these spaces. We have argued that existing practices produce indifference on account of the detachment, abstraction and lack of connection to people's lived experiences. In response to this, we have tried to identify a number of different lines of thinking which afford new approaches that we hope could help revitalise interest in this area. Such new lines of thinking depart from current assumptions in a number of respects. These involve reworking the grammar of becoming educated in RE in ways that have far-reaching epistemological, ontological and ethical consequences.

Firstly, we have given consideration to the educational in the sense of wanting to encourage what is transformative; those ideas, desires, perceptions, capacities, joys and skills that can be drawn out to develop or reveal something new and creative. Crucially, we contend, these are produced in and through engaging forms and types of difference, mediated through the widest possible range of knowledge practices. Such an openness to difference involves articulating new *conceptual personae* that better represent this given the significance of metaphors as regards styles of reasoning, and in Chapter Four, this was explored in relation to greater sensitivity to questions of gender. So being educational is about seeking to sustain and also actively to expand the kind of interdisciplinarity that was especially associated with approaches to RE advocated by Ninian Smart (1973). This, we contend, can only be achieved through becoming increasingly open to sense-making in different registers, deliberately courting difference (Lather and Smithies, 1997; Lather, 2007; 2010), seeking out the unfamiliar and being willing to remain unsettled (Braidotti, 2002). Such an orientation is, in other words, ready for the incoming of the new rather than simply a reiteration of, and alignment with, the already known. And so this is characterised by an openness and a resistance to practices that close things down into conveniently measurable forms that in turn sustain exclusionary zones. What we propose instead is the kind of edgework (Brown, 2005) that favours practising counterpoint as opposed to taking up positions that drown out other voices. In consequence, we have also tried to avoid spending too much time shouting

164 Remediation—Beyond Indifference?

down the opposition, using critical practices instead to facilitate, open up and make possible the perception of new or different perspectives so feminist theory, philosophy and dreams can be tools to transform and enlarge the notions of literacy that have emerged more recently within the professional field of RE, as explored in Part Two.

Of course, we have given over some time and space to diagnostic analysis, highlighting a tendency to compartmentalise RE so that practices under this heading in schools and colleges and even university departments of professional education sometimes seem only tangentially linked to the richness of resources still apparent within the academy. We have noted a failure of communication between these different RE contexts in contrast with the situation at the time of Ninian Smart's exciting innovations in the 1960s and 70s. His was an intellectual quest that, in foregrounding a radical understanding of experience that was in part drawn from phenomenology (see Chapter One), enabled a much broader educational focus than had hitherto been the case. Its impact—based on appropriation, adaptation and travel across educational levels—was hugely significant and rejuvenating, 'stealing other disciplines' most interesting questions', as Smart (1973) once put it and revealing a vision of RE as a kind of educational hub that drew purposefully on creative and dynamic knowledge practices so as to set up a wide variety of encounters with difference. And, in terms of the resources reviewed in this book, the approach also has potential affinities with a number of more recent trends within the academy. Spinoza's ethological approach, as taken up by Deleuze, for example, shares a radical openness to what actually happens in experience, whilst the process-oriented work of Whitehead, mediated through the writings of Latour, Stengers and Butler (2012), to name but a few, also chimes with new work on socio-material orientations (Law, 2009; Bennett, 2010; Fenwick and Landri, 2014).

However, much of the excitement of the original encounter between different institutional levels of RE that characterised the work of Smart has been lost through its routine translation in schools into formal educational structures which, over time, have been shown to be significantly limited, if not intellectually stifling. If the initiating dialogue between educational sectors might be characterised as incorporating a form of intellectual wayfaring (Ingold, 2011), it must be said that the interaction between professionals at all levels seems to have gotten stuck at the point of its first iteration. The trope of neutrality worked in the 1960s and 70s as an entirely legitimate means of addressing the particular challenges of the confessional model that had preceded it and had wider implications for both the academy and the population at large at a time of increasing encounter with difference through the impact of colonial immigration and the expansion of global trade, travel and communication. Since this time, there has been little sense of any ongoing work in terms of a tradition of inquiry (MacIntyre, 1984; 1988) that would have allowed this discussion to move beyond its initial terms in order sufficiently to register and engage with changes in the academy as well as in relation to broader currents of technological, demographic, social and

Teasing Out the Cross-Cutting Themes 165

philosophical concern. Instead, RE pedagogy and educational discourse more broadly has been restricted to delivering a substantially unaltered programme as effectively as it can, given the crisis of plausibility which we have already outlined in Part One. The kinds of re-thinking we envisage here involve a radical reshaping of the discourse that is drawn upon in thinking educationally, as in the substitution of diffraction for the metaphor of neutrality that so haunts the present settlement.

Work on instituting a tradition of inquiry might have helped address the sense, for example, in which RE and schools more generally still appear aligned with the values, systematicity and coherence of the modernist project (Toulmin, 1993; I'Anson, 2004). This aimed towards a single definition or account for everything in spite of a context of fragmentation, increasingly revealed through the work of theorists. Latour (1993) has even claimed that 'we have never been modern'; indeed, the unity and consistencies of perspective that inform modernity as a project are shown to be illusory once they are investigated empirically (Vries, 2016). Such an investigation suggests multiple fields of practice (such as law, religion, science etc.) characterised by discontinuous 'modes of existence' (Latour, 2013), all of which entail their own distinctive felicity conditions and language. It could be argued that schools have been implicated in sustaining the modernist illusion (Hartley, 2000), something that might have been avoided had ongoing communications between schools and universities been instituted more effectively; mechanisms have not been developed by either schools or universities to maintain ongoing dialogue and exchange beyond the terms of the settlement that had been achieved.

In present circumstances, without a pressing sense of a tradition of dialogue, there is little impetus for RE in schools—still framed by its originating tropes, methodologies and practices from the 60s and 70s (that continue to be cemented into place by current educational policy objectives)—to open itself up to a new set of contemporary problematics. A tradition of inquiry between the sectors might also have addressed the possibilities and risks of reclaiming the legacy of Smart for new educational purposes through proposing a radical return to experience, as discussed in Chapter Six. A radically empirical understanding of experience focuses on what is given rather than a somewhat arbitrary predetermined ordering which closes off significant aspects in advance. An open-ended empirical approach offers an opportunity to re-engage with educational questions in RE spaces beyond the terms of the current settlement.

Our view is that there is a need to acknowledge experiential registers so that they are not dismissed as 'just subjective' but are recognised as important determinants of value and sense-making, since they, too, are given in experience as much as anything else (see the discussion of Whitehead's development of James's radical empiricism in Chapter Six). A tradition of inquiry would increase awareness of the temptation to produce essentialised accounts from limited perspectives and of the importance of critique addressed to this complex subject (Mohanty, 1992; Taylor, 1998). What we

166 *Remediation—Beyond Indifference?*

hope to offer, then, is an invitation and encouragement to initiate such an ongoing tradition of inquiry. This would stage a serious conversation with a series of contemporary problematics that might include, for example, the incommensurability of ontologies, the unevenness of playing fields and the political challenges of sharing a planet. Such problematics might also include the complexities of translation, the issue of 'religion' itself as a power-category (Fitzgerald, 2015) and the challenges of negotiation, continuing, in other words, to steal all the best questions—but for educational purposes. Our examples of working with different theoretical styles and orientations should be seen in this light as attempts to encourage others towards new articulations of a field of inquiry characterised by theoretical openness and imaginative as well as pedagogic generosity.

To this end, we have tentatively contributed our heuristic (Chapter Six) to promote ongoing dialogue and new thinking comprising three inter-related elements: the critical, the ethical and the experimental. Linked to a radically empirical methodology, it is an invitation to think again in relation to a series of different traditions and to practice in new terms, which we suggest come under the rubric of becoming ethnographer. The educational aim of becoming ethnographer through a more radical turn to the material and empirical acknowledges the reality of the kind of negotiations that students make and to which the project of RE as a whole could be addressed as a process of refining these practices. So, for example, a student who is learning about Christianity from the perspective of becoming ethnographer will engage not only with the richness of texts but also (critically, experimentally and with due respect to the variance of situated practice) with people who claim to be Christians but whose accounts and behaviours will be divergent and frequently contradictory. In other words, this points towards the educational consequences of what we are suggesting for students at all levels (including our colleagues and ourselves) in terms of opening up a broader existential arena that presents new opportunities for engagements, encounters and negotiations.

The prospect of a new relationship between schools and higher education augurs far-reaching change both as regards knowledge practices and the kinds of thematics that are taken as constitutive of educational inquiry within this field. In other words, engaging in ways that are simultaneously, critical, experimental and ethical will have implications as regards both the substance and methodology of inquiry. For as we have argued above (Chapter Three), a relational and embodied perspective questions the tendency within RE to focus largely upon topics that involve death and the cessation of life over a concern with broader issues of natality: the coming into life and the conditions within which beings can thrive (e.g., Jantzen, 1998; Irigaray, 2004) or bring new projects to birth (Jasper, 2012). Likewise, a critical investigation of the *conceptual personae* that currently dominate ways of making sense might, in turn, give way to more relationally grounded metaphors that open pathways towards different priorities, such as a re-orientation of gendered hierarchies (Chapter Four).

Teasing Out the Cross-Cutting Themes 167

Such a re-thinking and re-orientation would also be necessary if that dialogue were to take up and engage with the kinds of ontological issues towards which a relational approach gestures. So, for example, a move beyond the bi-furcation of reality that was a key insight of Whitehead's (1920) work (Chapter Six) questions the manner in which inquiry is framed in terms of primary and secondary qualities in advance of analysis in ways that import an arbitrary privilege to 'nature' over 'cultural' renderings of sense. Moving beyond this framing potentially opens up inquiry within RE to engage new ecological perspectives that are not caught in this trap and that concern urgent issues of our time (Latour, 2015). And this also re-orientates analysis away from an exclusive concern with the past—with what has already come to pass and the ways in which this has been traced—to a new concern with that which might come to be and towards which the matters of concern engaged within the classroom might anticipate. This is where another ontological issue that we have considered touches down in ways that have immediate and significant consequence. For this is to make a distinction between an *actual* ontology that is concerned with the ways in which reality has in fact been determined and a *virtual* ontology that is concerned with the field of possibilities that might conceivably come to pass. Such a distinction makes it possible to overcome the excessive deference given within educational thinking to what has already been achieved (the actual) over what might become possible.

Within the classroom, such an ontological re-orientation might issue in both present- and future-oriented projects that encourage students to imagine different scenarios that involve different relational configurations (Harvey, 2006). Of course, the very possibility of such an imagining otherwise is fundamentally linked with the development of a range of critical literacies that might enable students to have a language with which to 'read' current situations and, through critical analysis, entertain other ways forward that instantiate different values. We have sought to draw attention to this particular gathering of practices and imaginative capacities under the rubric of a becoming ethnographer (Chapter Six). On this basis, it then becomes possible to reflect upon ways in which reality is 'mapped into knowledge' (Stengers, 1997)—on the one hand, becoming critical of ways in which metaphors privilege certain orientations over others whilst, on the other, promoting orientations that open up fresh ways of thinking, such as the significance of dreams (Chapter Five).

The development of our heuristic in terms of becoming experimental, becoming critical and becoming ethical has also prompted us to consider whether our diagnosis and remediation have implications for educational fields beyond that delimited by the subject RE. Calling for an ongoing critical approach gestures towards a broader educational agenda or theory. Certainly, we are not the first or only ones to point towards the compartmentalised condition of subjects or disciplines in schools (Chapter Two). Our own experience—of discussing with colleagues, students, teachers and

168 *Remediation—Beyond Indifference?*

engaging with other stakeholders within RE[1]—tells us that professionals and students commonly have to make considerable and sometimes unproductive adjustments when they step out of one compartment into another (in whichever direction) (I'Anson and Jasper, 2011), nor is the lack of connection between subjects in schools and the academy something that is confined to RE as a distinct subject area.[2] This would suggest that the themes of this book have broader implications beyond this particular subject area. For example, it could be said that the very term 'religion' is in fact one part of the problem insofar as this leads to forms of categorisation that marginalise particular kinds of experience.

So, how might we move beyond the present situation? Setting up an ongoing tradition of inquiry might enable both the articulation of new translations of practice and the construction of new agenda. Instituting such a dialogue across different levels of education might go some way towards moving beyond the harsh-seeming judgment that such translations are as inevitable as they are invariably negative. Thus, one of the key points at issue in our discussion of the school examination system (in Chapter Two) is that what tends to make this process really problematic is its invisibility: when we fail to notice all the processes and stages that actually intervene (Latour, 2013) and pay insufficient attention to virtual or potential resolutions (Deleuze, 1988). More positively, the emphasis on the contextual and relational that characterises more recent approaches within the academy is precisely a form of identifying some of the translations that might be produced, impacting on all our ongoing agenda and issuing in all kinds of new settlements. Here, especially, a commitment to approaches that are at once experimental, critical and ethical is more likely to promote a greater inclusivity and inventiveness. Additionally, of course, through this process, some new insight through greater generality is gained. Thus, it is not a simple choice between framings that are oriented to relationality or greater universality, as the discussion of 'transcendence incarnate' above (Chapter Four) indicates.

Another cross-cutting theme within the book that initiates discussion is metaphor (that is etymologically linked to translation and through its meaning to bridging). The critical refraction, redeployment or deliberate variation in metaphors is a tool we use and in whose skilful (and playful?) use we seek to encourage students to engage difference and to negotiate their way between levels and theories through a range of knowledge practices. The metaphorical tropes that we have considered act as key alternatives to that of neutrality, something to which we—in many ways—remain so resolutely attached, in spite of the many difficulties it raises. We suggest the conscious critical employment of different metaphors, such as, for example, diffraction, bridging, translation, becoming undone and re-imagining, could also help us acknowledge how engaging with the differences these metaphorical alternatives afford, affect us and—in educational terms—helps draw us out to facilitate transformations and change.

Given the strongly theoretical nature of the book as a whole, we have to admit that perhaps our greatest hope is that we can encourage more theoretical engagement; picking up the theory question, we want readers to recognise its resourcefulness for new imaginary thinking rather than reiterating agendas that have gone before. Although this may be unfamiliar territory for some practitioners, the aim is also to empower them to engage—and perhaps experiment with—new styles of reasoning rather than simply experimenting with pedagogy, that is, thinking through the rationale for the subject area which is usually assumed to be settled. Our research agenda would consider ways in which the subject is structured first and then address forms of pedagogy that are in accordance with that, rather than the other way around.

In this book, we have largely focused on some of the theories that might be drawn upon to sustain a new openness to difference in educational settings. We are also aware of how this opens up possibilities as regards research into the new gatherings of concepts, tropes, people, relational configurations, materials and objects collectively produced to express forms of difference. We also recognise, too, that this gestures towards a new research agenda in terms of mapping how such assemblages work in order to produce forms of difference.

In Conclusion

The present settlement in RE was the outcome of a major re-thinking about the purpose of the subject and its scope, and it was enormously influential in the UK and in a wide variety of international educational contexts. Under the sign of neutrality, a new approach to the subject area was inaugurated that offered a response to pressing issues of the times, one that had both an academic rationale and educational justification in its move beyond limited forms of confessionalism. The new approach involved far-reaching practices of translation that aligned RE with styles of reasoning and the distinctive concerns of modernity. Indeed, so successful was this translation that it was not considered necessary to inaugurate mechanisms through which that settlement might be reviewed, re-interpreted or adapted in the light of changing circumstances through any kind of on-going dialogue between the various stakeholders, educational and otherwise.

Arguably, the modernity that this approach anticipated was an illusion that could not come to pass (Latour, 1993), and the cultural, academic and policy contexts have also changed in the intervening years in ways that could not have been predicted. This has led to a situation in which, in our view, there is a serious question as to whether RE in its present form is fit for purpose. By offering a distinctive historical and spatial analysis of the heterogeneous assemblage of various practices, concepts and tropes that are, today, gathered under the name of RE, we have sought to provide some insight into how this subject developed the contours that it did. Such insight is

170 *Remediation—Beyond Indifference?*

insufficient if it does not lead to a re-thinking and re-imagining beyond these terms, however. We have therefore also offered a number of trajectories that might conceivably inform new ways of imagining RE. Certainly, these are speculative, but they are put forward in the hope that they might encourage researchers, practitioners and policy makers to return to the drawing board and to provide them with some new theoretical and conceptual resources that could help initiate that new discussion.

We have also sought to articulate ways in which an ongoing educational dialogue might be instituted that accords greater value to difference, relationality and materiality—whilst, of course, acknowledging the difficult kinds of ontological work that this will necessarily entail. Our contribution to such a way forward is to offer the educational heuristic in terms of critical, ethical and experimental elements, which we have articulated in the book, in conversation with a wide range of theoretical resources that include empirical philosophy, feminist theorising and STS, amongst others. This heuristic also affords and encourages engagement with conceptual resources and lexicons that derive from non-Western traditions of inquiry, and we offer some illustrations as to what this might mean in practice.

The implications of such a re-imagining are far-reaching—for it not only draws upon a wide range of theoretical traditions, but also impacts on the kinds of knowledge practices that students undertake. Here, under the rubric of becoming ethnographer, we have explored some of the consequences of such a new orientation for the class or seminar room, where we envisage students becoming equipped with new capacities for knowledge-creation: enabling them to think critically and sympathetically about situations, but also to envisage alternative relational possibilities to enable them to navigate and negotiate through the complex and challenging global contexts of the twenty-first century. These proposals are put forward in the hope that they may re-vitalise discussion about the future of RE; we remain hopeful for that future and the potentialities of the subject area beyond indifference.

Notes

1. We gratefully acknowledge the support of the Carnegie Trust in supporting our 2014 research project 'Religious and Cultural Difference in Educational Spaces: Engaging with Stakeholders' in this regard.
2. The acknowledgement of a gap between school and university contexts in relation to knowledge practices is not just something that is characteristic of RE, but is found in other subject areas, too. In view of this, the University of Stirling Initial Teacher Education programme introduced a new course that focuses specifically upon students developing a unit of work that takes a new thematic, methodology or framing that students have encountered at university and then translates this into a project for a particular stage in school: for example, in RE, introducing a unit of work for senior pupils on the ethics of cultural appropriation, raising awareness of this issue in relation to young peoples' consumption of music, fashion etc. Another project focused upon the Western invention of 'Hinduism', again, for pupils studying in the upper stages of the secondary school. Colonial understandings and

Teasing Out the Cross-Cutting Themes 171

representations of India, and whether the category of 'religion' is appropriate to such a cultural context, were also proposed as ways of introducing notions of ethnographic reflexivity and intersectionality. Through such means, students gained some initial experience of the kinds of work involved in introducing more critical, ethnographical approaches that problematised Western categories and tendencies towards generalised statements. Students are also encouraged to think through how the unit of work would be structured in practice and to articulate appropriate pedagogical approaches, including the kinds of assessment envisaged.

Bibliography

Bennett, J., 2010. *Vibrant Matter: A Political Ecology of Things*. Durham, NC: Duke University Press.

Braidotti, R., 2002. *Metamorphoses: Towards a Materialist Theory of Becoming*. Cambridge and Malden, MA: Polity Press.

Brown, W., 2005. *Edgework: Critical Essays on Knowledge and Politics*. Princeton and Oxford: Princeton University Press.

Butler, J., 2012. 'On this occasion'. In: R. Faber, M. Halewood and D. Lin eds., *Butler on Whitehead: On the Occasion*. Lanham: Lexington Books, pp. 3–18.

Deleuze, G., 1988. *Bergsonism*. 1991 ed. New York: Zone Books.

Fenwick, T. and Landri, P., eds., 2014. *Materialities, Textures and Pedagogies*. London and New York: Routledge.

Fitzgerald, T., 2015. 'Critical religion and critical research on religion: Religion and politics as modern fictions'. *Critical Research on Religion*, vol. 3, no. 3, pp. 303–319.

Hartley, D., 2000. 'Shoring up the pillars of modernity: Teacher education and the quest for certainty'. *Internationl Studies in the sociology of Education*, vol. 10, no. 3, pp. 243–260.

Harvey, D., 2006. 'The right to the city'. In: R. Scholar ed., *Divided Cities*. Oxford and New York: Oxford University Press, pp. 83–103.

I'Anson, J., 2004. 'Mapping the subject: Student teachers, location and the understanding of religion'. *British Journal of Religious Studies*, vol. 26, no. 1, pp. 41–56.

I'Anson, J. and Jasper, A., 2011. '"Religion" in educational spaces: Knowing, knowing well, and knowing differently'. *Arts and Humanities in Higher Education*, vol. 10, no. 3, pp. 295–314.

Ingold, T., 2011. *Being Alive: Essays on Movement, Knowledge and Description*. London and New York: Routledge.

Irigaray, L. 2004. *Key Writings*. London and New York: Continuum.

Jantzen, G. M. 1998. *Becoming Divine: Towards a Feminist Philosophy of Religion*. Manchester: Manchester University Press.

Jasper, A., 2012. *Because of Beauvoir: Christianity and the Cultivation of Female Genius*. Waco, TX: Baylor University Press.

Keller, C., 2008. *On the Mystery: Discerning Divinity in Process*. Minneapolis, MI: Fortress Press.

Lather, P., 2007. *Getting Lost: Feminist Efforts Towards a Double(d) Science*. New York: SUNY.

Lather, P., 2010. *Engaging Science: Policy From the Side of the Messy*. New York, Washington, DC, Baltimore, Bern, Frankfurt am Main, Berlin, Brussels, Vienna, and Oxford: Peter Lang.

172 *Remediation—Beyond Indifference?*

Lather, P. and Smithies, C., 1997. *Troubling the Angels: Women Living With HIV/ AIDS*. Boulder, CO: Westview Press.

Latour, B., 1993. *We Have Never Been Modern*. Cambridge, MA: Harvard University Press.

Latour, B., 2013. *An Inquiry Into Modes of Existence: An Anthropology of the Modern*. Cambridge, MA: Harvard University Press.

Latour, B., 2015. 'Telling friends from foes in the time of the anthropocene'. In: C. Hamilton, C. Bonneuil and F. Gemenne eds., *The Anthropocene and the Global Environment Crisis—Rethinking Modernity in a New Epoch*. London: Routledge, pp. 145–155.

Law, J., version of 29 December 2009. 'Collateral realities'. Available from www. heterogeneities.net/publications/Law2009CollateralRealities.pdf.

MacIntyre, A., 1984. *After Virtue: A Study in Moral Theory*. Notre Dame: University of Notre Dame Press.

MacIntyre, A., 1988. *Whose Justice? Which Rationality?* London: Duckworth.

Mohanty, C.T., 1992. 'Feminist encounters: Locating the politics of experience'. In: M. Barrett and A. Phillips eds., *Destablilizing Theory: Contemporary Feminist Debates* Stanford, CA: Stanford University Press. pp. 74–92.

Smart, N., 1973. *The Science of Religion and the sociology of Knowledge*. Princeton, NJ: University of Princeton Press.

Stengers, I. 1997. *Power and Invention: Situating Science*. Minneapolis, MN: University of Minnesota Press.

Taylor, M.C., ed., 1998, *Critical Terms for Religious Studies*. Chicago and London: University of Chicago Press.

Toulmin, S., 1993. *Cosmopolis: The Hidden Agenda of Modernity*. Chicago: University of Chicago Press.

Vries, G. de, 2016. *Bruno Latour*. Cambridge and Malden, MA: Polity Press.

Whitehead, A. N., 1920. *The Concept of Nature*, Cambridge: Cambridge University Press.

Index

Abell, S. K. 34
Actor Network Theory (ANT) 73
Acts, book of 129
Agabus 129
Al-Ghazālī 115, 119, 120, 126, 127, 128, 129
Alderson, R. 13
Allwright, D. 156
Althaus-Reid, M. 80
Anderson, B. 62
Anderson, E. 77
Anderson, P. S. 16, 67, 78–9, 81–8, 98
Anjum, O. 116
anthropocene era, the 141
anthropology of Islam 115–32; of the good 1
apophatic 148
Aquinas, Thomas 119
Arab Spring, the 121
Arendt, H. 32
Armour, E. T. 61
Asad, T. 117–21, 128
askêsis 70, 151–2
assemblage theory 139, 142, 169
Aupers, S. 13

Balberg, M. 152
Barad, K. 59, 69, 80, 135
Barnes, L. P. 14
Barry, A. 155
Battersby, C. 79
Baumfield, V. 143
Beattie, T. 96
Beauvoir, S. de 79, 85–8; *Memoirs of a Dutiful Daughter* (1958) 85
becoming ethnographer 1, 153–4, 167, 170; becoming undone 52, 81, 100, 111, 103, 108, 168
belief 17, 21, 23, 31, 40–3, 47–9, 50, 53, 60, 63–4, 78, 97, 117, 123, 126, 135–6, 137

Benjamin, S. 4
Bennett, G. 145
Bennett, J. 141, 164
Berger, P. L. 23–4, 95
Bergson, H. L. 149
Bertrand, M. 66
Besley, T. 98
Bhabha, H. 33
Bhugra, D. 123, 124
Bhui, K. 123, 124
Biesta, G. 21, 24, 87–8, 107, 116, 137, 149
Bilge, S. 79
Bloomer, M. 19
Boddy, J. 128
body, becoming queer masculine 104–6; disciplining 83; the lived 81–2, 85–7
Borges, J. L. 66
Bourdieu, P. 155
Bowker, J. W. 119
bracketing (*epochē*) 4, 35–9, 139, 141
Braidotti, R. 78, 90, 94, 99, 100, 103, 141, 150, 163
Brogan, M. 73
Brooks, R. 20
Brown, A. 14
Brown, C. G. 14
Brown, R. 2, 20
Brown, W. 78, 148, 163
Bruce, S. 13
Bruher, J. 144
Brunk, C. G. 156
Buddhism 46, 64, 76
Bush, J. A. 116
Butler, J. 16, 39, 67, 73, 78, 100–1, 103, 104, 107, 164

Caldwell, S. 46
Callan, A. 123
capabilities 82–5
Caputo, J. D. 37, 60, 148

174 Index

Carasso, H. 2, 20
care of the self 70, 96, 154
Carmichael, P. 42
Carrette, J. 2, 94, 95, 138, 139, 156
Carter, S. A. 77
Cartesian binary 85, 96
Certeau, M. de 16, 22, 33, 47, 48, 53, 154
Chakrabarty, D. 60
Chanter, T. 77
children's rights education 136
Christ, C. 78, 80, 98, 100
Christianity 14–15, 22, 47, 53, 63, 79,
 81, 88, 96, 100, 119, 153–4, 166
Church, R. 73
Clough, M. 96
Collini, S. 2, 20
complexity reduction 117, 149
conatus 67
conceptual personae 57, 78, 94, 108,
 138, 163, 166
confessionalism 15, 31, 169
Conroy, J. 14–16, 39, 52, 143
Cope, P. 34
counterpoint 148
Crang, M. 2, 47, 120, 135
Crenshaw, K. 16, 79
critique (Latour) 124, 147, 149, 165
Cunningham, A. 17
curriculum 14, 33, 44–5, 49–51, 144;
 Curriculum for Excellence (Scotland)
 23, 87, 97–8
Cush, D. 143–4

Daly Goggin, M. 77
Daly, M. 83–4, 102
Davies, B. 80, 150
Dawkins, R. 13
Defoe, D. 53; *Robinson Crusoe* 45
Dekoven, M. 5
DeLanda, M. 157
Deleuze, G. 23, 65, 67–8, 73, 87, 100,
 142, 149–50, 156–7, 164, 168
Dennett, D. C. 13
Dervin, F. 4
diagnosis (of present situation in RE
 through time) 1, 11–28, 29–30, 57,
 123, 136, 143, 145, 152, 167
difference 1, 3, 5, 15, 19–20, 22, 24,
 30–1, 33, 41, 51–2, 57, 59–60, 63,
 65, 68–9, 71–3, 78–81, 85, 88, 91,
 93–5, 100, 103–7, 115–16, 127, 133,
 135, 136–9, 148, 151, 163–4, 168–70
diffraction 59, 69–70, 80–1, 135, 165

dihlīz 115, 120, 126–7, 128–9
Dines, G. 102
disconcertment 38, 89–91, 93
discourse of religion 32–5, 78, 146, 157
doing ontics: *hadīth nafsī* 122; *hulm*
 122; in the Islamic tradition 121–2;
 in relation to dreams 3, 120–122,
 128, 129, 164, 167; in relation to
 Islam 126; in relation to Nigerian
 classroom 88–9; *ru'yā* 122
dreams as a matter of concern 120
Dressler, M. 34
Duffy, S. 65

Eddo-Lodge, R. 82
edgework 163
Edgoose, J. 136
Education 1, 14, 21–2, 24, 31, 33, 36,
 38–9, 41–45, 49, 51–2, 59, 62, 65, 67,
 72, 77, 82–3, 87, 89–92, 95, 99–100,
 102–3, 105–6, 108, 123, 133, 135–9,
 142, 145, 151–4, 163, 167, 169; Act
 of 1944 13, 96; (Scotland) Act of
 1945 13, 96; (Scotland) Act 1980 13;
 different sectors 11–2, 19, 23, 79,
 143–4, 164, 168; heuristic 2–3, 57,
 143, 170; matter of concern 4, 30,
 34; purposes of 29, 88, 166; Reform
 Act (England & Wales) 1988 13, 17,
 97; relationship with religion 32,
 78; research 20; revolutionary 100;
 teacher 5, 11–12, 167–8, 170
Edwards, R. 33, 42, 136
Eliade, M. 5
El-Zein, A. H. 117
embodiment 3, 57, 60, 81–2, 84, 86–7,
 96, 103–7, 120, 137
Equalities Act, 2010 83
Erricker, C. 96, 97, 100
Erricker, J. 96, 97, 100
ethics 122, 140, 151–2, 156, 170;
 Spinoza's 65–8
ethnography 18, 40, 133, 139, 153–5,
 166–7, 170–1
ethology 68
European Qualifications Framework
 (EQF) 44, 45, 53
Eve 85, 86, 87, 98, 99; sculpture by
 Gislebert 85–6
examination 11, 14, 17, 29, 38, 43–5,
 47–2, 136–7, 149, 168
Examined Life (Butler, J. and Taylor S.,
 2008) 107

experimental 1–4, 11, 17, 19, 68, 72, 78, 80, 90, 94, 98, 133, 141, 144–5, 148–52, 154, 156, 166, 167–70

Fanon, F. 62
Faubion, J. D. 151–2
felicity conditions 36–7, 39, 127, 165
feminist 72, 96, 98, 107; body 82; locational 81, 90; theology 80, 83, 102; theory/philosophy 1–3, 16, 20, 32, 57, 60, 64–5, 77–9, 91, 150, 170
Fenwick, T. 70, 136, 164
Fitzgerald, T. 13, 21–2, 49, 60, 78, 166
Flood, G. 31
Foucault, M. 3, 17, 23, 33, 59, 63, 70–1, 73, 96, 120, 146, 151–2, 154, 157
Fowkes Tobin, B. 77
Franke, W. 148
Fricker, M. 84, 86
Friedman, S. S. 81
Fuller, I. 52

Galileo, G. 140
Gardiner, M. 62
Gatens, M. 61, 65, 66, 73
Gearon, L. 36
Geertz, C. 116, 117
Gellner, E. 116, 117
gender 2–3, 57, 61, 63, 77–114, 146, 163, 166; dysphoria 103; essentialism 78
Gender Rebel (E. Epstein, 2006) 104
genealogy 29, 60, 138
generosity 108; pedagogics of 103–7, 166; politics of 73
genius 79; female 79, 88
Gilligan, A. 13
Gilsenan, M. 116
Gislebert 85, 86, 878
go-along together 89–93, 127
Good Samaritan, parable of 90, 94
Goodchild, P. 156
Gregory the Great 147; The Life St Benedict of Nursia 147
Grimmitt, M. 15, 17, 18
Guattari, F. 23, 87, 100, 149–50

Hacking, I. 2
Hadith (sayings of the Prophet) 118, 129
Hadot, P. 95
Hakkarainen, K. 150–1
Haltman, K. 69
Haraway, D. 59, 69
Harding, S. 16, 73

Hardt, M. 66
Harris, D. 155
Harrison, P. 68
Hartley, D. 165
Hartsock, N. C. M. 16
Harvey, D. 33, 153, 167
Heelas, P. 35, 122, 147
Henare, A. 69
Henderson, D. 148
Hersch, J. 85
heuristic 2–3, 12, 57, 133, 143–4, 156, 166–7, 170
higher education 1, 14, 22–3, 143–4, 153, 156, 166
higher examination – Religious, Moral and Philosophical Studies (RMPS) 44–5, 49
Hill Collins, P. 79
Hinduism 4, 46, 170
Hitchens, C. 13
Homer 38, 147
hooks, b. 82, 100
horizons of possibility 121, 145
Houtman, D. 13, 80
Hügel, F. von 157
human resources (HR) management 95
Hunter, I. 23
hypermasculinity 112

I'Anson, J. 2, 12, 15, 19–20, 23, 33–4, 38, 47, 52, 64, 68, 73, 93, 136, 143, 149, 153, 155–7, 165, 168
Ibn Hanbal, A. 119
Ibn Sīnā (Avicenna) 119
Ihde, D. 141
imaginary/imagination/imagining 1–4, 9, 30, 32, 35–7, 47, 51–2, 57, 59–68, 71–2, 77–81, 108, 115–16, 118–21, 126–8, 133, 135–6, 138, 140, 144–5, 150, 153, 156, 166–8, 170
indifference 4, 29–30, 51–2, 57, 77, 86, 94–5, 100, 133, 144, 147, 154, 163, 170
Ingold, T. 5, 63, 147, 164
interdisciplinarity 153, 155, 163
intersectional theory 78–9, 81, 171
intimate terrorism 79
Ipgrave, J. 18
Irigaray, L. 23, 32, 64, 88, 91–4, 99, 150
irrationality 78
Ishak, Y. 125, 127, 166
Isherwood, L. 82, 96, 98

176   *Index*

Islam 115–31; as discursive tradition 3, 115, 118–20
Islam anthropology of 115–29; as discursive tradition 117–9; as a matter of concern 116; possessed states in 115; 'world religions' approach to 115

Jackson, R. 15, 16, 18–19, 53, 154
James, A. 153
James, W. 138–41, 165
Jantzen, G. 32, 61, 64, 67, 96, 141, 150, 166
Jasper, A. 2, 12, 15, 19–20, 23, 32, 38, 47, 64, 78–9, 88, 93, 96, 108, 153, 156–7, 166, 168
Jesus 82, 90
Jewitt, C. 154
Jinn 116, 122–3, 125–7, 129; medical framings of 124; in relation to multiple ontologies 124
Johnson, M. 33, 79
Johnson P. C. 122, 124; as spirit possession 124
Judaism 22, 119; Rabbinic 152

Kant, I. 60, 146
Keller, C. 79, 146, 148, 150
Keller, M. 63, 122, 124
Kelly, L. 83
King, R. 94, 95, 156
King, U. 98
Kleinman, A. 123
Knight, S. 93
Knorr Cetina, K. 45, 48, 148
Knott, K. 33
knowledge, bi-furcation of 140–1, 167
Kress, G. 154
Kristensen, W. B. 5
Kristeva, J. 16, 79, 88
Kurttila, T. 63

Laing, A. 51
Lakoff, G. 33
Lambek, M. 127, 151
Land, R. 149
Landri, P. 164
Lather, P. 20, 163
Latour, B. 5–6, 18, 37–8, 40, 42, 78, 83, 86, 108, 123–4, 127, 138–9, 141, 147, 168–9
Law, J. 2, 19–20, 38, 47, 53, 63, 65, 69–70, 73, 77, 89, 136, 137, 157, 164–5, 167

learnification 24
Lederman, N. G. 34
Le Dœuff, M. 16, 61, 62, 77, 79, 85
Leeuw, G. van de 5
Lefebvre, H. 33
Leganger-Krogstad, H. 18
Lin, W-y. 2, 38, 65
lines of flight 105, 150
Lippy, C. H. 78
Littlewood, R. 123
livability 103, 106–7
Llewelyn, J. 73
Lloyd, G. 2, 16, 65–6, 73, 77
Lock, A. 122, 147
Locke, J. 61, 140
Long, C. H. 60
Lopez Jnr., D. S. 47, 63
Luke, Gospel of 90, 92, 94
Lyotard, J. 73

Ma Vie en Rose Berliner (1997) 103
MacArthur, E. 32
McCabe, R. 123, 124, 129
McCutcheon, R. T. 21, 35, 49
McFague, S. 80
McGettigan, A. 2, 20
McGushin, E. F. 71–2, 152
MacIntyre, A. 117–18, 146, 164
McIvor, J. 13
MacMurray, J. 62–3
Maimonides, M. 119
Mandair, A.-P.S. 34, 60
Mannheim, K. 24
Mannion, G. 155
mapping into knowledge 19, 69, 136–9, 142, 144–5, 149, 151, 153–4, 156
Marten, M. 20
Masefield, P. 14
Masschelein, J. 4, 30, 32, 155
Massey, D. 33, 36
matter of concern 3–4, 6, 18, 30, 34, 38–9, 51, 57, 69, 115–17, 120, 128, 135, 167
May, T. 138
Meinert, L. 136
Ménil, A. 63
Merleau-Ponty, M. 85
messiness 4, 20, 36, 43, 47, 89
metaphor 29, 33, 37, 42, 57, 59–64, 68, 71–3, 77–82, 84–8, 90–93, 100, 108, 119–20, 141, 148, 150–1, 163, 165–8
Millar Report, the 36
Mishnah (rabbinic legal texts) 152
Mishnah 152

Mittermaier, A. 120–2, 128–9
mode of existence 37, 127, 165
modern project 127; modernist 22, 115, 165
Mohanty, C. T. 79, 165
Mol, A. 41, 63, 65, 77
Monro, S. 77, 101
Moosa, E. 119, 120, 126
Morten, N. 83
Moumtaz, N. 118, 120, 128
Mu'tazila 119
Mubarak, H. 121
Müller, M. 5
multi-modal readings 24, 154
Myers, M. 155

natality 32, 52, 67, 166
National Association of Standing Advisory Councils on RE (NASACRE) 23
National Curriculum (England and Wales) 23
Natkin, R. 52
Negri, A. 67
Neighbourliness 88, 90–4
neutrality (methodological) 15–16, 29–31, 34–8, 41, 52, 59–62, 64, 69, 71, 73, 77–81, 108, 135–6, 140, 152, 156, 164, 168–9
Newman, E. 82
Nicolson, A. 38

Office for Standards in Education (Ofsted) 23
Ogilvy, K. C. 93
ontics, doing 65, 126–8
ontology 15, 31, 53, 126–7, 136–7, 142, 149; of the actual 146, 167; dragons 147; dreams 122; educational 144; multiple ontologies 125–6; of the virtual 141, 167
Osberg, D. 116, 149
other, the 5, 15, 17, 20, 38, 44, 52, 71, 79, 85, 88, 90–2, 94, 101, 104–5, 136
Otto, R. 5
outdoor learning 93

Paavola, S. 150–1
Paechter, C. 33
palpating reality 138
Pals, D. 34
Parrinder, G. 5
Patel, V. 123
Patton, G. 13

Paul, the apostle 129
pedagogy 103, 105, 107, 143–4, 165, 169
Pedwell, C. 2
performativity 101
phallicity 78
phenomenology 2, 5, 15, 139, 141
philosophy of education 1, 39, 155
Plaskow, J. 98
politics 61, 65; category of 21; of difference 103; of imaginative generosity 73, 108; in Islam 117; of location and marginality 33
pornography 102
possession, possessed states 115, 122, 124–8
post-colonial theory 22, 60, 62, 65, 72, 79, 81, 90
Price, J. 2
Priebe, S. 123–4, 129
Prout, A. 153
Punch, S. 136
Pussy Riot 99
Putin, V. 99
Qu'ran, the 118–19, 125–6, 129
qualifications 44–5, 50, 143
queer 91, 103–6

Rabinow, P. 145
Radford, J. 83
radical empiricism 138–141
Rambelli, F. 64
RE 1–5, 9, 11–24, 29–31, 33–4, 37–8, 41–4, 49–52, 57, 59, 60, 62–3, 65, 68–9, 71–2, 77–8, 81–3, 87, 89–90, 92–3, 95–8, 100, 103, 106–7, 120, 133, 135, 137–9, 141, 143–5, 148, 152–4, 156–7, 163–9, 170; dialogical approaches 18; official account of 13–15, 19–20, 23, 30, 37, 81, 83, 98, 100; orientation to practice 142
Readings, B. 40
reductionism 35, 117
re-enchantment 141
Reeves, J. 33, 73
religion, associated with feminine 78; category of (western) 21–2, 47, 49, 60, 166, 171; definition of 21, 31, 117, 165; dimensions of 15, 20, 31; material 36, 61, 154; mode of existence as 37, 139
Religious, Moral and Philosophical Studies (RMPS) 44–5, 49
Religious Observance (RO) 12–13, 97–8

178 Index

remediation 133–62, 167
revisioning 78
rhetoric 38, 60, 64, 71, 77–9
Rich, A. 98
Richardson, H. 13
Richardson, L. 73
Ripley, C. 6
Roberts, R. 95
Robinson, C. 143–4
Rodriguez, N. 103–8
Rose, N. S. 51
Rothenberg, C. 128
Royal Anthropological Institute 154
Ruether, R. Radford 98, 102
Rumens, C. *This 'Holiness Crap'*
(2012) 99

Sabry, S. S. 129
Sámi, the 63
Santo, B. 39
Sarroub, L. K. 5
Sartre, J.-P. 85–6
Schielke, S. 128
Science and Technology Studies (STS) 60
Scolnicov, S. 73
Scott, D. 120
Scott, S. 125
Scottish Credit and Qualifications
Framework (SCQF) 54
Scottish Qualification Authority (SQA)
23, 44–9, 53
Scrima, A. 148
secular 13–4, 21, 30, 39, 78, 95, 139,
147
Seneca, L. A. 32
Serano, J. 102–3, 106–7
Serres, M. 32
Sfard, A. 150
Sheldrake, P. 95–6, 98
Shildrick, M. 2
Shopen, G. 64
Singh, S. P. 123, 125
Skeie, G. 154
Smart, N. 2, 14–5, 17, 19–20, 22, 31,
34, 35, 39, 52, 60, 139, 163–5
Smith, B. K. 46
Smithies, C. 20, 163
socio-material practices 11, 33, 47, 51,
65, 69–70, 77, 137–8, 148, 152–3,
164
Soja, E. W. 33
Sørensen, E. 136–7, 155
Souriau, E. 157
Souza, M. de 15

space 3, 12, 18, 23–4, 29–56, 60, 63,
67, 71, 78, 81–2, 87, 89, 90–3, 95,
98–100, 102–7, 120, 128–9, 136,
150, 163, 165; spatial 2, 9, 29–30,
32–7, 42, 45, 51, 59, 69, 91–2, 120,
133, 169
Spencer, D. 73
Spice, R. C. 82
Spinoza, B. 57, 59–60, 65–73, 77, 81,
96, 142, 149–51, 164
spirituality 70–2, 78, 81, 94–100, 156
Spivak, G. C. 33, 79
Stack, T. 14, 21–2, 49
Standing Advisory Council on RE
(SACRE) 13, 23
Standish, P. 39
Stausberg, M. 34
Steiner, G. 4
Stengers, I. 18, 108, 137, 140, 148, 153,
156, 164, 167
Stewart, F. 154
Strathern, M. 142
Strenski, I. 5
Strhan, A. 4, 30, 43, 47, 135, 139
Stuart, E. 82, 96, 98
St. Ville, S. M. 61
style(s) of reasoning 2–4, 52, 57, 60, 62,
66, 72, 77, 79–80, 82–3, 87, 89–90,
95, 98, 100, 108, 115, 120, 133, 135,
149, 163, 169
subjectification 88, 107, 152
subject position 41, 50, 52, 69, 87, 91,
94, 100, 107–8, 154
Suhr, C. 129

Taguchi, H. L. 69, 80
Taylor, C. 62
Taylor, M. C. 165
Taylor, S. 107–8
telos 151, 156
Thatcher, A. 97
Thatcher Ulrich, L. 77
thinking/imagining otherwise 57–132,
167
Thomas, D. 119
Thompson, L. 78
three elements of education 144–5,
152–3, 157, 166
threshold concepts 149
Thrift, N. 2, 72, 108, 120, 137
Tiele, C. 5
Tisdall, E. K. M. 136
Toulmin, S. 165
traditions of inquiry 52, 119, 146, 170

Index 179

transcendence incarnate 78, 81, 85, 87–8, 90, 98, 168
transgender 91, 100, 103, 105
translation 38, 40, 42, 83, 86, 127, 149, 164, 168–9
Trible, P. 79
truth 2, 4, 16–18, 35–6, 38–9, 44–5, 50–1, 61, 64, 66–7, 70–2, 80, 104–5, 127
Tweed, T. A. 21, 33

Usher, R. 33
Ussher, J. M. 83–4, 100

Valentin, K. 136
Vansieleghem, N. 155
Verran, H. 1, 65, 88–92, 94, 126
via negativa 148
violence against women 79, 83
visual 62–3, 71, 89; visual orientation 64–5, 77
Vries, G. de 165
Vygotsky, L. 144

Wach, J. 5
Walls, A. 5
Wangarr ('dreamtime') 126
Warwick project 154
Weiss, J. 73
Weldon, V. 13
Wender, W. 36; *Wings of Desire* (1987) 36

western metaphysics 79
Whatmore, S. 138
Whitehead, A. N. 39, 140–1, 164–5, 167
Whitworth, P. 90
Wiebe, D. 14
Wildman, W. J. 23, 31
Williams, R. 38
Williams, Z. 19
Wings of Desire, film 36
Winnicott, D. 128–9
Winquist, C. E. 22, 122
Wittgenstein, L. 5
Womanspirit Rising (1979) 98
Woodhead, L. 14
Woolgar, S. 40
word-world settlement 83, 137, 142, 146–7
work on the self 17, 71
Working Paper 36 (Schools Council, 1971) 12, 14
Wright, A. 15–6, 19, 53, 97
Wynne-Jones, J. 13
Wyschogrod, E. 66

Yolngu, the 126
Yoruba, the 89
Young, I. M. 82
Young, J. O. 156
Young, S. H. 64